September 2004

to our English/California friends
Come Home Soon!

Love, the Hubbards

" The hills (of San Francisco) in all directions were covered with tents and the streets crowded with people from all parts of the world anxious to make their fortunes in a few days in this golden land of promise…"

S. SHUFELT, MARCH 3, 1850, PLACERVILLE,
EL DORADO COUNTY, CALIFORNIA

Joan Irvine Smith

Jean Stern

FOREWORD BY James L. Doti

TIMELINE BY James Irvine Swinden

CALIFORNIA

This Golden Land of Promise

CHAPMAN UNIVERSITY PRESS ❖ THE IRVINE MUSEUM

© 2001 The Irvine Museum

12th Floor, 18881 Von Karman Avenue

Irvine, California 92612

www.irvinemuseum.org

ISBN 0-9714092-0-X

LCCN 2001135809

Edited by Jean Patterson

Designed by Lilli Colton

Printed in Italy by I.G.E. Musumeci

through Overseas Printing

All measurements are in inches, height precedes width.

FRONT COVER: William Wendt, *Along the River Bed*, oil on canvas, 30 x 40 inches, Private Collection, courtesy of The Irvine Museum

END SHEETS: *French Miners Working the Long Tom*, engraving, Private Collection

FRONTISPIECE: Granville Redmond, *Poppies and Lupine*, oil on canvas, 25 x 29 inches, Private Collection, courtesy of The Irvine Museum

CONTENTS

William Wendt, Along the River Bed,
oil on canvas, 30 x 40 in., Private Collection,
courtesy of The Irvine Museum

My father, James Irvine, Jr., died in 1935 when I was two years of age, and my mother, Athalie Irvine Clarke and I lived in Los Angeles with her parents. One of my most vivid childhood memories is driving with my mother and grandparents to San Juan Capistrano, to visit the mission, where I loved to feed the great flock of white pigeons that fluttered about the fountain in the court-yard and along the garden paths. Occasionally, one of the birds would fly high above my head into the sky, and my mother would tell me that was where my father had gone. Even to the present day, when I walk through the mission grounds, my recollections reach me at a deep and personal level, far beyond that of just a beautiful and historic monument.

During the summer, my mother and I stayed in a small tenant house on the Irvine Ranch, at Irvine Cove, that my father had moved to the site in the 1920s. It was set well-off the old coast road, on a cliff overlooking the beach. I spent hours exploring the tide pools and caves, looking for shells and other sea life, and searched the sage-covered bluffs for Indian artifacts. At other times during the year, I visited my grandfather, James Irvine, at the ranch house in Tustin, where I spent my days playing with the dogs, or accompanying him when he inspected his wells, irrigation ditches and lakes, and field crops, orchards, and packing houses.

My grandfather had a great love of nature, a sentiment uncommon to most of his contemporaries. If an oak tree intruded upon a projected road widening, he would re-route the road rather than remove the tree. I often rode with the cowhands, when they moved cattle through the majestic oaks and sycamores in the San Joaquin Hills and the Santa Ana Mountains. Every spring, my grandfather held a round-up on the ranch to brand the calves, which was reminiscent of those held a century before on the early ranchos. As a child, I had the unique opportunity to see the land as Portolá must have seen it, over two centuries ago, and loved it as my grandfather did.

For more than ten years, I have been collecting California plein-air art, not only for its beauty and artistic merit, but for the images it evokes of my childhood, many of which have passed into history. It has long been my intent that these magnificent landscape paintings would raise public awareness to the urgent need to preserve our imperiled environment.

I also have been collecting paintings, drawings and etchings of the Mission San Juan Capistrano, as well as the other twenty California missions. As time passed, my interest in California history grew and deepened when Harvey Smith, who is married to my cousin Linda Irvine Smith, started the Capistrano Pageant Foundation. They commissioned a lovely musical play about Mission San Juan

Capistrano that outlines the history of California, from its first native inhabitants to the arrival of the Spanish and Mexican colonizers, to California becoming a state in 1850, and ending with the mission being de-secularized in 1865.

To complement the first presentation of the Capistrano Pageant in 1999, a group of concerned organizations, including the Mission San Juan Capistrano, The Irvine Museum, the Nature Conservancy, the City of San Juan Capistrano, the County of Orange and my own Joan Irvine Smith & Athalie R. Clarke Foundation, produced an informative pamphlet that further acquainted the reader with the fascinating history of our Golden State. This illustrated pamphlet, entitled *California's True Gold*, not only enhanced the experience of the pageant but also rectified the sad fact that in the California public education curriculum, a student gets one brief opportunity to learn of our state's history in the fourth grade. There is no further California history taught until the college level, and then only as an elective course.

The title page of our book lists two authors, myself and Jean Stern, Executive Director of The Irvine Museum. It also lists my son, James Irvine Swinden, as the compiler of our historical timeline. Yet, as in any significant endeavor, there are a large number of individuals and organizations that have generously contributed their time and special knowledge to make this book a reality. Many of these will be mentioned by Jean Stern in his introductory statement, but I would like to personally express my deep appreciation to our co-publisher, Chapman University, and its President, Dr. James L. Doti. In addition, I want to thank Professor Leland L. Estes, Chair of the Social Sciences Division of Chapman University, who organized a select group of scholars to review our text for factual accuracy. In addition to Dr. Estes, our editorial board included Professors Lynne M. Pierson Doti, Robert A. Slayton, and James C. Miller, all of Chapman University, and Phil Brigandi, a noted Orange County historian.

From the beginning of this project, our history of California was aimed at the general reader, and we freely recognize that we owe a great intellectual debt to a number of noteworthy and meticulous historians. Our book is simply the telling of a wonderful story, a narrative drawn from selected parts of the books, articles and informational Web sites that are listed in our bibliography. We strongly recommend that people continue their quest for historical knowledge by reading these and many other sources to get a fuller sense of California's rich and colorful past.

Where our book differs, however, is in its superb selection of illustrations. We have searched countless museums and public and private collections of historical paintings throughout the country to locate images that illustrate the fascinating and colorful story of California. The unrivaled merit of the illustrations in our book, we feel, will make the narrative clear and enjoyable, and as a result, the lessons taught by the history of California will be lasting ones. ❧

JOAN IRVINE SMITH
PRESIDENT
THE IRVINE MUSEUM

William Wendt, Oaks and Sycamore,
Irvine Ranch, *oil on canvas,* 24 x 32 *in., Private
Collection, courtesy of The Irvine Museum*

FOREWORD

When I think of "history," I do not just recall facts and figures. I also think of the visual images that are indelibly etched on my mind. Those visual images accompanied some of the most memorable historical works I have read. Indeed, my recollection of history is most vivid when I can associate a fact or figure with the imprint of an historical image. So when I recall the Civil War, I think of a remarkable pen and ink drawing in Peter Townsend's *Our America* depicting endless columns of Lee's soldiers marching toward Gettysburg. When I think of World War II, I think of *The Holocaust Chronicle* and its haunting images of the people who experienced the horrors of that war.

In a similar way, California history comes beautifully to life in this book, and it comes alive in a very special way. Not only is *California, This Golden Land of Promise* a cogent, well-researched and highly readable narrative, it is also illustrated with over 300 works of art and images that will etch California's remarkable history in the minds of all those fortunate to experience this book. I use the word "experience" rather than "read" to convey my belief that this book's art and images are as important as the narrative in conveying a sense of the scope and grandeur of California's historical development.

From the time people first entered California more than 12,000 years ago to the 1870s, *California, This Golden Land of Promise* presents a comprehensive history that includes the people, social and cultural forces and environmental issues that helped shape a state that now has the sixth-largest economy of the world. The various historical epochs are made real in one's mind by many wonderful paintings. Among them are scenes of the Battle of San Pasqual, painted at the battlefield by William H. Meyers. Charles Christian Nahl's evocative paintings help shed light on the rancho period and Gold Rush era. And Alexander Harmer's exquisitely rendered paintings give us a period view of California missions as well as the life and times surrounding those missions. These are only a few examples of the artwork that will give readers a new look on California.

The final chapter, on the beginnings of the Irvine Ranch in southern California, sets the stage for the next volume, which will bring California's history to the present. Until then, the present volume is obviously a labor of love of Joan Irvine Smith, whose guiding spirit and passion has brought the public a magnificent historical work—a work that advances our understanding of a great land's ancestry. She and Jean Stern are to be congratulated for expanding the frontiers of knowledge and doing it in such an aesthetically pleasing way. As president of Chapman University, it is an honor and privilege to have our press's imprimatur on it. ❧

JAMES L. DOTI

Joseph Kleitsch, Bougainvillea, Mission San Juan Capistrano, *1923, oil on canvas, 30 x 24 in., Private Collection, courtesy of The Irvine Museum*

Paul de Longpré, Poppies in an Indian Basket,
watercolor, 15 x 21 in., The Irvine Museum

INTRODUCTION

*T*his book came about as a result of Joan Irvine Smith's determination to produce a highly readable, popularly appealing and richly illustrated history of California, her native state. When she and her mother, the late Athalie R. Clarke, founded The Irvine Museum in 1992, they endowed our institution with a significant collection of paintings that show California as it looked between 1890 and 1925, a time when California changed forever, from an idyllic ranching and farming setting to one of growing cities and burgeoning population.

Making full use of our versatile collection, supplemented by paintings borrowed from important private collections, we have endeavored to offer exhibitions that raise awareness of the uniquely beautiful and fragile environment that makes our state such an attractive place to live. At the same time, among the many exhibitions at The Irvine Museum as well as those that have traveled throughout California and the rest of the country, we have displayed a large number of historical paintings of the California missions. In fact, one of our most popular traveling exhibitions was entitled *Romance of the Bells: The California Missions in Art.*

Thus, it followed that, as part of our role as an educational institution, our museum could produce a book on the history of California and illustrate it quite successfully with paintings. That initial idea evolved beyond using only works that have appeared in our exhibitions, to a dedicated effort to locate and secure images of the most important and beautiful historical paintings of California wherever they may be found.

Even though the aim of producing this book was to write and illustrate an introductory-level history, we nevertheless needed to have our text checked for factual accuracy, and for this we turned to the History Department at Chapman University, our co-publisher in nearby Orange, California. We are greatly indebted to Professors Leland L. Estes, Lynne M. Pierson Doti, Robert A. Slayton, and James C. Miller, all of Chapman University, as well as Phil Brigandi, Orange County historian, for reading the manuscript and making appropriate and insightful suggestions.

History does not take place in a vacuum; every important event in any part of the world is either affected by or causes an effect on other events in various parts of the world. To fully appreciate the global circumstances that paralleled our own historical events in California, James I. Swinden, Vice-President of The Irvine Museum, has compiled an interesting and informative timeline that lists major political, social and artistic developments. As you read through these notable events and human achievements, you will better appreciate the circumstances that have shaped our own history.

To the many other museums, historical societies, libraries, corporate and private collections and individuals who allowed us to reproduce their treasured masterpieces as illustrations to the text, we are grateful and each is noted next to the image they contributed.

Others who facilitated our project with additional guidance and moral support include, by institution in alphabetical order, Darlene A. Dueck of the Anschutz Collection, Denver; James H. Nottage, Chief Curator, Autry Museum of Western Heritage, Los Angeles; David Belardes, of the Blas Aguilar Adobe, San Juan Capistrano; Kevin Shoaf of Bluebird Gallery, Laguna Beach; Ed and Yvonne Boseker, the Boseker Collection, Santa Ana; Dr. Peter Keller and Dr. Armand Labbe, of the Bowers Museum of Cultural Art, Santa Ana; Scot M. Levitt, Butterfield & Butterfield, Los Angeles; William Horton and Jann McCord, at the California Club, Los Angeles; Scott A. Shields, Curator of Fine Arts, California Historical Society, San Francisco; Dr. Kevin Starr, California State Librarian, and Helen Harding, of the California State Library in Sacramento; Staci Otte, Director, and Jeannine L. Pedersen, Collections Manager, Catalina Island Museum, Avalon; DeWitt Clinton McCall, of DeRu's Fine Arts in Laguna Beach; Tom Gianetto, of Edenhurst Gallery, Los Angeles; Barbara J. Blankman, First American Title Insurance Collection, Santa Ana; Morton H. Fleischer and Donna Fleischer, the Fleischer Collection, Scottsdale; Tony Forster, of the Forster Family Archives at the San Juan Capistrano Historical Society; John Garzoli and Joel Garzoli, of the Garzoli Gallery, San Rafael; Pam Ludwig, Joan Irvine Smith Fine Arts, Laguna Beach; Ellen K. Lee, historian and Director of the Helena Modjeska Foundation; Harvey L. Jones, Senior Curator, the Oakland Museum of California; Judy Liebeck Gauntt, Orange County historian at the Irvine Historical Society; Merika Adams Gopaul, Christine Leedom and Judy Thompson, of The Irvine Museum; Whitney Ganz, of William A. Karges Fine Art, Los Angeles and Carmel; Dr. Oscar and Trudy Lemer, the Lemer Collection, San Francisco; Dr. Patricia Trenton, of the Los Angeles Athletic Club Art Collection; Lynn C. Kronzek, and the Los Angeles Conservancy; Sandra Heaphy of Maritime Heritage Prints Boston; Colleen and Mark Hoffman of Maxwell Galleries, San Francisco; Lynn A. B. Voorheis, Mission Inn Museum and Foundation, Riverside; Gerald J. Miller, Administrator, Alana Jolley, Curator, Jaqui Nuñez, and Sandy Wheeler, of the Mission San Juan Capistrano; Lisa Peters and Peter Fairbanks of Montgomery Gallery, San Francisco; Elisabeth Waldo-Dentzel and Paul Dentzel, at the Multicultural Arts Studio, Northridge; William Doty and Ann Cummings, at the National Archives, Pacific Region; Dr. James L. Powell, President and Director, and Beth D. Werling, historian, Natural History Museum of Los Angeles County; Jessie Dunn-Gilbert and Alfred Harrison of North Point Gallery, San Francisco; Don Tryon, of the O'Neill Museum and the San Juan Capistrano Historical Society; Don Dobmeier, of the Orange County Historical Commission, Santa Ana; the Orange County Historical Society; Nicholas M. Magalousis, Archaeologist, Rancho Santiago College; Ray Redfern, Redfern Gallery, Laguna Beach; Margaret N. Dykens, Librarian, San Diego Natural History Museum; David Bisol, Curator, Santa Barbara Historical Museum; Linda M. Agren, Santa Barbara Museum of Natural History; Dr. William Hendricks, historian and Director, Sherman Library, Corona del Mar; Alicia Egbert, Stanford University Art Library, Palo Alto; Nan Chisholm, Sotheby's, New York; Kim Walters, of the Southwest Museum, Highland Park, Los Angeles; George and Irene Stern, of George Stern Fine Arts, Los Angeles; John Stobart, artist and maritime historian; and Bill Vose, Vose Galleries, Boston.

The following individuals also provided much appreciated support to our project: Pamela Hallan-Gibson, Orange County historian; Joan Hedding of the William Wolfskill family; Roy C. Rose, Avalon; Jim Sleeper, Orange County historian; Doris I. Walker, author and historian; Colonel Charles Waterhouse, U.S. Marine Corps artist; and Christopher Bliss, principal photographer. We are grateful to all these people.

In memory of Hubert H. Bancroft, Robert Glass Cleland and Norman Neuerberg. We also remember Mark Hoffman, of Maxwell Galleries, San Francisco, who passed away just prior to the publication of this book.

The writing and production of this book required the dedication and hard work of numerous photographers, editors, and designers, most of all Lilli Colton, our long-time graphic designer and production coordinator.

Finally, there are two special people whose roles in this project were indispensable: Katrina Lutge, who was our constant colleague in planning sessions and historical field trips and regularly offered judgment on the merits of various phrases and images as this book was brought to life; and my Laura, whose love and wisdom has sustained me through this exhausting but uniquely rewarding effort. ❧

(Mr.) Jean Stern
Executive Director
The Irvine Museum

Duncan Gleason, Ning Po
(Chinese Junk)*, oil on canvas, 20 x 16 in.,*
Catalina Island Museum

CHAPTER 1

THE FIRST SETTLERS

T he question of when ancient peoples first entered the North and South American continents has been debated among scientists for many years. Until recently, archaeologists believed that human beings entered North America no earlier than about 12,000 years ago. The principal evidence for this dating was a series of remarkable finds of ancient stone spear points of a distinct style, first found in 1926 and 1928 in direct association with the remains of extinct bison that had been killed and butchered for food by early peoples at sites near Folsom and Clovis, New Mexico. Unlike other Indian arrowheads, these very ancient or "Paleo-Indian" stone points all have a unique and distinctive shape, being thin blades with characteristic flutes, or long grooves, chipped down the center on both sides. In the years that followed, Clovis points were established as the earliest-known stone points found in North America, with superb examples being found at mastodon kill sites thought to be up to 14,000 years old.

Paleo-Indian stone artifacts of the Clovis and Folsom cultures have since been found throughout the United States, with a large number from various California locales. Ancient sites at Tulare Lake, in the southern San Joaquin Valley, and China Lake, in Kern County, have produced many examples.

One outstanding group of California Clovis points, from a site at Borax Lake, were made of obsidian and thus could be dated using the obsidian hydration measurement method. Obsidian, a natural volcanic glass, is porous and absorbs moisture at a very slow but constant rate. When a piece of obsidian is broken or flaked off in the process of toolmaking, the newly exposed surfaces start to hydrate, and over time, that outer layer of exposed obsidian gets a thicker and thicker covering of hydration. The obsidian tools from Borax Lake were dated to be about 12,000 years old.

For many years, it was believed that there was no significant human presence in North America older than the Clovis culture. However, beginning in the 1970s, scientists began to date older and older material from excavations at various places throughout the Western Hemisphere. Among the most noteworthy of these recently discovered sites are a rock shelter at Meadowcroft, Pennsylvania, dating back 17,000 years, and a site called Cactus Hill, in Virginia, that may date to 18,000 years ago.

Most interesting are a series of ancient sites in South America, including two in Peru, dating back 12,000 years, and Monte Verde, a settlement in southern Chile thought to have been occupied up to 12,500 years ago. While these sites are not as old as some found in North America, their existence gives rise to at least two

TOP: *Bighorn Sheep Petroglyph, Coso Range, CA, photo by David S. Whitley;*
BOTTOM: *Clovis points, casts, 4⅝ in. (longest), Lithic Casting Lab*

William Ritschel, Purple Tide, *oil on canvas,
36 x 40 in., Private Collection, courtesy of
The Irvine Museum*

intriguing interpretations. Their distance from the generally accepted point of entry—the Bering land bridge, exposed across the present-day Bering Strait during a period of glaciation—is very great. Thus, the dates from Peru and Chile suggest a very early date of entry, early enough to allow for migration over such a great distance. Secondly, as these sites are all near the Pacific coast, they present the possibility that early humans entered South America by sea.

However they arrived, the people who first populated North America were nomadic groups who obtained food by fishing and hunting, and by gathering fruits, nuts, berries, roots and leaves of edible plants along their annual migration routes. They lived off the land, taking only what they could readily use before moving to a new area. In this manner, the land recovered quickly, and thus rejuvenated, provided more sustenance for all living creatures that made up the local ecosystems.

In time, the people of what is now called the New World spread south and populated the entire Western Hemisphere. With the development of agriculture, many cultures established great cities and remarkably advanced civilizations. In the present-day United States, great metropolitan and ceremonial centers developed in the Mississippi Valley and the Southwest, although the most advanced and complex pre-Hispanic cultures were in Mexico and Central America and on the Andean Plateau in South America.

It is theorized that Chinese and Japanese ships first visited the west coast of North America perhaps 1,500 years ago. Although the trip would have been more than 7,000 miles, large, flat-bottomed, oceangoing junks could have reached America by riding the Japanese Current across the Pacific Ocean. Using this current, a junk might have traveled 75 to 100 miles per day across the ocean, landing perhaps on the coast of present-day Oregon. From there, it would have sailed south, along the California coast to Mexico, before catching the westerly trade winds back to Asia.

Evidence for this trans-Pacific contact is scant. Ancient Chinese texts mention a land called "Fusang," which may have been the west coast of North America. Fusang was described as a distant land rich in gold. Further evidence is provided by some ancient Chinese coins found in an archaeological site in the Pacific Northwest and numerous glass globes, used to hold up fish nets, that washed up on the shore in California. Most interesting are the large, doughnut-shaped stone objects that are occasionally retrieved, thought to be 3,000-year-old devices used by ancient Chinese sailors to clean seaweed off anchor lines. One of these stone objects was found off Palos Verdes, in southern California, and another was recovered off Point Conception in 1972.

In early Spanish times, a wrecked junk was found at the mouth of the Carmel River. Chinese marine technology and ship-construction methods were far ahead of those of any Spanish vessels. Oceangoing junks were equipped with compasses and sophisticated star charts for navigation. Moreover, junks were able to survive rough seas due to their tightly sealed bulkheads. European ships would flood with the first large wave. In the first century of Spanish colonization of California,

Chinese Junk, *c. 1880, stereoscope photograph, Private Collection*

a number of junks were observed off the coast, leading noted historian Charles Edward Chapman to estimate that more than 60 Oriental ships had landed in California between 1700 and 1900.

What would be of such great interest to people from the Orient as to risk a long, dangerous voyage? California was rich in otters and seals, animals whose fur was in great demand in the Orient. Additionally, Chinese traders put a great value on abalone meat and shells. As late as 1850, Chinese fishermen were taking 1,000 tons of abalone per year from California's coastal waters. This massive harvest ended when laws were passed in the early 1900s to protect the dwindling population of abalone. In response, Chinese fishing boats simply went farther south to the waters off Baja California.

Other than possible, and as yet, unproven, ancient European migrations to the New World, the first modern Europeans to encounter and colonize North America were the Norse, commonly called the Vikings. Ancient Norse sagas tell of sailing vessels going off-course and spotting an unknown coastline. Indeed, the oldest European settlement in the New World is a small Norse site at the northern tip of Newfoundland, Canada, called "L'Anse aux Meadows." There, around the year 1000, Leif Eriksson founded a small village in a place the Norse called "Vinland," or Wineland, for the abundance of wild grapes they found. The site has the remains of a few buildings, several loom weights, a Celtic bronze pin and an iron forge, all identified as distinctly Norse.

Because L'Anse aux Meadows is situated near the coast on a rocky point with little potential for agriculture, it is thought that the settlement functioned as a guidepost for Norse ships coming from Greenland. Perhaps Vinland was planned as a base camp for a permanent settlement and farming community at some other inland site. In any event, L'Anse aux Meadows seems to have been occupied for no more than ten years before being abandoned. ❧

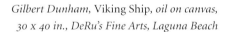

Gilbert Dunham, Viking Ship, *oil on canvas, 30 x 40 in., DeRu's Fine Arts, Laguna Beach*

William Ritschel, Land's End, *oil on canvas,*
30 x 40 in., Private Collection, courtesy of
The Irvine Museum

CHAPTER *2*

PEOPLE OF THE OAKS

INDIANS OF CALIFORNIA

The Indians of California lived in harmony with the land, and the natural environment provided all the necessities of life. In fact, the environment was so abundant and diverse that it supported a native population far greater than any equal area in the United States.

Indian life was, for the most part, a peaceful existence. However, as was the case throughout the United States, California Indians occasionally practiced war and attacked neighboring villages, killed their enemies, took scalps and captured women and children as slaves. In view of the natural bounty that surrounded them, these limited conflicts were not waged to conquer territory but most often to avenge a personal wrong, such as the theft of an object or an affront to an ancestor.

Everyday life was built around village and family, and time was occupied by the ageless tasks of food gathering, hunting and fishing. As only those tribes in the southeastern portion of California practiced agriculture, other Indians were dependent on food sources that conformed to a seasonal cycle, such as when a particular tree would give seeds, fruits or nuts. They migrated to the hills and valleys, to gather acorns, nuts, berries, roots and seeds, and to the coast, to catch fish and gather shellfish. In this sense only, they were "nomadic," always staying within traditionally defined areas.

Of the several types of trees that are native to California, the oak, of which there are 18 species that make up 30 distinct varieties, was the most important to native populations. The acorn, the seed of the oak tree, was the basic vegetable food

OPPOSITE:
John Greenleaf Cloudman, Pomo Indians of California, *Zaplin Lambert Gallery, Santa Fe*
RIGHT:
Albert Bierstadt, Untitled (California Indian Village), Zaplin Lampert Gallery, Santa Fe

Percy Gray, Oak Tree and Poppies, *watercolor, 12 x 15 in., Private Collection, courtesy of The Irvine Museum*

for most California Indians. Nearly every tribe living west of the Sierra Nevada Mountains, or more than three-fourths of all native Californians, harvested acorns. Each group used specialized methods—handed down from one generation to the next—to gather, prepare and cook acorns. Furthermore, the wood, bark, roots and galls of oaks were used in one way or another in Indian life.

When picked from an oak tree or gathered from the ground, acorns were naturally bitter and could not be readily eaten. First, the acorns had to be hulled, parched in the sun, then ground into a powder. The acorn meal was then leached to remove the poisonous tannic acid. Once safe, the meal was cooked, either by boiling or roasting, and then consumed on the spot. More often, acorns were stored in baskets for later use.

Modern studies have demonstrated that acorn meal is an excellent source of nutrition. Some species of oak produce acorns that are up to 18% fat, 6% protein and 68% carbohydrates. By comparison, modern wheat and corn, which require intensive cultivation, are 2% fat, 10% protein and 75% carbohydrates.

Steps in the gathering and grinding of acorns; The Bancroft Library, University of California, Berkeley (left); San Diego Historical Society (center); Mission San Juan Capistrano (right)

In areas where more than one species of oak was available, Indians developed preferences for those that were tastier or easier to prepare. In the north coastal areas, the Hupa and Yurok looked for tanbark (or tanoak) acorns, which in fact come not from a true oak but an acorn-bearing variety of the beech family. Tanoaks grow well among redwoods and evergreens. In southern California, the Luiseños and Juaneños of Orange and San Diego counties derived nearly half their diet from six species of oak, favoring the black oak and live oak. Less desirable were acorns from canyon oaks, which have hard hulls and nutmeat that is difficult to grind. As a last resort, the Indians would gather acorns from scrub oaks, a low-lying variety that often takes the form of a dense, low-spreading shrub.

This dependence on acorns as the primary source of food is unique to California Indians. In parts of California where the oak is sparse or absent, as in the desert regions along the Colorado River, the traditional pre-Hispanic trio of corn, beans and squash were cultivated to meet the needs of basic nutrition, and people made great use of mesquite, yucca and agave, which occur naturally.

CLOCKWISE FROM TOP LEFT:
Albert R. Valentien, Canyon Oak, Black Oak,
Coast Live Oak, Tanbark Oak,
San Diego Natural History Museum

In addition to gathering food from the large variety of plants in their environment, California Indians were skillful hunters of the myriad of game in their habitat. Deer, antelope and mountain sheep were the largest game hunted by California Indians. Although they would be hunted year-round, all three were very difficult to bring down. Usually, most hunting was restricted to small animals and birds, using bows and stone-tipped arrows, throwing-sticks, or by trapping small animals in snares and nets. Rabbits, squirrels, field mice, rats, snakes and even coyotes were killed and eaten.

Thomas Hill, Deer Trail, *oil on canvas, 34 x 27 in., Butterfield & Butterfield*

Many California tribes had specific food taboos. As a rule, bears and mountain lions were not hunted, as they were believed to be inhabited by powerful spirits and were to be carefully avoided.

Ducks, geese and other waterfowl were hunted using decoys to lure the prey, which was taken with a net or a bow and arrow. Other times, the birds were taken alive and kept for eggs. Mallards and Canada geese were the most desirable egg-layers. The Chumash made basketry decoys with a duck head attached. Wearing these on their heads, they would wade into the water and slowly approach the birds in order to catch them. Another method employed by the Indians was to float a number of wild gourds downstream, past where ducks were feeding. When the birds no longer paid attention, an Indian would float down with his head in a gourd and grab one by the feet, pulling it underwater in order not to frighten the other ducks.

The California quail and band-tailed pigeons were also important food resources. The Pomo Indians caught these using long, tubular basketry traps, similar to those used to catch fish. Tribes in the Sierra Nevada Mountains laid noose snares made of human hair. Quail would be driven into a series of these snares, set in bushes and low-lying shrubs.

Miguel Costansó, the engineer and cosmographer on the ship *San Carlos* of the Portolá expedition of 1769, observed a group of San Diego Indians hunting

CLOCKWISE FROM TOP LEFT:
Jean-François La Pérouse, "Quail," from Voyage de La Perouse, *California History Section, California State Library; Acagchemem (Juaneño) duck decoy, rabbit stick, bow with polychrome decoration and arrow, Mission San Juan Capistrano*

near the bay. He described their weapons as follows: *"Their quivers, which they stick between the belt and the body, are made of the skins of the wildcat, coyote, wolf or deer, and their bows are two yards long. In addition to these arms, they use a sort of throwing-stick of very hard wood, similar in form to a short curved saber, which they throw edge-wise, cutting the air with great force. They throw it farther than a stone, and never go into the surrounding country without it. When they see a snake or other noxious animal, they throw the throwing-stick at it, and generally cut the animal in two."*

Costansó also noted that they were adept fishermen: *"Fish constitutes the principal food of the Indians who inhabit this port, and they consume much shell-fish because of the greater ease they have in procuring them. They use rafts made of reeds, which they manage dexterously by means of a paddle or double-bladed oar. Their harpoons are several yards long, and the point is a very sharp bone inserted in the wood; they are so adroit in throwing this weapon that they very seldom miss their mark."*

Prior to Spanish colonization, the most common native craft on inland waterways was the reed boat, made by lashing bundles of tules or reeds in the form of a low, open canoe. This type of craft was found throughout California and was paddled or poled in rivers and lakes. The Spanish called these boats *balsas*, as they shared a remarkable similarity to native boats they had previously seen on Lake Titicaca in South America.

Coastal Indians, such as the Chumash of the Santa Barbara area, made excellent seagoing boats and canoes. One type of canoe, called a *tomol* in the Chumash language, or *ti'at* in Gabrielino, was made of wooden planks lashed together with rope and made watertight with a natural tar or asphaltum that washed up on the beach in southern California. *Tomols* and *ti'ats* were quite seaworthy and were used to navigate between the mainland and the Channel Islands. These canoes were often noted by early explorers along the Channel Islands.

TOP: *Stages in making fish hooks, Catalina Island Museum;*
BOTTOM: *Chumash whale effigies, whalebone, Santa Barbara Museum of Natural History*

CLOCKWISE FROM TOP LEFT:
Seal effigy, pelican effigy, steatite, Catalina Island Museum;
Chumash shark, killer whale, steatite, Los Angeles County Museum of Natural History

Building a Tomol, *1912, photograph,*
Santa Barbara Museum of Natural History
BELOW, LEFT TO RIGHT:
Gabrielino plank canoe fragments, wood and
asphaltum; Gabrielino fishing spear and hooks;
Catalina Island Museum

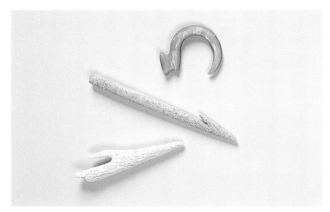

RIGHT:
Louis Choris, Bateau du Port de
San Francisco, *colored lithograph, 6¾ x 10 in.,*
Santa Barbara Museum of Art,
Gift of Carol Valentine
BELOW:
Reed boat (modern reconstruction),
Blas Aguilar Adobe, San Juan Capistrano

Of the 135 or more small tribes or tribelets of Indians in California, nearly all lived in small communities. Of the 46 native language groups recognized in the United States, 22, or nearly one-half, were found in California, and of those, only six extended beyond the present-day borders. Since many of these 135 tribelets were isolated by hilly and mountainous regions, which favored independent development, many spoke a distinct dialect that was nearly unintelligible to others.

Native Californians did not identify themselves as tribes or tribelets, but rather looked for association through local villages or home communities. The Spanish colonizers were the first to divide natives into groups, and those efforts were based largely on language affinity. This approach caused many problems, as native languages were often interrelated.

Dialects of the Chumash language group, for example, were spoken by people from San Luis Obispo Bay south to Malibu, including the islands of Santa

Tolowa
Karok
Yurok
Whilkut
Hupa
Chimariko
Wiyot
Bear River
Mattole
Lassik
Sinkyone
Kato
Nongatl
Wailoki
Yuki
Pomo
Coast Miwok
Wappo
Wintu
Wintun
Lake Miwok
Shasta
Modoc
Achomawi
Atsugewi
Yana
Yahi
Maidu
Northern Paiute
Washo
Interior Miwok
Mono Paiute
Owens Valley Paiute
Monache
Panamint Shoshone
Costanoan
Yokuts
Esselen
Salinan
Tübatulabal
Kawaiisu
Chumash
Vanyume
Chemehuevi
Kitanemuk
Alliklik
Serrano
Mohave
Fernandeño
Gabrielino
Luiseño
Juaneño
Cupeño
Cahuilla
Halchidhoma
Yuma
Dieueño
Kamia

0   50   100   150   200
MILES

A. L. Kroeber, Indian Tribes of California
(from R.F. Heizer, Languages, Territories, and
Names of California Indian Tribes*, 1966)*

Cruz, Santa Rosa and San Miguel, as well as the Santa Maria, Santa Inés and Santa Clara valleys, to the eastern slopes of the coastal range. Within the large, heavily populated area, there were at least seven distinct dialects spoken, and another one was yet so different that it may be considered a separate language by itself.

Immediately adjacent to the southern Chumash area, people spoke dialects of the Shoshonean, or Uto-Aztecan, language group. This large group included the Kizh, or Tobikhar, (later called Gabrielino, after missionization) dialect and several dialects that overlapped outside California into Arizona, including Piute, Ute, Comanche and Pima, as well as related dialects from present-day Mexico, such as Yaqui and Taraumari, spoken in Baja California, and Nahuatl, spoken by the Aztecs in Central Mexico. Gabrielino territory included the Santa Monica-Santa Ana plain and the three adjacent valleys around present-day Los Angeles: San Fernando, San Gabriel and San Bernardino.

Other southern California languages that were distinct dialects of Shoshonean/Uto-Aztecan and closely related to Gabrielino were Kechi (later called Luiseño) and Acagchemem (later called Juaneño), which included the areas of present-day Orange County and the northern part of San Diego County; Cahuilla or Kawia, spoken along the eastern slopes of the San Jacinto Mountains and the Salton Sea; Panakhil, spoken in inland parts of San Diego County; and Serrano, from the San Bernardino Mountains and the Mojave River Valley.

Most California Indians lived in villages of 12 to 15 to as many as 50 to 60 families. A tribe or tribelet took the form of several villages occupying a defined area. Members of a tribelet stayed on their own land and respected the territory of other tribelets. The chief lived in the principal village of the tribelet. He did not have power of life and death over the community and only served as long as he kept the trust of the rest of the group.

Houses were simple dwellings usually made of brush and reeds gathered in the immediate area or wood obtained from fallen trees. What these houses looked like and how they were built was essentially determined by the region and climate.

In the central part of California and toward the northwest, houses were built onto partly dug round pits, with sides and roofs made of heavy wooden planks. Having the houses partly underground helped keep them warmer in winter and

Thomas Hill, Indian Camp, Yosemite, *oil on canvas, 20½ x 13½ in.,* Dr. & Mrs. Edward H. Boseker

LEFT: *Jules Tavernier,* A "Mucca" in the Forest, *pastel on canvas, 36 x 20 in., Maxwell Galleries, San Francisco;* RIGHT: *Herman Herzog,* Indian Hogans in the California Sierras, *oil on canvas, 36¼ x 48¼ in., The Anschutz Collection*

cooler in summer. Houses of this type were built by the Coast Miwok people, who inhabited the coast and hilly region north of San Francisco. In the mission period, the Coast Miwoks were forced to relocate into the Mission San Rafael.

Another group of Miwoks lived in the Sierra Nevada Mountains. There, they faced a climate with particularly cold winters. These Miwoks built warm houses of wood with layers of bark as insulation against the frigid weather.

In the southern part of the state, in present-day Orange and San Diego counties, the climate was relatively mild, and Indians were generally unconcerned with very cold winters. Most of the year, they lived in lean-to structures made with branches, reeds and brush piled up to protect against the wind. In the winter, however, they built distinctive semi-circular structures—called *kiitkas* in the Acagchemem, or Juaneño, language of San Juan Capistrano—using a framework of bendable branches, arranged around a shallow pit dug about 18 inches into the ground, and covered with thatched reeds or deer weed, tied by strands of yucca. Generally, houses were not built for permanent occupation, as many southern California Indian groups continually moved from summer areas to winter areas in search of food.

Each village had a *temescál*, or sweat house, where the men would meet on a daily basis for a ritual steam bath. This special lodge differed in appearance from one tribe to another, but each one was built around a pile of stones that was heated and doused with water to produce steam. Following their steam bath, the men would run out of the *temescál* and jump into a cold stream or pond.

TOP:
Carl Von Perbandt,
Pomo Indians at Fort Ross, *1886,*
The Oakland Museum, Kahn Collection
BOTTOM:
Acagchemem (Juaneño) Kiitka (modern
reconstruction), reeds and willow branches,
Mission San Juan Capistrano Museum

Like every other Indian group in the United States, California Indians had no knowledge of the wheel, no metal tools, no system of writing and subsisted in a level of development equivalent to that of the Late Stone Age. Pottery was absent in northern and central California, with the notable exception of tribes in southern and desert areas. In San Diego County, for instance, pottery vessels were an essential part of Indian material culture, and artifacts include cooking pots, water bottles, portable canteens, large pottery vessels for the storage of acorns, pipes and religious effigies.

In the greater part of California, the basic container was made of basketry. The justly famous California Indian basket exhibits a wide range of shapes and purposes, including cooking and, because many baskets were so tightly woven, storing water. As for beauty and refinement, California basketry was, and remains to this

TOP, LEFT TO RIGHT:
Kumeyaay (Diegueño) water bottle, c. 1700, clay, Private Collection; Chumash presentation basket, c. 1820, diam. 24 in., Santa Barbara Museum of Natural History; watertight coiled basket, Mission San Juan Capistrano Museum; Woman Making a Coiled Basket, c. 1915, photograph, Mission San Juan Capistrano Archive.
RIGHT:
Grace Carpenter Hudson, Our Home (Yath Chow) *or* The Money Maker, *1920, oil on canvas, 16 x 22 in., Maxwell Galleries, San Francisco*

day, superior to all other regions of the United States. In addition, California Indians were experts at chipping stone. The items they made—points, blades and scrapers, often made of obsidian—are among the most beautiful stone tools known.

California Indians were generally open in demeanor and gregarious by nature. They welcomed the first Spanish explorers with food and gifts. Early contacts between Indians and the Spanish were marked by dancing and chanting that went far into the night, so much so that the Europeans complained of having little opportunity to sleep.

Dancing and chanting were an important part of life for California Indians. Moreover, many of their rituals and ceremonies were expressed in dances. There were dances to welcome visiting Indians, to mark the birth of a child, to prepare for war and to celebrate peace. There were dances to mark seasonal hunting and

food-gathering: the tribes of the northwest had a first-salmon dance; others had a first-eel dance and a first-acorn dance. Some of these "first" dances have a function similar to that of the Puritans' Thanksgiving feast in New England.

As was the case in pre-Hispanic cultures, the religious system of California's Indians was rich and complex. Most of what survives of their oral literature was recorded by people of the same outside cultures that tried to destroy it. Much of it survives in the memories of descendants of tribelets and thus avoided extinction.

Like other native peoples of the New World, California Indians believed that all of nature was interconnected and possessed a sacred power. People were to respect that power by following a set of carefully prescribed guidelines for every aspect of daily activity. Hunting down and killing an animal, drinking from a spring or entering a cave required a ritual act in advance, however simple, as a sign of respect and affirmation. As Native-American historian Edward D. Castillo of the Cahuilla-Luiseño tribe wrote, "*The religious beliefs and traditions of the Indians of California teach that the blessings of a rich land and a mild climate are gifts from the Creator. The Indians show their love and respect for the Creator—and for all of creation—by carefully managing the land for future generations and by living in harmony with the natural environment.*"

The spiritual leader of the village was the shaman, or healer. The shaman was usually a man, but among the Indians of northwest California, occasionally a woman. The shaman would heal by means of elaborate rituals, with chanting and the use of natural remedies. Sometimes the shaman would cure an illness by going into a trance and then "pulling out the disease."

The following is a narrative told by a shaman of the Yuma Indians, explaining his power to cure:

> *I had my dreams first when I was quite young, but I did not try to cure until I was an old man. I remembered them quite clearly always and never forgot anything in them.*
>
> *If I hear of a sick person, something tells me whether his illness is one I would be good for. This may happen even if I have not had a dream and power especially for his sickness. If I feel right, I know I will be able to cure the man. When I have a good feeling, I am very strong inside…The patient and the relations know too, for I seem to draw the sick man to me…When I work on the patient, it does not tire me at all and it makes me very happy.*
>
> *Sometimes I feel quite different about it, I don't get any good feeling and though I do my best, I do not often cure [in these circumstances]…And when I go away from the sick man I don't want to return to him. I feel heavy and tired and very sleepy that night. I cannot keep my mind on the sick man. I know it is really no good me trying to help him, even if I have had a dream for his sickness.*

Grace Carpenter Hudson, Indian Baby, *oil on board, 5 ½ x 4 ½ in., Maxwell Galleries, San Francisco*

Juaneño shaman, c. 1910, photograph, Mission San Juan Capistrano Archives

In the southern part of the state, shamans made use of the highly poisonous *Toloache* plant or jimsonweed (*Datura meteloides*) to make a powerful drug. When taken for ceremonial purposes, Datura induced a hallucinogenic trance. Shamans used the drug to enhance their powers; it was also administered as part of the juvenile initiation ritual. Boys who took this drug were rendered unconscious for several hours and were expected to have visions and thus gain "power" of some kind, perhaps in hunting or other useful skills. Datura is a very dangerous drug, and on occasion, boys would die from being given too large a dose.

The use of Datura was related to the cult of Chinigchinich, the creator deity of the Gabrielinos and Juaneños. The Chinigchinich religion was an elaborate belief system with complex rituals. In addition to Chinigchinich, the central figure and creator deity, it included a number of lesser deities, each with a specific function and level of importance. The religion was maintained by an elite class of priests or shamans who performed all ceremonies and supervised a sacred site within the community. In this highly moralistic religion, daily life for all its followers was governed by a strict code of behavior.

The Kumeyaay, or Diegueño, of southern and inland San Diego County, are part of the Yuma Indian group. Their traditions were recorded in the 1920s and 1930s by Dr. Malcolm Rogers, who interviewed Indian people still living in remote parts of San Diego County and published his findings through the San Diego Museum of Man. Although nearly all California native cultures had elaborate death rituals, Rogers found that the Kumeyaay never spoke of death and made no reference to it in their mythology. Instead, their songs and stories present a spirit world filled with everyday little animals who take on human qualities. Kumeyaay stories of how the world began and of the struggle between good and evil are acted out by coyotes, rabbits and other small animals.

In the northern part of San Diego County, the Luiseño people (Indians native to the region around Mission San Luis Rey, in Oceanside) are part of the

Datura, *colored engraving, Private Collection*

Shoshonean or Uto-Aztecan language group and differ slightly in traditions from their southern cousins of the Yuma group. To them, death was very mysterious and people spent many years preparing for it. There were complicated ceremonies when a person died, at which offerings were made and all the dead person's belongings, including the house, were burned. This was done to insure that the departed one would have all of his or her own possessions and would have no reason to return.

In the Luiseño story of creation, all was empty space in the beginning, and Ké-vish-a-tak-vish was the only being. Thereafter came a period of upheaval, when things came into shape:

Dance of Indians at Mission San Jose,
The Bancroft Library, University of California, Berkeley

> *Then Ké-vish-a-tak-vish made a man, Tuk-mit, the Sky, and a woman, To-mai-yo-vit, the Earth. There was no light, but the two became conscious of each other.*
>
> *"Who are you?" asked the man.*
>
> *" I am [the Earth]. I am stretched, I am extended. I shake, I resound. I am diminished, I am earthquake. I revolve, I roll, I disappear. And who are you?"*
>
> *"I am [the Sky]. I am night. I am inverted. I cover, I rise. I devour, I drain [by death]. I seize, I send away the souls of men. I cut, I sever life."*
>
> *"Then you are my brother."*
>
> *"Then you are my sister."*
>
> *And by her brother, the Sky, the Earth conceived and became the mother of all things.*

(Constance G. DuBois, "Mythology of the Mission Indians," in *American Indian Prose and Poetry*, ed. Astrov)

The poetry of the California Indians is touching and gentle, and deals with universal and timeless themes. The following, from Constance DuBois' *The Religion of the Luiseño Indians*, is the Luiseño "Song of the Spirit," dealing with the inevitability of death:

*Maurice Braun, The Oak, oil on canvas, 14 x 18 in.,
Private Collection, courtesy of The Irvine Museum*

> *At the time of death,*
> *When I found there was to be death,*
> *I was very much surprised.*
> *All was failing.*
> *My home,*
> *I was sad to leave it.*
> *I have been looking far,*
> *Sending my spirit north, south, east, and west,*
> *Trying to escape death,*
> *But could find nothing,*
> *No way of escape.*

From the neighboring Apache Indians of Arizona, this is a wedding benediction:

Now you will feel no rain,
For each of you will be shelter to the other.
Now you will feel no cold,
For each of you will be warmth to the other.
Now there is no more loneliness for you,
For you have each other.
Now you are two bodies,
But there is only one life before you.
Go now to your dwelling place,
To enter into the day of your togetherness.
And may your days be good and long upon the earth!

The physical appearance of the California Indians varied in different regions. Although some whites had found other North American natives to be noble and admirable in appearance, many were critical of California's Indians. When writers described other Indians of North America, they noted their skin as being red or bronze-colored. In California, writers told of people with dark-brown and black-colored skin. A miner in 1849 wrote a letter home to his relatives, saying that the term "redskin" did not apply in California, as the Indians were more of a "dark chocolate-brown."

Later writers referred to the California natives as "digger Indians," probably because of the time spent digging for roots, a considerable part of their diet. But the term "digger" had many adverse connotations, as it reinforced the widely held notion that Indians lived in dirt. Moreover, their diet included foods thought to be repulsive, such as snails, caterpillars, crickets, grasshoppers, worms and grubs, all of which sickened those with non-Indian sensibilities.

From ancient times, the California Indians did more than arrive at a harmonious adjustment to their idyllic environment—they flourished. Any criticism regarding their failure to develop agriculture fades away when taking into consideration their abundance of natural resources, most of all oak trees, the source of their staple food, the acorn.

Grace Carpenter Hudson, Indian Summer, *1905, oil on canvas, 16 x 20 in., Maxwell Galleries, San Francisco*

Furthermore, when one considers the extreme culture shock of rapidly coming from a virtual Garden of Eden to near slavery at the hands of the Spanish, it is remarkable that Indians of the mission system were able to quickly learn the Spanish language and become proficient at speaking it. Similarly, mission Indians were compelled to acquire and practice Roman Catholicism, a complex religious system, not unlike their own Chinigchinich religion.

Unlike previous Spanish conquests in the New World, in which the natives were subjugated by the military before being turned over to the church, the mission system in California replaced the military as the way of subduing the natives. The missionaries generally accompanied the military whenever Spanish presence was extended into a new region. On some occasions, they preceded the military, as when they were part of expeditions of exploration.

Alice Coutts, Playmates of the Desert,
oil on board, 11¼ x 8½ in., The Irvine Museum

Alice Coutts, Indian Girl with Cat and Dog,
oil on canvas, 12 x 10 in., The Irvine Museum

The principal object of the missions was to convert and civilize the native inhabitants. In a more strategic way, the missions assisted the military by keeping the local Indians peaceful and under subjugation. This accomplishment made it easier for Spain to control large amounts of territory with as few soldiers as possible, a cost-effective benefit that did not go unnoticed by the royal administrators.

When the Spanish entered a territory, the missionaries would begin by attracting native inhabitants into the mission on a voluntary basis, offering gifts as inducements. Once baptized and in the mission system, the Indians were no longer free to leave, and the duration of their stay was determined by the time necessary for them to become "civilized." Indians who were reluctant to enter the system voluntarily were forced into a mission village called a *reducción.* Areas that had once contained a number of native villages were essentially deserted, as their populations had been herded into mission villages. The few individuals that eluded the roundup were forced into hiding in outlying areas, out of reach of the missionaries. To lessen the chance of escape, walls were built around the missions and Indians were locked in at night. The ones who escaped were hunted down and brought back.

Not only were entire villages missionized, but subsequently entire regions. In what is now Santa Barbara County, there were more than 100 identifiable Chumash villages that were destroyed when their residents were brought into that mission. The mission system also tried to eliminate all original native group names or tribelet designations. Thereafter, Indians were referred to by only one cultural group, named for the mission in that particular region. Indians in the jurisdiction of the Mission San Diego were to be called "Diegueños." Those attached to the Mission San Gabriel were "Gabrielinos," and the Mission San Juan Capistrano, "Juaneños," no matter what they originally called themselves.

DECLINE OF THE NATIVE POPULATION

Although California was perhaps the most densely populated region of the United States prior to European contact, there was no effective resistance to the nearly complete destruction of Indian life. California Indians had no way of withstanding the overwhelming variety of diseases and epidemics brought by the Spanish in the late 1700s. Nor could they counter Mexican institutional policies and later, the large number of Americans and other Europeans who came for the Gold Rush. Independent by nature, the many small groups of Indians had no organization for alliances and confederacies, as was the case in the plains and eastern woodlands. Thus, the process of dispossession of the California Indians and the destruction of their way of life happened relatively quickly.

Under Spain and Mexico, the native population in California dropped from an estimated 300,000 in 1769 to less than 100,000 at the time of the American occupation of California in 1846. Tragically, the coming of hundreds of thousands of Americans after 1850 greatly accelerated the decline of the Indian population to less than 30,000 in 1870, and then only about 15,000 by 1900. The largest cause of death among Indians was disease to which they had no resistance, accounting for

William Keith, California Alps, *Mission Inn Foundation and Museum, Riverside, CA*

nearly 60% of Indian deaths. The next leading cause of death was starvation and malnutrition, which took a toll of approximately 30%. Finally, physical assaults such as military and civilian shootings accounted for about 10% of the decline in the Indian population.

In the end, the root cause of the destruction of some of the most vibrant and flourishing Indian cultures of North America may have been, indirectly, their serene isolation and their success at natural adaptation to their environment. Theirs was a gentle, peaceful life that was in harmonious balance with the environment. It required no centralized organization, no warfare, and no suspicion of strangers, whom they welcomed openly, and it flourished for thousands of years before the Spanish came in the late 1700s and changed it forever.

Nonetheless, California Indians have survived in the general community and on more than 105 reservations, more than in any other state. They have consciously preserved many aspects of their traditional cultures and are working to restore knowledge of their languages. As traditions and customs are passed from one generation to another, the ancient cultures of the California Indians survive. ❧

Virgil Williams, Landscape with Indians, *oil on canvas, 18 x 30 in., The Irvine Museum*

William Ritschel, Conquest of the Corsair *or* Days of the Spanish Main, *oil on canvas, 24 x 29 in., Private Collection*

CHAPTER 3

SPANISH EXPLORATION OF CALIFORNIA

For more than a thousand years prior to the discovery of the New World, there existed a rich and active trade between Europe and the Orient. Using age-old caravan routes that traced across Central Asia, through Constantinople (now called Istanbul, Turkey) then into the deserts of the Middle East and across the Mediterranean Sea to ports like Venice and Genoa, exotic goods such as spices, silk, porcelain, amber and perfume were imported from China, India and the Spice Islands (now called the Mollucas) to satisfy European demand.

By the late 1300s, the growing dominance of the Ottoman Empire, a Moslem state and staunch adversary of Christian Europe, began to impede this trade by subduing many of the traditional routes. In due time, prices for Oriental goods rose and a search began for alternate routes to the east. Finally, after many years of warfare, the Ottoman Turks conquered the Byzantine Empire, and with the fall of Constantinople in 1453, all overland trade routes to the east fell under their control.

To find a sea route to the Orient, Portugal, under the direction of Prince Henry the Navigator (1394–1460), began to send naval expeditions south along the west coast of Africa as early as 1418. The information derived from these voyages, including geographical and astronomical data, led to the production of accurate maps, which proved crucial in precise navigation. This growing store of information, coupled with improved ship designs, gave the Portuguese a decided advantage in navigation and allowed them to dominate trade in the last half of the 1400s.

Portugal's stature as a naval power attracted sailors and adventurers from all over Europe. One of those was Christopher Columbus (1451–1506) who, in 1481 in the service of King John II of Portugal, had made a voyage to the Gold Coast (now called Ghana) in Africa.

With the novel idea of reaching India by sailing west instead of east, Columbus calculated that the distance of such a voyage would be about 1,000 leagues, or approximately 2,600 miles. In 1484, he petitioned King John II for men and ships to pursue this theory. A royal panel studied the proposal and determined the distance to be at least four times longer and thus too far to reach. In retrospect, the Portuguese calculations of the distance from Portugal to India by sailing west on the Atlantic Ocean were correct, but of course neither they nor Columbus foresaw the existence of the American continents in between.

Columbus next tried to sell his plan to Spain. He presented his project to King Ferdinand and Queen Isabella, who likewise appointed a commission to study the idea. However, Spain was too busy fighting the Moors in the southern part of the country and had no resources to spare for exploration.

In 1488, Bartolomé Diaz (1450?–1500), a Portuguese mariner, became the first European to sail around the Cape of Good Hope, at the southern tip of Africa. However, once he was certain he had gone around the southern tip of Africa, Diaz returned to Portugal to announce his discovery. In 1497, his countryman Vasco da Gama (1460?–1524) set off on a two-year voyage that led him around the Cape of Good Hope and into the Indian Ocean to the city of Calicut, in India. Vasco's voyage made him a rich man, and the wealth from trade with the Indies made Portugal the most powerful country in Europe.

Earlier in 1488, Columbus had been called back to Portugal by King John for a review of his proposal. Unfortunately, soon after his arrival, Diaz returned to Portugal with the news of his successful rounding of Africa. Columbus was promptly dismissed, as Portugal was no longer interested in his untested and risky plan to reach India.

In 1492, Granada, the last Moorish city in Spain, fell, and Columbus was granted a second audience at the Spanish court. Wanting to challenge Portuguese domination of the seas, King Ferdinand and Queen Isabella agreed to supply Columbus the ships he required.

On August 3, 1492, Columbus sailed from the Spanish port of Palos with three ships, the *Santa Maria*, the *Pinta* and the *Niña*. Three days later, the *Pinta* lost its rudder and Columbus was forced to stop at the Canary Islands, off the northwest coast of Africa. There, the men fitted a new rudder on the *Pinta*, and the sails on the *Niña* were modified to improve her speed. After a month of delay, the expedition set sail once more on September 9.

With the wind at his back the whole distance, Columbus had quick sailing. At a point where he believed he had sailed approximately 1,000 leagues across the Atlantic Ocean, he sighted land, an event that in his mind must have vindicated his calculation of the distance to India. He came ashore not in the Indies but on one of the Bahama Islands. However, thinking he had reached the Indies, he called the natives "Indians," a misnomer that has remained to this day.

Thereafter, Spanish expeditions successfully established bases, at first on islands in the Caribbean Sea, and using these as stepping-stones, onto the mainland.

LEFT: Columbus before Ferdinand and Isabella; *RIGHT:* The Landing of Columbus; *photogravures, Private Collection*

LEFT: Columbus' *Santa Maria, photogravure*; RIGHT: The Fleet of Columbus Approaching the New World, *engraving; Private Collection*

These military expeditions were driven by two motives: the prospect of finding new sources of wealth, and at the same time, the belief that they were pursuing a sacred duty to systematically convert the native inhabitants to Christianity.

Vasco Núñez de Balboa (1475?–1519) came to the New World in 1501 as part of an expedition to Venezuela. He explored the Caribbean Sea and established himself on a plantation on the island of Hispaniola (now Haiti and the Dominican Republic). When his plantation failed, he went to Panama to escape his creditors. In 1513, following native reports of a great sea to the west, Balboa led an expedition across the isthmus. After nearly a month of difficult travel through hot, fever-infested jungle, Balboa reached the shore of the Pacific Ocean, which he named "Mar del Sur" (South Sea).

Juan Ponce de León (1460–1521) came to the New World in search of the Fountain of Youth, a fabled spring whose water was believed to restore youth. On Easter Sunday 1513, he landed on the east coast of Florida, so named for "Pascua Florida," or the Flowery Feast, the Spanish name for Easter Sunday. He came ashore at what is now St. Augustine but established no permanent presence there. He continued his search, sailing into the Gulf of Mexico, and on his return trip to Florida, was wounded during an Indian attack and died in Cuba in 1521.

In 1565, the settlement of St. Augustine was established by Pedro Menéndez de Avilés (1519–1574). It is the oldest continuously occupied European city in North America.

RIGHT:
Vasco Núñez de Balboa Takes Possession of
the Mar del Sur *(Pacific Ocean), from* Dogs of
the Conquest, *University of Oklahoma Press,*
1983, photo courtesy of Sherman Library
and Gardens, Corona del Mar, CA;
BELOW:
Thomas Moran, Ponce de León in Florida,
The Cummer Museum of Art & Gardens,
Jacksonville, FL

Frank Cuprien, The Dream Ship,
oil on canvas, 20 x 30 in., Private Collection,
courtesy of The Irvine Museum

First Cavalry Charge Headed by Cortez, *from Harper's Monthly,* December 1855, Sherman *Library and Gardens, Corona del Mar, CA*

Cabeza de Vaca and His Companions,
1880, engraving, Private Collection

HERNANDO CORTEZ AND THE CONQUEST OF MEXICO

The first significant Spanish entry in the North American mainland occurred on February 10, 1519, when Hernando Cortez set out to conquer the Aztec Empire in what is now Mexico. His small army was made up of about 600 soldiers, of whom 32 were crossbowmen. He also brought along 14 cannons and 16 horses. Cortez's weapons—steel swords, armor, cannons and crossbows—were far more effective than any arms the Aztecs had, but the warhorse was perhaps Cortez's most valuable military asset, as it had never before been seen by native peoples, and the sight of a charging horseman completely terrified large numbers of opposing troops. In the end, Cortez was consistently able to defeat a significantly larger force of arms by taking advantage of his weapons of war and arranging a series of alliances with other native states that were eager to see the Aztecs defeated.

A few years after the conquest of Mexico, Spain began to reach out toward the periphery of its new empire. In 1528, a force of about 300 men, led by Fánfilo de Narváez, landed on the coast of present-day Louisiana. Modeling his expedition on Cortez's, Narváez expected to find a civilization much like the Aztecs, with enormous amounts of gold. As his troops moved inland, they looted and destroyed a series of Indian villages, none of which contained any gold.

In due time, the Indians fought back. Narváez was attacked and his army all but completely destroyed. The few survivors were forced to retreat to the sea, near present-day Galveston, Texas. There, the desperate men built crude rafts and sailed toward Mexico. They were caught in a storm and shipwrecked, and a few unfortunate survivors were captured by Indians. Eventually, all the Spaniards were killed or died of disease except four: Álvar Núñez Cabeza de Vaca, two other members of the crew and a black slave named Estabán. After two years of captivity, the four men escaped and spent the next six years making their way through Texas and northern Mexico ending up, in 1536, entirely across the continent at the Pacific coast near Culiacán, in the state of Sinaloa. Upon his return, Cabeza de Vaca was taken to Mexico City, where he reported to Cortez a fantastic story he had heard of the existence of a great civilization in the American Southwest, with seven cities of gold called "Cíbola."

Having completed the conquest of Mexico, Cortez was commissioned by the king of Spain to find the Strait of Anián, the mythical "Northwest Passage" that would supposedly greatly shorten the voyage to China and the Indies. Cortez was convinced that this passage could be found to the north of Mexico's Pacific coast. Not content with all the fame, power and riches he had amassed in the conquest of Mexico, he was certain that a similarly rich empire lay hidden, just waiting to be conquered.

Indeed, just such a wealthy kingdom had been found by another bold adventurer, Francisco Pizarro (1476–1541), who conquered the Empire of the Incas in Peru in 1532. As Cortez listened to the report by Cabeza de Vaca, he was enthralled, as it confirmed his belief in the existence of yet another rich empire.

From their earliest voyages along the Pacific coast, Spanish explorers believed Baja California to be the southern tip of a large island, an island they called "California," after a mythical land described in a novel written in 1510 by Garcí Ordoñez de Montalvo. This story, *Las Sergas de Esplandian* (The Exploits of Esplandian), gained wide popularity, especially among soldiers and sailors who were seduced by the adventure and romance in the story. One of the most interesting characters in Montalvo's book was a beautiful black Amazon queen named Calafía, who ruled a kingdom "on the right-hand side of the Indies…an island named California, which was very close to the earthly Paradise." According to the book, Calafía and her female warriors were experts with the long bow. Furthermore, they wore armor of gold and jewels, as her kingdom was immensely wealthy, especially with pearls. It is not surprising that the legend of Calafía and her enormous wealth stirred the imagination of many adventurers who sailed for the New World.

With little or no accurate information regarding the Pacific coast of North America, people had no reason to doubt the existence of Queen Calafía. As Baja California, a place reputed to be rich with pearls, appeared to be the southern tip of a large island, and on their maps it was on the right-hand side of the Indies, therefore, those early explorers believed, they had found "California." As a place name, "California" appears in documents as early as 1542, and although it was in general use by explorers and navigators for many years, it was not officially adopted until the early part of the 1600s.

In 1532, Cortez sent two small ships on an ill-fated expedition in the Gulf of California. In addition to the search for the Strait of Anián, he was acting on reports of great quantities of beautiful pink pearls along the coast in Baja California. However, when the expedition landed near present-day La Paz, the Spaniards were attacked and massacred by the natives.

The following year, Cortez sent two more ships, which landed on the southern tip of Baja California. Thinking it to be the island of Queen Calafía, they too

La Granbatallaq tuboel Alm.te con el Rey Guarionex. y cienmil yndios enla Vega Real

Battle between Spanish and Native Americans, *from* Dogs of the Conquest, *University of Oklahoma Press, 1983, photo courtesy of Sherman Library and Gardens, Corona del Mar, CA*

were attacked, not by Amazon women but by hostile Indians, who killed 20 of the men. The few Spaniards who made it back to Cortez nevertheless reported having seen great quantities of precious pearls.

Finally, Cortez went to see for himself. In 1535, he led an expedition to the southern tip of Baja California and founded a settlement near the present-day city of La Paz. On the beaches, Cortez found mounds of discarded oyster shells. The natives cooked the oysters whole, ate the meat and discarded the shells. Usually, the cooking process marred any pearls that may have been inside, but occasionally some survived unblemished. It was these pearls that were traded among the Indians and eventually came to the attention of the Spanish.

Cortez was able to locate several oyster beds offshore in about 30 feet of water. However, the suspicious and hostile natives were unwilling to dive for the Spanish, so Cortez had to gather what pearls he could from the discarded shells and whatever oysters washed up on shore. In the end, the pearl fishery didn't produce enough to justify the expense of constantly re-supplying the settlement, and as the settlers could not grow food on the arid land, the colony was abandoned.

Pueblo of Moqui, *engraving, Private Collection*

Having given up on finding pearls, Cortez nevertheless persisted in his search for the long-sought Strait of Anián. In 1539, he sent Francisco de Ulloa with three small boats to explore the eastern coast of Baja California in an effort to find Anián. From Acapulco, the principal Spanish port on the west coast of Mexico, Ulloa sailed north in the Vermilion Sea (now called the Sea of Cortez, or the Gulf of California) and followed the eastern coast all the way to the Colorado River, where the coast turned south again to form the western side of the sea. They had come all the way along the coast to La Paz and found no northern outlet to the ocean.

Ulloa had proved that California was not an island after all, but because his voyage was considered a failure—as he did not fulfill his mission to find the Strait of Anián—his findings were not widely circulated and only Spanish maps were updated to show California as a peninsula. However, most European maps merely copied existing maps, and as late as 1784, most maps perpetuated the misinformation of the "island" of California.

Envious of Cortez, who claimed the right to continue his conquests in areas north of Mexico, Don Antonio de Mendoza, the Viceroy of New Spain (Mexico), took up the search for Cíbola, the fabled cities of gold that Cabeza de Vaca had reported. To that end, he sent Marcos de Niza, a Franciscan priest, to investigate Cabeza de Vaca's tales. Accompanied by Estabán, the black slave who had been with Cabeza de Vaca, Niza crossed Sonora and Arizona and went near the Moqui Pueblos of New Mexico before being attacked by Indians. Estabán was killed and Niza retreated back to Mexico, where either in an outright lie or under the influence of a wild imagination, he confirmed the existence of large, wealthy cities.

Niza's report caused great excitement in Mexico. In response, Mendoza authorized two expeditions: in 1540, he sent Francisco Vásquez de Coronado by land to find Cíbola, and when that effort failed, he sent Juan Rodríguez Cabrillo by sea in 1542 to find the Strait of Anián.

Map of North America Showing California as an Island, *Paris, 1699, Sherman Library and Gardens, Corona del Mar, CA*

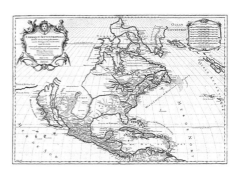

James Swinnerton,
Sunset in Monument Valley, *oil on canvas,*
30 x 40 in., The Irvine Museum

Angered that Mendoza had stripped him of his authority to explore the American Southwest, Cortez returned to Spain in 1540 to plead his case. There, he was ignored by court officials, who were envious of his glory. Cortez never returned to the New World and died in 1547, without vindication.

Early in 1540, Coronado led his army into the Southwest, looking for Cíbola. His expedition included the adventurous cleric Niza, who went along as a guide and to tend to the Indians' souls. In April, they reached the first of the "fabled cities." Cíbola turned out to be one of the Zuni Pueblos in New Mexico, which to the Indians of the poorer desert tribes appeared to be fabulously wealthy. Undaunted, Coronado sent out scouting parties to the other pueblos. One party went to the Colorado River and followed it north until they encountered the Grand Canyon. Other parties returned with unfavorable reports, and in the end, no gold was found.

Gunnar Widforss, Grand Canyon, *watercolor,*
23 x 20 in., Private Collection,
courtesy of William A. Karges Fine Art,
Los Angeles and Carmel

Learning of an even greater city called "La Gran Quivira," which lay to the east on the vast plains beyond the mountains, Coronado crossed into what is now the High Plains of the Texas Panhandle and into Oklahoma. In his journal, Coronado described vast herds of bison and noted that the High Plains were *"bare of landmarks, as if [they] were surrounded by the sea. Here the guides lost their bearings because there is nowhere a stone, hill, tree, bush, or anything of the sort."* To keep from getting lost in this bleak land, all bearings were taken by compass, and Coronado detailed one of his men to count and write down the number of footsteps taken every day.

The mythical Quivira was eventually found to be simply a settlement of a few Indian dwellings, with no gold whatsoever. After nearly two years of arduous searching, Coronado reached present-day Kansas before finally turning back to Mexico empty-handed.

JUAN RODRÍGUEZ CABRILLO

Juan Rodríguez Cabrillo, a Portuguese adventurer, was actually named João Rodrígues. The name "Cabrillo" in Spanish, or "Cabrilho" in Portuguese, has come down in history as his last name, but it probably indicated the town of his birth, perhaps Cabril.

He had considerable experience in the New World, having come in 1520 to serve in the army of Fánfilo de Narváez. Soon after they landed in Veracruz, Narváez and his troops were directed by the Governor of Cuba to find and punish Cortez, who had violated orders by taking command of the expedition and advancing into Mexico without waiting for the governor. Forewarned of Narváez's arrival, Cortez halted his march into Mexico and turned back to deal with him. In a surprise attack, Cortez routed Narváez, who then fled back to Veracruz. As a gesture of amnesty, Cortez, who needed as many soldiers as he could get, offered Narváez's men a chance to join his expedition. The accounts of Cortez's successful campaign were sufficient to entice many, including Cabrillo, to switch sides.

In the battles that followed, Cabrillo displayed bravery and leadership and was continually promoted by Cortez. On August 13, 1521, Cabrillo was at the head of his battalion when the city of Tenochtitlán (present-day Mexico City) fell, marking the end of the Aztec Empire.

With two other veteran officers of the Mexican campaign, Pedro de Alvarado and Francisco de Orozco, Cabrillo continued south and participated in the Conquest of Guatemala. After the war, he was rewarded with vast estates in Guatemala and became very wealthy through gold mining. He married and settled into a comfortable life as a provincial governor.

The lure of adventure, however, would soon find him and lead him to his destiny. In 1536, Cabrillo agreed to join Alvarado in an expedition to explore the

Russell A. Ruiz, Artist's Conception: Indian Village, *1790, watercolor, 9 x 11¾ in., Santa Barbara Historical Society*

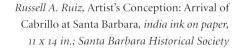

Russell A. Ruiz, Artist's Conception: Arrival of Cabrillo at Santa Barbara, *india ink on paper, 11 x 14 in.; Santa Barbara Historical Society*

Pacific Ocean and began to build a fleet of ships for the venture. The fleet of 13 ships was completed, and on Christmas Day 1540, Cabrillo and the fleet arrived at the port of Navidad (in the Mexican state of Colima, about 20 miles north of present-day Manzanillo). However, the following year, before the Pacific campaign got underway, Alvarado was killed fighting an Indian revolt in Jalisco, in western Mexico (Guadalajara is the capital of Jalisco). Mendoza took possession of the fleet, leaving Cabrillo in command as admiral.

Viceroy Mendoza liked Cabrillo, considering him to be "very skilled in matters of the sea." With the promise of great rewards, Cabrillo accepted an assignment from Mendoza to explore the coast of California in search of the Strait of Anián.

On June 27, 1542, Cabrillo and his pilot, Bartolomé Ferrelo (or Ferrer), left the Mexican port of Navidad with two of the ships he had constructed, the *San Salvador* and the *Victoria*. The *San Salvador*, Cabrillo's flagship, was most likely a coastal galleon, a smaller version of the large, oceangoing galleons so commonly associated with images of Spanish naval power. It was about 100 feet long, having one mast with square rigging and three masts with lateen, or triangular, sails, one in front of the large square sail and two more behind. The stern, or back of the ship, had a high sterncastle; as captain, Cabrillo's quarters would have been there. The *Victoria* was a much smaller vessel and had no deck.

On September 27, 1542, after three months at sea and many of his crew starving or dying of scurvy, Cabrillo became the discoverer of California when he reached, according to his journal, *"a port, closed and very good, which [we] named San Miguel"* (now called San Diego Bay). The next day, Cabrillo landed and became the first European to set foot in California.

Cabrillo's journal continues, *"Having cast anchor in [the bay we] went ashore where there were people. Three of them waited, but the rest fled. To these three [we] gave some presents and they said by signs [sign language] that in the interior, men like the Spaniards had passed…that they were bearded and clothed and armed like [us]…[with] crossbows and swords…and they [the Indians] ran around as if they were on horseback."* The accounts and descriptions given by the San Diego natives (of the Kumeyaay, or Diegueño, group) were clearly of the Coronado Expedition, which two years earlier had ventured to the Colorado River. The Yuma and Mojave Indians that Coronado encountered were closely related to the Kumeyaay, being in the same language group.

Cabrillo charted the California coast northward as far as Cape Mendocino, which he named after his patron, Viceroy Mendoza. He came upon numerous Indian villages in his travels along the coast. Near present-day Santa Barbara, he encountered a group of Chumash Indians, noting, *"They were dressed in skins, and wore their hair very long and tied up with long strings interwoven with the hair, there being attached to the strings many trinkets of flint, bone and wood."* Friendly and open to strangers, the Chumash came to greet the ships in *tomols*, or *ti'ats*, ocean-worthy, wood-plank canoes, ranging from 10 to 30 feet long. In his log,

Edward Borein, Conquistadores Entering California, *etching, 9⅞ x 11¹³⁄₁₆ in., Private Collection*

Duncan Gleason, The *San Carlos* Entering the Golden Gate, *Courtesy of the Estate of the Artist*

Cabrillo wrote of seeing many *"fine canoes each holding twelve or thirteen Indians…always there were many canoes because all the coast is heavily inhabited, and there came many Indians to the ships."* Of the many villages he encountered, he found no evidence of great wealth.

In October, on the return trip, he explored an island that he named after his flagship, "San Salvador" (the island is now called Santa Catalina). As he looked across a large bay, he could see columns of smoke from numerous Indian campfires, floating motionless in thin spirals in the air. This unique phenomenon, caused by the natural inversion layer, led him to call it the Bay of Smokes (now called Santa Monica Bay).

Continuing his exploration of the Channel Islands, Cabrillo landed on an island he named "La Posesión" (now called San Miguel Island), where he was seriously hurt in a fall. The wound became infected, and three months later, as he lay dying, he transferred command of the expedition to Ferrelo, with instructions to continue the survey. Cabrillo died on January 3, 1543. His crew buried him on San Miguel and renamed the island "La Isla de Juan Rodríguez."

With Ferrelo now in command, the expedition turned north once again, charting the coast above Cape Mendocino. It went as far as what is now Oregon, in March 1543, before turning back toward Mexico.

Arthur E. Beaumont, Adventure, *1931, etching, 8⅞ x 7⅜ in., Private Collection*

In the end, all who were sent to explore California's coast found nothing resembling the Aztec or Incan Empires, and after Coronado and Cabrillo, no further efforts were made to seek Calafía, Cíbola or Anián. In fact, no attempts were made to settle or colonize the region for 200 years. Spain was finding greater wealth in the conquest of South America, and all further attempts to colonize North America were scaled down.

THE MANILA GALLEONS

Following Cabrillo, the only Spanish activity in California was the traffic of the Manila Galleons, engaged in the highly lucrative China Trade. The galleon was the main Spanish war vessel, a large, bulky craft that was loaded with row upon row of cannons. For the China Trade, special galleons were built as merchant ships, with far fewer guns, leaving more space devoted to cargo.

Spanish silver coins, 8 reales (Charles III); Mexico City Mint, 1788, obverse (left), reverse (center); Mexico City Mint, 1777, with Oriental chop marks (right)

For hundreds of years prior to the Spanish, large oceangoing Chinese boats, called junks, brought silks, ivory and porcelain to the Philippine Islands to trade for perfume, spices, amber and sandalwood. When Spain colonized the Philippines in 1565, it regulated the China Trade and greatly enriched the royal treasury by taxing the merchants who ran the trade. At the time, the Philippine Islands were administratively a part of Mexico, so this commerce came under the rule of the Viceroy of Mexico.

At first, the Manila merchants ran as many as four large, oceangoing Spanish galleons a year in the round-trip voyage between Manila and Mexico. From the Philippines, Chinese goods were sent to Acapulco, on the west coast of Mexico, where they would be off-loaded. There, merchants would divide the goods. A small part of the cargo would be sold in Mexico, to wealthy officials and ranchers from various parts of the New World. The profits from just the sales in Mexico were often enough to pay for the entire shipment. The rest of the cargo would be carried by wagons across Mexico to Veracruz, the principal port on the east coast, and sent to Spain, where it would be sold at tremendous profit throughout Europe.

On the return trip to Manila, the ships would be loaded with cocoa, produced in Mexico, and silver, in the form of bullion and coins from the mines of Mexico, Bolivia and Chile, as silver was the only medium of exchange the Chinese would accept as payment. The basic large Spanish silver coin was the ocho reales (eight reales, about the size and weight of a silver dollar) that was made in the mints of Mexico City, Mexico, and San Luis Potosí, Bolivia. The Spanish eight reales, or "piece of eight," was accepted all over the world and served as legal tender in the United States until the middle of the 19th century. The Manila-bound galleons would also carry priests to the Orient, where they were needed for the growing number of churches and missions there.

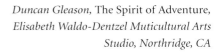

Duncan Gleason, The Spirit of Adventure, Elisabeth Waldo-Dentzel Muticultural Arts Studio, Northridge, CA

At first, the Spanish government placed no restrictions on the Manila Trade. It was a risky, dangerous voyage, and those willing to take the chance were rewarded with substantial profits. Later, between 1587 and 1593, Spain decided to bring order to this wild bonanza. The number of trips made by Manila Galleons was reduced to two, then to only one per year, to keep from flooding the European market with Chinese goods and to minimize the drain of Spanish silver to China. To counter this restriction, merchants began to build larger and larger ships. By the late 1590s, each slow and unwieldy galleon carried nearly 1,000 tons of valuable merchandise. It was a lucrative trade that lasted more than 250 years, as the last Manila Galleon sailed in 1815.

The voyage from Mexico to Manila was relatively quick. The galleons caught the northeast trade winds south of Acapulco, which pushed them across the Pacific Ocean to the Philippines in a trip lasting 60 to 90 days.

The return trip, however, was much longer and more difficult, often up to nine months of misery, starvation and scurvy. First, the ships had to weave their way through the myriad of islands that make up the Philippines group to reach the open sea. This part alone could take up to one month. Then they would sail hundreds of miles north along the eastern coast of Asia to catch the Japanese Current, which took them even farther north to the west winds, which carried them across the Pacific, landing somewhere near the northern limits of Spanish California at about the Oregon border. The final part of the journey was the quickest, to sail south with the prevailing winds along the California coast to Mexico.

By the time the galleons reached California, water supplies were low and stagnant, and any fresh food on board had long run out, leaving only dry, coarse food to eat. Furthermore, perhaps half the crew or more would be sick or dead from scurvy, a dreaded disease caused by vitamin-C deficiency. One of the more horrendous effects of scurvy was the loss of teeth and the occurrence of raw, painful

Alson S. Clark, Spanish Galleon,
oil on canvas, 38 x 51 in., Bluebird Gallery,
Laguna Beach, CA

sores in the mouth. These, in turn, caused victims to starve to death because they could not eat the hard, dry food that remained toward the end of the voyage. At their first opportunity after crossing the Pacific Ocean, the Manila Galleons would stop in California for fresh water, meat and whatever fruits they could obtain.

SIR FRANCIS DRAKE IN CALIFORNIA

Along the California coast, the presence of slow, richly laden Spanish ships, manned by a nearly defenseless, sick crew, was an irresistible target for Spain's enemies, not the least of which was Sir Francis Drake (1543?–1596), the English privateer. In all, Drake made three voyages to the New World. On his first trip, in 1572, he explored the Caribbean, landed on the Atlantic side of Panama and crossed the isthmus to the Pacific Ocean. He thus became the first Englishman to see the Pacific Ocean. He plundered several Spanish settlements in the Caribbean, where on one raid he narrowly escaped capture. His exploits made him rich, and his victories earned him respect, even from the Spanish, who, in grudging tribute to his exploits, called him by the fearsome nickname of "El Draque" (The Dragon).

On his second voyage, from 1577 to 1580, Drake was sponsored in part by a company of English merchants who hoped to increase their profits by having him find the fabled Northwest Passage. With the secret support of Queen Elizabeth I, who wished to break the Spanish monopoly on Pacific trade, Drake, a severe taskmaster who demanded unquestioned discipline from his men, set off with five ships to reach the Pacific Ocean. However, when the fleet reached the southern tip of South America and attempted to enter the perilous Straits of Magellan, only the *Golden Hind* made it to the Pacific side. The others either sank in the rough waters or turned back to the Atlantic.

While in the Pacific, he raided coastal settlements in Chile and Peru and captured several Spanish vessels carrying vast amounts of treasure. With his little ship, the *Golden Hind*, loaded with treasure, and fearing that the Spanish fleet would be waiting for him on his return to the Atlantic Ocean, Drake decided to continue west and reach England by traveling around the globe, as Ferdinand Magellan had done 50 years earlier. He headed the *Golden Hind* north along the Pacific coast, perhaps looking for the Northwest Passage that would safely get him back to England.

From June 17 to July 23, 1579, Drake anchored the *Golden Hind* probably in what is now called Drake's Bay, several miles north of San Francisco. Drake landed and claimed the territory for England. As the chalky white cliffs that surround the bay reminded him of Dover, he named the region "New Albion."

While Drake beached his ship and attended to much-needed repairs, his crew went out and explored the countryside. At first, they expressed great disappointment at the dry, dirt-brown appearance of the summertime landscape. But once they ventured inland, the country became green and lush and the men found it very pleasing.

Sir Francis Drake, *engraving, from* The Life and Death of Sir Francis Drake, *1671, The Bancroft Library, University of California, Berkeley*

The coast was teeming with large numbers of sea otters, whose fur brought a good price in Europe, but the men paid little attention to them. They noted, however, the easy abundance of deer and other game, and particularly the very large colonies of "connies," or gophers and ground squirrels, which abounded everywhere they went.

Drake and his men also encountered a village of Coast Miwok Indians, who at first believed the Europeans to be spirits returning from the land of the dead. In his diary, Drake observed that *"the men, for the most part, go naked, and the women take a kindle [cluster] of bulrushes, and combing it after the manner of hemp, make themselves thereof a loose garment, which being tied about their middles, hangs down about the hips, and so affords them a covering of that, which nature teaches should be hidden. About their shoulders, they wear also the skin of a deer with the hair upon it."*

While in northern California, Drake is said to have left a brass plaque on shore as proof of his landing. In 1934, such a brass plaque was found near Drake's Bay bearing a crudely inscribed text claiming New Albion for England. Long a point of contention over its authenticity, the plaque was finally proven to be a forgery in 1977, when an analysis of the metal showed it to be a modern alloy.

Though no attempts were made by England to settle and colonize northern California, the name New Albion nevertheless remained on British and non-Spanish maps for another 200 years, and English claims to northern California were not given up until the Oregon Treaty between the United States and Great Britain in 1846.

In the fierce competition between Spain and England for mastery of the seas, Drake's exploits in the Pacific proved greatly embarrassing to Spain. In reward for his deeds, Queen Elizabeth named him Vice Admiral of the British navy. In 1588, he led them to a critical victory against the Great Armada, a fleet of Spanish ships sent to invade England. Drake died on his third voyage to the New World, off Panama, in 1596.

Sir Francis Drake in California, Shearman Collection, History Collections, Los Angeles County Museum of Natural History

Thomas Hill, San Diego Bay from Point Loma, *1907, oil on canvas, Maxwell Galleries, San Francisco*

For all his victories and captured vessels, Drake never encountered one of those rich treasure ships from Manila. However, in 1587, a Manila Galleon was captured by the English captain Thomas Cavendish off Baja California. The galleon *Santa Ana* was returning from the Philippines when she was taken by Cavendish as she rounded the point of Cabo San Lucas, the southern tip of Baja California.

Sebastián Vizcaíno

By one of those unique bits of historical coincidence, the cargo of the *Santa Ana* belonged to Sebastián Vizcaíno (1550?–1615), who was on board at the time of its capture. Vizcaíno was a Spanish Basque soldier and adventurer who had fought for Spain in Flanders, a medieval European country that was an important part of the Spanish Empire.

By 1583, Vizcaíno was in the New World, looking for opportunities to enlarge his wealth. A man of action and enterprise, Vizcaíno turned to the Manila Trade and made a fortune as a merchant. By 1587, most of Vizcaíno's fortune was in the form of a large cargo of valuable goods bound for Mexico on the *Santa Ana*.

Cavendish stopped the galleon with a few well-aimed cannon shots. He then set the crew and passengers ashore with only a small store of supplies and transferred all the merchandise and treasure from the *Santa Ana* to his own ship, and before leaving, set the *Santa Ana* on fire. The burning hulk drifted ashore, and Vizcaíno organized a party to board the ship and put out the fire. With just a few quick repairs, Vizcaíno and his party were able to sail across the Gulf of California to the mainland, where they were rescued. For his brilliant leadership and resourcefulness, Vizcaíno received a commendation from the Viceroy of New Spain.

Paul Dougherty, Rocks and Surf, *oil on canvas, 36 x 48 in., Private Collection, courtesy of The Irvine Museum*

Looking to recoup his fortune, Vizcaíno made a second voyage to Manila in 1590, this time successfully returning to Mexico. On his initial investment of 200 gold ducats, Vizcaíno made a profit of 2,500 ducats.

Always interested in opportunities to enrich himself, Vizcaíno heard of places in Baja California that yielded beautiful pink pearls. He formed a company and applied for a permit from the Viceroy of New Spain to start a colony to pursue a pearl-fishing venture. The license was granted, and in March 1596, Vizcaíno set out from Acapulco with three ships for Baja California. In the middle of August, he landed at a bay where he found peaceful Indians who welcomed him and his men. Vizcaíno named the bay "La Paz" (Peace) and founded his settlement there. However, when they ventured north along the coast in search of pearls, they were attacked by Indians, and several of his men were killed. Forced to return to La Paz, he found the colony nearly out of food. In October, he abandoned the site and returned to Acapulco.

Meanwhile, news of the taking of the *Santa Ana* by Cavendish had reached Europe. Threats by other raiders, especially the Dutch, to find and capture these special ships caused great consternation in Spain and Mexico. To protect her treasure ships, Spain decided to establish a safe harbor in California where the Manila Galleons could stop and re-supply without threat of attack.

In 1599, Vizcaíno applied for a second permit to return to Baja California. The disastrous results of his first attempt at starting a colony caused his request to be delayed for more than two years. Finally, in 1602, the Viceroy of New Spain, Don Gaspár de Zúñiga y Acevedo, Count of Monte Rey, offered Vizcaíno a chance to return to sea. He granted a license, but only for a thorough survey of the California coast from Cabo San Lucas north to Cape Mendocino. Vizcaíno was not to enter the Gulf of California, on penalty of death. Furthermore, he was to make no settlements, and was to take great care to avoid conflict with the Indians. The Viceroy made it clear that this voyage was for exploration of the coast of California with the purpose of finding a safe harbor for the Manila Galleons.

Vizcaíno accepted, and on May 5, 1602, he and a party of 200 men set out from the Mexican port of Navidad with three ships, the *San Diego*, the *Santo Tomás* and the *Tres Reyes*. On November 10, after six months of difficult sailing, his expedition arrived at San Miguel Bay, discovered by Cabrillo in 1542. Vizcaíno renamed it San Diego Bay, both after his flagship and after the feast of San Diego de Alcalá (November 12).

While in San Diego Bay, Vizcaíno's men took the opportunity to relax and recover from the rigors of the voyage. The climate was mild and the land productive. Furthermore, Vizcaíno wrote in his journal that they found *"a great variety of fish, as oysters, mussels, lobsters, soles, etc. and in some of the rocks up the country were found geese, ducks, and quails; rabbits and hare were also here in great numbers."*

Of the local Indians, Vizcaíno noted, *"[They] came peaceably and took us to their rancherías [villages] where they were gathering their crops…They had pots in which they cooked their food, and the women were dressed in skins of animals."* Before leaving the villages, gifts were exchanged between the Spanish and the Indians.

As he sailed north, Vizcaíno charted and renamed many of the places previously found by Cabrillo, including San Clemente and Santa Catalina islands, the Santa Barbara channel and Carmel. Early in December, his ships sighted Point Conception, north of Santa Barbara, named after the Feast of the Immaculate Conception (December 8). On December 16, 1602, Vizcaíno entered a harbor that he named Monterey, after his patron the Viceroy, Count of Monte Rey. On the shore of the bay, the Carmelite friars who accompanied Vizcaíno said mass *"in the shadow of a large oak tree, some of whose branches reached the water."* Perhaps in his haste to meet his obligation and return to pearl fishing, Vizcaíno recorded the harbor of Monterey in these glowing terms: *"We found ourselves to be in the best port that could be desired, for besides being sheltered from all winds, it has many pines for masts and yards, and live oaks and white oaks, and [fresh] water in great quantity, all near the shore."* Thus, he recommended it as an ideal anchorage for the Manila Galleons.

By the time the expedition reached Monterey, 16 men had died of scurvy and a large number were ill from the disease. Vizcaíno was forced to send the *Santo Tomás* back to Navidad with the sick men. Upon their return to Navidad, 25 had died and only nine remained alive.

Meanwhile, Vizcaíno, on the *San Diego*, continued north toward Cape Mendocino, but he went no farther. He was forced to turn back to Baja California as only six of his men were fit enough to man the ship. The third vessel, the *Tres Reyes*, had gotten separated in a storm. It continued north hoping to rejoin Vizcaíno, and went possibly as far as the Oregon border before turning back to Baja California. When it finally returned to Navidad, the crew of the *Tres Reyes* consisted of only five men.

Although Cabrillo had previously mapped and given names to many of the same places, Vizcaíno's voyage received great public interest when it was published in 1606, and the place names he ascribed became permanent notations on Spanish maps.

In 1612, Vizcaíno made one more voyage of discovery, looking for two mythical islands called Rica de Oro (Rich in Gold) and Rica de Plata (Rich in Silver), said to be located near the coast of Japan. Very little is known of this trip. Vizcaíno probably died off the coast of Mexico in 1629, the result of a battle with a Dutch fleet.

Even though Vizcaíno's voyage was well received and his discovery of a "superb" harbor at Monterey was just what the authorities wanted to know, no more ships were sent north to California, and no attempts were made to build a defensible port there for the safety of the Manila Galleons. The threat of pirates and privateers, particularly the *Pichilingues*, or Dutch pirates, who would wait in ambush along the California coast, was sufficient to drive all Manila Galleons away. As soon as these treasure ships sighted any indication of the coast, they immediately turned south. They would rather face the deadly scourge of scurvy than risk their precious cargo in search of fresh food and water.

Moreover, the voyages of exploration of the previous century had convinced the Spanish that there was absolutely no treasure to be found in the entire region of California except for the pearls that came from the coast along the Gulf of California. As such, Baja California became the focus of all Spanish activity in the 1600s, to the exclusion of all other parts of the province.

By the 1680s, Spanish adventurers had exhausted all attempts to find pearls, and plans to exploit Baja California were abandoned, as the few pearls that were gathered hardly paid for the expense of the expeditions. The lasting legacy of the treasure hunters was a leery and hostile population that considered all Spanish visitors to be slavers and murderers. The wrath and antagonism visited upon the Indians of the Baja California peninsula in the 1600s would later be reaped by the Jesuit missionaries of the 1700s. ❧

Guy Rose, Point Lobos, *c. 1918,*
oil on canvas, 24 x 29 in., Private Collection,
courtesy of The Irvine Museum

John Frost, The Flowering Desert, *1922,*
oil on canvas, 27 x 32 in., Private Collection,
courtesy of The Irvine Museum

CHAPTER 4

FATHER KINO AND THE JESUIT MISSIONS

*A*ll through the 1600s, Spain made repeated attempts to start colonies in Baja California. Unfortunately, the main incentive for exploration of Baja California was pearl fishing, and all attempts at founding settlements at that time were merely fronts for fortune hunting. In the latter part of the century, Spain made a decided effort to establish legitimate colonies by appointing Isidro Atondo y Antillón, a soldier and navigator, to start a permanent settlement. In 1683, Atondo set out with three ships, 100 men and three Jesuit priests. One of those Jesuits was Father Kino.

The Society of Jesus, commonly called the Jesuits or the "Black Robes," was the largest all-male order in the Roman Catholic Church. It was founded by Saint Ignatius of Loyola in Paris, France in 1534. A former army officer, Loyola organized the Society of Jesus along military lines, requiring of his followers pledges of chastity, poverty and above all, obedience. The most important of the founding members was Francis Xavier, who would himself later be made a saint. The Society of Jesus was officially approved by Pope Paul III in 1540.

Almost from the first, the Jesuits became an important force in education and missionary work. They founded colleges throughout Europe and sent missionaries to all parts of the world, particularly the Orient and the New World. As such, they were one of the strongest tools against the rising tide of Protestantism in Europe. By the mid-1700s, there were almost 23,000 Jesuits working in missions throughout the world.

Father Eusebio Francisco Kino (1645–1711) was an Italian Jesuit, educated in Germany. A brilliant mathematician who had been trained in mapmaking, he had come to Mexico City as the Royal Cosmographer. His new assignment was to accompany Atondo and start a series of missions in Baja California.

When the Atondo expedition reached La Paz, on the Gulf of California in Baja California, in 1683, they found the natives to be hostile, as they associated all Europeans with the mistreatment they had received at the hands of the pearl hunters of the previous century. It took a long time and many small gifts before they would once again accept the presence of Spanish colonists. In spite of the success with the natives, by July the critical lack of water in the region proved too big an obstacle, and Atondo reluctantly abandoned his settlement in La Paz.

In October, Atondo tried again, this time in San Bruno, about 50 miles north of La Paz. There, the Indians were less hostile and Father Kino was readily able to start a mission. At first, the mission thrived and Kino was able to explore the area, walking across to the Pacific Ocean side. To their dismay, Atondo and Kino

Raymond Dabb Yelland, Sea of Cortez, *1878,*
oil on canvas, 28 x 48 ¼ in., Garzoli Gallery, San Rafael, CA

found this region to be arid and barren as well, and the colony continued only because of massive aid from outside. In time, San Bruno was also abandoned, as it never reached a basic level of self-sufficiency.

After the failures in Baja California, Kino was sent to Pimería Alta (Upper Pima Land), a Spanish province in Northern Mexico that included the northern portion of the state of Sonora and the southern part of present-day Arizona. Kino founded the first Jesuit mission in Sonora in 1687.

From 1692 to 1701, Kino explored the Southwest and founded missions in New Mexico and Arizona. The beautiful Mission San Javier del Bac, near Tucson, was established in 1700; the following year, Kino crossed the Colorado River to work with Indians of the delta. Although there were no serious attempts at establishing a permanent presence there, Kino wrote reports and produced maps of the region. It was Father Kino's precise charts that finally proved conclusively that Baja California was not an island, but in fact, a peninsula.

Some of these first missions in Pimería Alta were barely struggling to survive and rarely achieved a large number of Indian converts. Many were situated in desert-like regions with poor agricultural acreage. As such, they were continually dependent on outside aid and could not support a large number of residents. With little food for the converts, the more isolated missions were subject to frequent revolts by the local Indian population. Furthermore, these places were vulnerable to constant attacks by Apaches and Comanches, who regularly ventured south from Arizona to raid villages and missions.

In 1697, the Jesuits secured permission to return to Baja California to try once more to establish missions and settlements. Father Juan María Salvatierra, a Jesuit of Italian-Spanish descent who had worked with Kino in Sonora, was charged with the task of going to Baja California. The site Salvatierra chose was located on the gulf side of Baja California, about one-third of the way up the coast. In November 1697, the presidio and Mission de Nuestra Señora de Loreto were founded. This was the only presidio in Baja California until 1736, when a second presidio was established in the recently re-founded settlement of La Paz, which became the capital of the province.

A contemporary description of the Mission at Loreto reveals the bleakness and desolation of the outpost and region:

> Loreto lies only a stone's throw from the California Gulf. The dwelling
> of the missionary is a small quadrangle of not more than one story,
> of unburnt brick and having a flat roof. One wing of the quadran-
> gle, which alone is partly built of stone and lime, constitutes the
> church. The other three wings contain six apartments, each about
> 20 feet square, and having each one opening toward the beach or
> sea; these serve for sacristy, kitchen, and a small store room. Near
> this quadrangle are four other walls in which are kept very lean beef,
> also tallow, lard, soap, wheat, corn and several millions of black

Elmer Wachtel, Colorado River, Grand Canyon, *oil on canvas, 36 x 24 in., Private Collection*

Leland Curtis, The Desert Road, *oil on canvas,*
30 x 40 in., Charles Sands

John Frost, Desert Evening, *oil on canvas, 26 x 30 in., Private Collection, courtesy of The Irvine Museum*

William H. Meyers, U.S. Squadron at Loreto, *1848, watercolor, Franklin D. Roosevelt Library, Hyde Park, NY*

Paul Grimm, Desert Flowers *(detail),*
oil on board, 12 x 16 in., Private Collection,
courtesy of The Irvine Museum

bugs which are generated in the grain and other articles.... The whole
garrison of the presidio, including the captain and lieutenant, some-
times consists of six or eight men, but never more than twelve or
fourteen....Moreover, towards the setting sun, one sees two rows of
huts made of mud, in which big and little, men and women, all
together, dwell 120 natives. No foliage of any kind, no shade except
that formed by buildings, no water except that obtained from holes
or wells dug in the sandy soil....All this forms Loreto, the capital of
California.

The Loreto Mission became the "mother mission" for Baja California, from which all others were founded, including Nuestra Señora del Pilar de la Paz (La Paz) in 1720, Santiago de los Coras del Sur (Santiago) in 1721 or 1723, San José del Cabo de San Lucas in 1730, and Todos Santos in 1733 or 1735. In all, 24 Jesuit missions were founded between 1697 and 1767. Many of these missions were short-lived; others, although recorded as "missions," were in fact only small chapels temporarily set up in native villages. Their exact names and founding dates are uncertain, as some were later moved to more advantageous locations. Today, nearly all towns and villages in present-day Baja California del Sur are situated at or near mission sites.

By the late 1700s, the fervor and effectiveness of the Jesuits began to breed hostility and resentment in several European courts. Unlike most religious orders, the Jesuits were made up of well-educated men, and their strict, military-like discipline made them seem immune to any governmental control. Moreover, much of the activities of the Jesuits had come into conflict with other religious orders, which maneuvered behind the scenes to have the Jesuits' power and independence suppressed.

Fearing the growing power of the Order of Jesus, the King of Portugal expelled the Jesuits from his country and all his colonies in 1759. France did the same in 1764. On June 24, 1767, the Viceroy of New Spain received secret orders from King Carlos III to arrest all Jesuits and expel them from Mexico and the Philippine Islands. By 1773, the Order of Jesus was itself dissolved, by order of Pope Clement XIV. By 1814, however, demands that the Jesuits be allowed to resume their educational and missionary work led to the restoration of the order by Pope Pius VII.

In 1767, the assignment of expelling the Jesuits from Baja California was given to the newly appointed governor, Don Gaspar de Portolá. After that, all missionary activity in New Spain, including the American Southwest and Baja California, was turned over to the Franciscan Order.

When the Franciscans assumed control over the missions of Baja California, only 14 or 15 Jesuit missions were still in operation. The Franciscans founded one mission in Baja California, at San Fernando de Velicata, about 300 miles south of San Diego Bay, in 1769, and closed several of the older Jesuit outposts, which were deemed unproductive.

While Spain was busy colonizing Baja California, other nations began to explore the coast of Alta California with an eye toward establishing their own colonies. In 1724, Captain Vitus Bering (1681–1741), a Danish navigator, was commissioned by Peter the Great, Czar of the Russian Empire, to survey the coast of Siberia to see if Russia and Alaska were connected by a common coastline. Bering

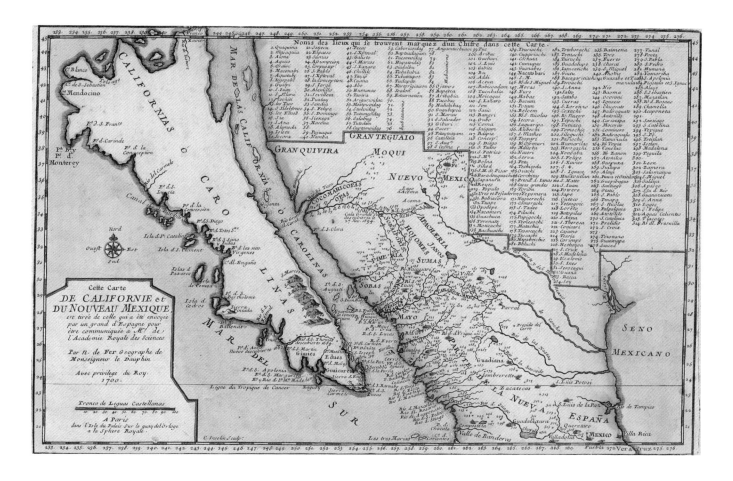

Map of California, Paris, 1700, Sherman Library and Gardens, Corona del Mar, CA

discovered that these lands were separated by the body of water that now bears his name, the Bering Strait. His exploration of Alaska constituted the basis for the Russian claim to the region and opened Alaska to Russian fur trappers.

Later, in 1741, Bering headed another expedition along the coast of Alaska. The Russian Empire wanted to consolidate its monopoly on the fur trade by establishing a series of forts and trading posts along the coast. Bering found the land rich in natural beauty and full of fur-bearing animals. His findings heightened Russia's desire to colonize the west coast of North America. On the return voyage, he discovered the Aleutian Islands. Bering died when his ship wrecked on one of these islands, now called Bering Island. ❧

CHAPTER 5

THE PORTOLÁ EXPEDITION

*F*rom as far back as the early 1540s, Spain had started exploring the coast of California, and Spanish expeditions had landed and made numerous contacts with native inhabitants. The motivation had always been the search for wealth, but no treasure had ever been found. Alta California was essentially abandoned, and consequently, it was not until 1769 that Spain moved to establish permanent colonies in California.

The impetus for this abrupt change came as a result of the Seven Years' War of 1756 to 1763 (called the French and Indian War in the United States), a conflict that pitted France, Austria and Russia against Great Britain and Prussia. The British, who had just defeated the French in North America, had taken sole possession of Canada and were casting aspirations southward into Oregon and beyond. Furthermore, the Russian Empire was expanding its base of operations in Alaska and the Pacific Northwest.

These outside threats to the Spanish Empire in the New World were evaluated by the Viceroy of New Spain, Antonio Bucarelli. Hearing reports that the Russians had already penetrated California from Alaska, and that the British had extended westward from Hudson's Bay, Bucarelli dismissed any suggestions that California might have to be abandoned. The Russian threat to colonize California, he surmised, was possible but would be extremely costly. As for the British, Bucarelli wrote in 1774, *"This seems to me a very distant prospect which does not at the present time impose new cares upon us; indeed it has the same appearances of invention as the pretended passage from [Hudson's Bay] to our South Sea [Pacific Ocean], of which public accounts have spoken so much."*

Nevertheless a careful man, Bucarelli ordered a series of exploratory voyages along the California coast, from 1774 to 1776, to determine if any foreign power had actually established settlements. Coastal expeditions by Juan Pérez, Bruno de Heceta and Juan Francisco de Bodega proved that neither the Russians nor the British had established themselves in California. The way was clear for Spain to establish settlements in Alta California.

To protect this distant part of the Spanish Empire, King Carlos III of Spain ordered José de Gálvez, the Visitador-General (Inspector General) of Spain, to prepare a plan for the establishment of a number of missions, pueblos (towns) and presidios (forts) throughout California. Gálvez was a man of great energy. As the personal representative of the King of Spain, he was intent on protecting the crown's rights and property in the far-away colonies.

Arthur F. Mathews,
Discovery of San Francisco Bay, 1896,
oil on canvas, 70¼ x 58½ in., Garzoli Gallery,
San Rafael, CA

Signature of Fr. Junípero Serra, *Mission San Juan Capistrano*

From Spain, Gálvez traveled to San Blas, the principal supply port on the Pacific coast of Mexico, to prepare his plan. He found that he had been deceived about provincial finances by being given a too-favorable view of the circumstances by incompetent and dishonest officials in Mexico. To make things right, he needed men of the highest reputation, people he could trust. He selected Father Junípero Serra, a Franciscan priest, to establish the missions, and Gaspar de Portolá, the governor of Baja California, to secure a military presence with the presidios. The trio then went to La Paz, in the southern part of Baja California, to organize the expedition.

Junípero Serra (1713–1784) was born in Petra, a small village on the island of Majorca, Spain. He was baptized under the name Miguel José Serra. His father, who worked as a quarryman or sometimes as a farm worker, was Antonio Serre (the name varies from Serre in the Majorcan dialect, to Serra in Catalán, to Sierra in Spanish) and his mother was Margarita Ferrer. His paternal grandmother was named Juana Abram, most likely from a Jewish family that had converted to Catholicism during the Spanish Inquisition.

Serra joined the Franciscan Order in 1730, and after a year of probation, took the vows of poverty, chastity and obedience and took the name Junípero after Brother Juniper, the constant companion of St. Francis of Assisi. A man to whom his religion was everything, Serra turned away from nearly every source of life's pleasures and had long ago rejected the joys of earthly love. He did not drink alcohol and ate only small amounts of simple foods. He was rarely seen laughing and it is said that he never once told a joke. To the contrary, as was common in many religious orders of his day, Serra engaged in various forms of penance, such as whipping himself, putting a torch to his chest or beating his chest with a stone at the end of his sermons. Over the years, he suffered gravely from the ill effects of such practices, but he never complained. Always true to his vows, his manner was quiet, humble and austere.

Serra became a deacon in 1736 and a priest in 1737. From 1739 to 1743, as a doctor of theology, he taught at the Lullian University in Majorca. Among his students were Juan Crespí and Francisco Palóu, who would later accompany him to California.

In 1748, Serra learned that the College of San Fernando de Mexico was recruiting missionaries for the New World. In 1749, he and Palóu wrote to the Administrator for Franciscan Affairs in the Indies for permission to go to the New World as missionaries. They were accepted but put on a stand-by list, as the boat going to Mexico was full. As it happened, several of the Spanish missionaries were afraid to get on board the tiny ship, allowing Serra and Palóu to board after all. On Easter Sunday, April 6, 1749, Serra preached before his father and mother for the last time, in the church where he had been baptized, then left Petra, never to return.

The crossing from Palma to Malaga on the mainland took 15 days. Then they took a freighter for Cadiz, the main Spanish port, arriving on May 7. On August 29, Serra and Palóu sailed on the *Villasota*, taking 100 days to cross the Atlantic

Ocean, arriving in Puerto Rico in late October. The most difficult part of the crossing, Serra wrote many years later, was the shortage of drinking water. During the last two weeks of the crossing, they were restricted to only a half-pint per day. Yet he never complained, and Father Palóu wrote of the voyage, *"One would have said he was the only person not suffering from thirst."* When the *Villasota* finally arrived in Veracruz, Mexico on December 3, the ship was blown back into the open sea and began to founder. The missionaries aboard prepared to face death, and prayers were made to various saints. The name of Santa Barbara was cried out and the sea grew calmer and gentle winds blew the ship safely into the harbor. Of the privations and perils of the crossing, Serra, in characteristic humility, would state, *"There were only a few. The most serious thing of all is that I did not manage to bear them with patience."*

Upon his arrival in Mexico, Serra was 36 years old. As a youth, he was described as frail, short and weak. When he joined the Franciscan Order, it was said that he could not even reach the lectern to turn a page, but he credited his devotion to the priesthood as the reason for a sudden period of growth and strength. In 1943, his bones were exhumed and measured, and his height was determined to have been no more than five feet, two inches.

Even though he could have ridden the 270 miles from Veracruz to Mexico City, Serra asked to walk the distance, perhaps as an act of devotion or penitence.

Father Junípero Serra,
Mission San Juan Capistrano

During the long trip, as he was asleep one night, Serra was stung on his left foot by a scorpion. His condition worsened as he continually scratched the wound and spread the poison up his leg. The result was a debilitating leg affliction that would leave him partially crippled for the rest of his life.

From 1750 to 1767, he worked at missions in various parts of Mexico. Assigned to the missions of Sierra Gorda, a few hundred miles north of Mexico City, Serra insisted on walking the whole trip, in spite of his painful leg. One of his duties was to build the church of Santiago de Xalpan, which still stands today. He learned to speak the local language and devoted himself to teaching the Indians agriculture and stock-raising.

According to Father Palóu, Serra's biographer, during one of his sermons, Father Serra *"took out a chain and after lowering his habit so as to uncover his back, having exhorted his hearers [audience] to penance, he began to scourge himself so violently that the entire congregation broke into tears. Thereupon, a man from the congregation arose and hurriedly went to the pulpit…took the chain from the penitential father…uncovered himself to the waist and began to perform public penance. So violently and merciless were the strokes that, before the whole congregation, he fell to the floor, they judging him dead. After he received the last Sacraments where he fell, he died."*

When the Jesuits were expelled from Mexico in February 1768, and the Franciscans were ordered to manage all missionary activities, Serra was sent to Baja California to direct the former Jesuit missions. On April 1, 1768, at the age of 54, Serra arrived in Loreto to become Father President of the missions in California.

Working together, Serra and Gálvez initially proposed to build four missions in Alta California, starting in San Diego, proceeding almost immediately to Monterey and then putting two more in between. Having noted Vizcaíno's glowing description of Monterey as a superb harbor, Gálvez planned to make it the principal mission in Alta California, with San Diego as the midway point to Loreto, the principal mission of Baja California. The long-term goal was to have a chain of missions and presidios stretching from north to south to facilitate control of California. The presidios would protect the region from foreign invasion and Indian uprisings, while the settlers would develop and exploit the land and the missions would convert the natives and prepare them as the labor force. They would all be connected by El Camino Real (The Royal Road or Highway), which linked the missions in Baja California and would soon stretch from Loreto to Monterey.

The military commander of the expedition, Gaspar de Portolá (1717?–1784?) was born in Balaguer, Spain. After 30 years of service in the Spanish army, Captain de Portolá was promoted to Governor of Baja California in 1767. One of his first duties was to expel the Jesuits from Baja California, an assignment he fulfilled with great reluctance. When the order came to survey Alta California, he welcomed the adventure. His expedition's task was to scout, identify and map potential sites for construction of presidios and to assist the padres in selecting locales for the missions.

Gálvez had divided the expedition into four separate parts, two parties by ship and two parties by land. The plan was to reach San Diego Bay with 300 men and all the supplies needed for the trip. On January 9, 1769, the advance group of 62 people left La Paz on the *San Carlos*. Aboard were Lieutenant Vicente Villa, captain of the ship, Miguel Costansó, official cartographer and surveyor, Father Fernando Parrón, and Lieutenant Pedro Fages, overall military commander of the seagoing expeditions. Fages was the leader of a unit of 25 men from the Compaña Franca del Voluntarios de Cataluña (Free Company of Catalonian Volunteers), a select group of Spanish soldiers recruited from Barcelona. Also known as the "Blue Coats," they were fusiliers, or light infantry, armed with rifles.

The second ship, the *San Antonio*, carried probably 28 people, including Captain Don Juan Pérez, who had formerly commanded a Manila Galleon, Fathers Juan Vizcaíno and Francisco Gómez, as well as various sailors, carpenters and blacksmiths for the pueblos. The two ships were supposed to travel together, but a storm caused a delay in the rendezvous from Mexico, so the *San Carlos* sailed first, on January 9.

The sea voyage from La Paz to San Diego took 110 days, as Miguel Costansó noted in his journals, *"on account of the prevalence of north and north-west winds, which, with little interruption continue throughout the year and are directly contrary to the voyage, as the coast bears northwest to southeast."* The ceaseless headwinds blew the *San Carlos* off-course on numerous occasions. Furthermore, the map

Manuel Valencia,
Sunny Day, El Camino Real, *oil on canvas,*
24 x 30 in., June and Joe La Mantia

coordinates recorded by Vizcaíno were inaccurate, causing both ships to miss the port on their first passing. The delays caused more and more people to succumb to scurvy, the dreaded, deadly disease of sailors.

The *San Antonio* left La Paz a month later on February 15, but arrived in San Diego on April 11, more than two weeks before the *San Carlos*. The *San Antonio* had also been blown off-course, wandering along the Channel Islands for a few days before turning south toward San Diego. Finally, on April 28, both ships were in San Diego Bay, but more than half of the passengers and crew had died of scurvy before reaching their destination.

Of the land expedition, the first group was led by Captain Fernando Rivera y Moncada and Father Crespí. In a letter to Father Palóu, Crespí wrote: "*The first section of the expedition…is made up of…twenty-five leather-jacketed soldiers…three muleteers…and about forty-two Christian Indians from our farthermost missions.*"

They followed El Camino Real north to the farthest mission, Santa María de Los Ángeles, built by the Jesuits "on the borders of heathendom," according to Father Crespí's diary. It was in deplorable condition and had no resident priest, but was in a good locale, "*situated on a creek between very high, rugged hills that here makes a small valley, with many tall palm trees round about. There are a good many waterholes throughout the vicinity with very fine delicious waters.*"

Of the Christianized Indians who accompanied the expedition, Crespí wrote, "*Many of them did not get even as far as Santa María, but ran away, and some of these who did reach here, reached here ill; I am sorry for it and wonder how those poor souls will stand the journey ahead.*" The Rivera group reached San Diego on March 24.

The 25 *soldados de cuera*, or "leather-jackets," from Loreto under Rivera's command were frontier soldiers, many of whom were born in the New World, untrained in the finer aspects of the military arts and generally undisciplined. They did, however, have spirit and stamina, as well as Indian fighting skills that were lacking in regular Spanish soldiers. Generally older than the regulars, the frontier soldiers were usually married, often to Indian women, had children and tended small plots of land for crops and livestock.

Their first line of defense, and the military gear that gave them their name, was a cuirass, or leather armored vest made of six or seven layers of thick deerskin, shaped like a coat without sleeves. This would protect them against arrows shot at close range. In addition, when mounted, they wore *armas de vaquita*, an apron-like leather guard attached to the front of the saddle and hanging down on both sides, to protect their legs as well as the horse. To ward off arrows and spears, they carried a round shield of thick leather strapped to the left arm. With all their armor, the leather-jackets were experienced, self-contained fighters, prepared for any circumstance.

All this protection, however, added greatly to the load the horse had to bear. Besides the woolen uniform, which weighed 18 pounds, the heavy leather vest weighed an additional 18 pounds. Moreover, the shield, *armas de vaquita*, musket,

Model of Spanish Colonial leather shield,
History Collections, Los Angeles County Museum of Natural History

two pistols, shot and powder, sword, lance, saddle, saddle blanket and pad, bridle, spurs and a full canteen of water added an extra 123 pounds. For food, each soldier carried 22 pounds of biscuit, 12 pounds of *pinole* (toasted and ground corn or grain) and a copper vessel that was used for heating water. In total, a fully readied leather-jacket burdened his horse with an extra 165 pounds above his own weight.

To carry all this equipment over long, dry stretches of open country, each *soldado de cuera* was required to have, according to the military regulations of 1772, six horses, one mule and a colt. Even so, to counter losses from fatigue, drought, stampede, and most commonly, theft by Indians, the leather-jacket on active duty needed three additional new horses per year. Inevitably, the large number of horses kept in the presidio corrals were a constant attraction to marauding Indian bands, and the soldiers were rarely able to keep their herds intact.

At first, Indian attackers charged headlong into units of mounted leather-jackets, shooting arrows that stuck but did not penetrate the armor. In return, they were met by overwhelming firepower from muskets and pistols, followed by deep thrusts of seven- to eight-foot lances, and if they survived to get close enough to the soldier, slashes from the short broadsword. After such initially disastrous experiences, Indians chose stealth, cunning and swiftness when fighting the well-armored horsemen.

Costansó showed great admiration for the *soldados de cuera* and wrote, *"Their offensive arms are the lance, which they handle adroitly on horseback, the broadsword, and the short musket which they carry securely fastened in its case. They are men of great fortitude and patience…and we do not hesitate to say that they are the best horsemen in the world."*

The journey from Baja California to San Diego and the subsequent expedition to Monterey was marked by continual rivalry between Rivera's "leather-jackets" and the Catalonian soldiers under the command of Lt. Fages. The Spanish soldiers looked down on the "leather-jackets" as provincial ruffians, but in a skirmish with Indians, the *soldados de cuera* would prove to be superior fighters.

The second land group left Loreto with Governor Portolá, Father Serra, 11 soldiers and several civilians and Indians. Knowing the risks and perils that lay

Jose Cardero, Indian Manner of Combat, *The Bancroft Library, University of California, Berkeley*

LEFT TO RIGHT:
Spanish Colonial helmet, mid to late 1700s, Elisabeth Waldo-Dentzel Muticultural Arts Studio, Northridge, CA; iron breast plate, c. 1770, Mort and Donna Fleischer Collection; flintlock rifle, 1700s, Mission San Juan Capistrano Museum

Lloyd Harting;
TOP: First Sighting of California, from the Highlands of Baja California, 1769; BOTTOM: The Raising of the Cross on Presidio Hill at San Diego; *The James S. Copley Library, La Jolla, CA*

ahead, Father Serra was anxious about the coming journey. In his diary, Serra wrote, *"I trust that God will give me the strength to reach San Diego, as He has given me the strength to come so far. In case He does not, I will conform myself to His most holy will. Even though I should die on the way, I shall not turn back. They can bury me wherever they wish and I shall gladly be left among the pagans, if it be the will of God."*

When the second group reached Mission Santa María de los Ángeles, Father Serra lingered a few days to minister to the few Indians who lived there. Then they proceeded 40 miles north to a place called Velicatá, where Serra founded the first Franciscan mission in Baja California. One of the padres was left behind with several Christianized Indians to build the mission.

From here north, it was all unknown territory. With no missions or white settlements to turn to, the expedition faced its gravest period. In his journal, Portolá recalled this part of the trip: "*In a few days we saw with extreme regret that our food was gone, with no source of supplies unless we should turn back. As a result, some of the Indians died, and the rest of them deserted from natural necessity. So I was left alone with the cuirassiers; without stopping the march, we went on, lamenting, now to the mountains to kill geese and rabbits, now to the beach for clams and small fish, and then in search of water, which we did not find for three or four days, the animals going twice that long without drinking, as we ourselves did sometimes.*"

Much of the journey through Baja California was over steep and rocky terrain under the blazing hot sun. At night, Portolá had to post sentries, as during most of the journey, "*we saw footprints of the gentiles [Indians] but not one was seen.*" On one occasion, Portolá wrote of other dangers, "*For the last four nights a roaring lion quite close to us kept us awake. May God guard us from it, as He has until now.*"

On one occasion, the expedition was met by a large group of Indians, armed with bows and arrows. "*Time and again they made as if to shoot their arrows,*" Father Serra wrote in his diary, "*They paid no heed to the peaceful overtures from our side, but, so indignant were they, that we could not calm them...We spent much time patiently trying to send them away in a friendly way. It was all in vain, no use whatever, and we feared bloodshed. By order of the Governor [Portolá], four soldiers, mounted on horses, forming a line, forced them to retreat.*"

Portolá's group arrived in San Diego on May 15. Between them, the two land parties had brought 200 head of cattle, the ancestors of the great herds that would later roam California. By the time all parties and ships reached San Diego, about 100 men who had come by sea had died of scurvy and most of the Indians from Baja California had deserted.

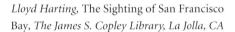
Lloyd Harting, The Sighting of San Francisco Bay, *The James S. Copley Library, La Jolla, CA*

Charles Arthur Fries, Looking Down Mission Valley, Summertime, *oil on canvas, 18 x 28 in., The Irvine Museum*

THE SEARCH FOR MONTEREY

The expedition to find Monterey set out from San Diego on July 14, 1769, with Portolá in command. The party numbered 64 in total, with Father Juan Crespí and Father Francisco Gómez as spiritual advisors. Among the expedition were men who would make California history, with names like Ortega, Amador, Alvarado, Carrillo, Serrano and Yorba. Father Serra stayed in San Diego because his infected leg had taken a turn for the worse. Sergeant José Francisco Ortega, the chief scout, and seven soldiers went ahead to mark the path. Their destination was the harbor at Monterey, discovered by Vizcaíno 167 years earlier. Along the way, they charted potential locations for missions, presidios and pueblos throughout California.

Presidio sites needed to be defensible and were usually on higher ground, overlooking the harbor or principal route of supply. For purposes of protection, the missions were, at first, placed nearby, but only if the following three requisites were met: availability of water, good soil for agriculture and a large population of local Indians. It is thought that in 1769, the native population of southern California may have been as large as 130,000, by far the largest concentration of Native American population in the United States.

On the first day on the trail, Father Crespí wrote: *"We set out from this port of San Diego on this day of the seraphic doctor, San Buenaventura, about four in the afternoon. On some parts of the road there are rosemary and other small bushes not known to us, and on the right hand we have a mountain range, moderately high, bare of trees, of pure earth well covered with grass. We saw many hares and rabbits, for this port abounds with them. At about two leagues [about five miles], we came to a very large village of heathen [on the east shore of present-day Mission Bay]…as soon as they saw us approaching, they all came out into the road, men, women and children, as though they came to welcome us, with signs of great pleasure. We gave them such presents as we could."*

By contrast, Portolá was not interested in describing the country. His first priority was the safety of the expedition. Of that first day, his diary says only, *"We marched for three hours. Much pasture, but no water for man or beast."*

On July 18, 1769, the expedition entered a pleasant valley north of San Diego. It was one of the first sites that the expedition mapped. In his diary, Father Crespí wrote: *"A little after three in the afternoon, we set out to the north. We climbed a hill of good soil, all covered with grass, and then went on over hills of the same kind of land and pasture. We must have traveled about two short leagues [a league was about 2.6 miles], when we descended to a large and beautiful valley, so green that it seemed to us to have been planted. We crossed it to the north and pitched camp near a large pool of water. At the extremities of the [valley] there are two large villages. The Valley is all green with good grass, and has many wild grapes, and one sees some spots that resemble vineyards. I gave this valley the name of San Juan Capistrano, for a mission, so that this glorious saint, who in life converted so many souls, may pray God in heaven for the conversion of these poor heathen."*

Spanish explorers generally named places in honor of the saint whose feast day it was when a particular place was discovered. Moreover, the missionaries in the New World were Franciscans, and they preferred using saints from their own order, favoring the most important ones. For this site, Father Crespí selected the name San Juan Capistrano, after a Franciscan saint of Italian descent, Saint Giovanni of Capistran (1385–1456), who had distinguished himself in battle against

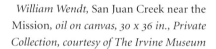

William Wendt, San Juan Creek near the Mission, *oil on canvas, 30 x 36 in., Private Collection, courtesy of The Irvine Museum*

the Turks in defense of Belgrade. The name San Juan Capistrano would later be re-appropriated for a more important locale; this valley is now called San Luis Rey Valley, after Saint and King Louis ix of France.

Continuing north, on July 22 they entered what is now Orange County, where Father Crespí baptized two Indian children not far from present-day San Clemente, at a spot the soldiers called "El Cañon de Los Cristianitos" (the Canyon of the Little Christians). Crespí wrote, *"The scouts [Ortega and his men] informed us that on the preceding day, they saw in the village two sick little girls. After asking the commander [Portolá] for some soldiers to go with us to visit them, we went, and found one which the mother had at her breast apparently dying. We asked for it, saying that we wished to see it, but it was impossible to get it from its mother. So we said to her by signs that we would not do it any harm, but wished to sprinkle its head so that if it died it might go to heaven. She consented to this, and my companion, Fray Francisco Gómez, baptized it, giving it the name of Maria Magdalena. We went to the other, also small, who had been burned and was apparently about to die. In the same way I baptized it, giving it the name of Margarita. We did not doubt that both would die and go to heaven."*

While scouting the mountains north of the valley, one of Portolá's soldiers accidentally dropped a *trabuco* (matchlock rifle) into a deep ravine. This was a serious mishap and the soldiers spent a long time looking for the gun, but moved on without ever finding it. The mountains where the gun was lost came to be known as "Sierra del Trabuco" (now called the Santa Ana Mountains). The gun (or one very much like it) was eventually found, many years later, in what is now called Trabuco Canyon, and is displayed in the Bowers Museum of Cultural Art in Santa Ana.

On July 23, they arrived at another place that met all requirements as a

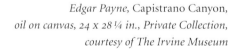

Edgar Payne, Capistrano Canyon, *oil on canvas, 24 x 28¼ in., Private Collection, courtesy of The Irvine Museum*

potential mission site. Father Crespí described the site as follows: "*A little before eleven we came to a very pleasant green valley, full of willows, alders and live oaks and other trees not known to us. It has a large arroyo, which at the point where we crossed it, carried a good stream of fresh and good water, which, after running a little way, formed into pools in some large patches of tules. We halted there, calling it the valley of Santa Maria Magdalena.*" (The stream is now called San Juan Creek.)

On July 26, the expedition came to a large river that they found difficult to cross. As it was the Feast Day of Saint Anne, Portolá named the river "Rio de Santa Ana." The party camped by the river for a couple of days, during which time they experienced a series of earthquakes. These events alarmed the Spaniards and compelled the padres to rename the river "Rio de Jesús de los Temblores" (River of Jesus of the Earthquakes), but the soldiers continued to refer to the river as well as the valley as Santa Ana.

On August 1, Crespí celebrated the feast of Nuestra Señora la Reina de Los Ángeles de Porciúncula (Our Lady, the Queen of the Angels at the Small Portion), one of the most important feast days in the Franciscan order. Early in the life of St. Francis of Assisi, about 1212, he was given a small, ruined chapel by the Benedictines for his repair and eventual use near Assisi, where he later died. It was on a very small piece of property, a "small portion" (porziuncola, in Italian). A fresco was painted on the wall behind the altar depicting the Blessed Virgin Mary surrounded by angels. Thus, this chapel, the cradle of the Franciscan Order, took the name "Saint Mary of the Angels at the Small Portion." Later, this place of worship became a center of pilgrimage, devotion and repentance. Today, the small stone chapel can be seen inside a large church called Santa Maria degli Angeli, which was built over the site.

The following day, the party camped by a river, which they named "Rio de Nuestra Señora la Reina de Los Ángeles de Porciúncula," and the site was recorded as ideal for future settlement. Years later, on September 4, 1781, El Pueblo de Nuestra Señora la Reina de Los Ángeles de Porciúncula was founded. (The name of the city was eventually shortened to "Los Angeles.")

As they continued north, the Portolá expedition stayed near the coast whenever possible, in hope of spotting the supply ship that was to meet them in Monterey. By August 14, they had reached the present-day site of the city of Ventura and a few days later came to a large native village where the Indians were making a *tomol* or *ti'at*, a seagoing, wood-plank canoe. Father Crespí noted in his diary, "*The Indians have many canoes, and at the time were building one, for which reason the soldiers named this town La Carpinteria [The Carpenter Shop], while I christened it with the name of San Roque.*"

On August 18, the expedition reached what is now Santa Barbara. Then they climbed a steep pass (now called Gaviota Pass), which Crespí named "San Luís Rey de Francia" (St. Louis, King of France), but the soldiers called it "La Gaviota" (The Seagull) because they had killed a seabird on the trail. At the top, they could see the Channel Islands and Punta Concepcíon (Point Conception), where Cabrillo and Vizcaíno had noted strong crosswinds.

John Gamble, Santa Barbara Landscape,
oil on canvas, 24 x 36 in., Private Collection,
courtesy of The Irvine Museum

Bruce E. Nelson, The Summer Sea, *1915,*
oil on canvas, 30 x 40 in., The Irvine Museum

When they reached what is today San Simeon, on September 13, they were forced to turn inland, as the coastal plain disappeared as the range of rugged mountains, the Sierra de Santa Lucia, named by Vizcaíno, turned directly into the ocean. In his diary, Portolá described these mountains as the *"very high, rough and long Sierra de Santa Lucia, which begins here [near San Luis Obispo] and ends at the mission of Carmelo, near Monterey."* Upon entering the sierra, the weather turned cold and the men spent about two weeks looking for ways to cross the mountains.

They emerged in the Salinas Valley, and following the Salinas River northward for several days, Portolá and his men reached a hill that overlooked a large, open bay. Although Portolá and his men had unknowingly found the Monterey Peninsula, they concluded otherwise, as the harbor did not meet Vizcaíno's magnificent description. Thinking Monterey was yet to the north, the expedition continued to present-day San Francisco. Finally, on November 2, a group of soldiers who had been sent out to hunt deer reached the northern tip of the San Francisco Peninsula and became the first white men to see the estuary now called the Golden Gate. On November 11, Portolá was forced to turn back due to the generally poor health of the group and their inability to cross San Francisco Bay.

They retraced their steps to Monterey, remaining there from November 27 to December 10, still trying to find Vizcaíno's harbor. The weather grew miserable and supplies were dwindling. Discouraged by his apparent failure to complete his mission, Portolá ordered an immediate return to San Diego.

In their journey, Portolá and Ortega were the first Europeans to set foot in what are now the major cities of California. They passed through a remarkably rich and diverse environment, a true "earthly Paradise" inhabited by gentle and docile people. The expedition encountered endless vistas of rolling, grassy plains, verdant hills covered with extensive timber, and ranges of snow-covered mountains. The land contained a myriad of wild game, including antelope, deer and bear, as well as birds and waterfowl of all kinds. The lakes, rivers and coastal waters were full of fish and shellfish. They had come upon a temperate, hospitable land with seemingly endless sustenance, all theirs for the taking. ❧

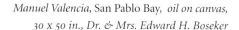

Manuel Valencia, San Pablo Bay, *oil on canvas, 30 x 50 in., Dr. & Mrs. Edward H. Boseker*

TOP:
Douglass Parshall, San Simeon Canyon,
oil on canvas, 36 x 40 in., Private Collection;
BOTTOM:
Herman Herzog, Monterey Pines with Bears,
30 x 36 in., Dr. & Mrs. Edward H. Boseker

Alexander Harmer, Garden of the Mission San Luis Rey,
Elisabeth Waldo-Dentzel Muticultural Arts Studio,
Northridge, CA

CHAPTER **6**

THE MISSIONS OF CALIFORNIA

*I*n 1769, while Portolá and Ortega were in the north, looking for Monterey Bay, Junípero Serra, who had stayed behind in San Diego, founded the first mission and named it after San Diego de Alcalá. This particular "San Diego," whose name in Latin is Saint Didicus, was born in Seville sometime around 1400 and died in 1463. He was a Franciscan monk who worked as a cook at the Capuchin Convent in Alcalá de Hernares, a small town near Madrid that was known for its university and later, as the birthplace of Miguel de Cervantes.

It was reported that while cooking one day, Diego, a pious man, was so enraptured as to be lifted in the air while angels continued his work. He was made a saint as a result of a miracle that occurred about 100 years after his death. In 1562, Prince Carlos of Spain, who was attending the university in Alcalá de Hernares, fell down a flight of stairs and was found unconscious. Although he appeared to be recovering quite well, he fell into a coma ten days later. Just then, a procession of Franciscan Friars was carrying the cadaver of Diego for re-interment. Hearing of the Prince's condition, the Franciscans explained that Diego was credited with having performed several miracles. They placed the corpse next to the Prince and suddenly, he awoke, fully recovered. In 1588, Pope Sixtus v made Didicus a saint.

The first task of the newly founded Mission San Diego was to care for the sick and dying crewmen of the *San Carlos* and the *San Antonio*. At the same time, the priests visited Indian villages in the hope of recruiting neophytes for conversion, but the local Indians were unimpressed and refused to go to the mission. More than one year would pass before the first Indian would be baptized in San Diego.

Mission of San Diego, *from* Reports of Explorations and Surveys, 1853–54, *U.S. House of Representatives, 1856, lithograph, Sherman Library and Gardens, Corona del Mar, CA*

James E. McBurney;
TOP: Junípero Serra Praying for
Return of Relief Ship;
BOTTOM: Junípero Serra
and Gaspar de Portolá at Monterey;
oil on canvas mounted on panel, Mission Inn
Foundation and Museum, Riverside, CA

Upon Portolá's return to San Diego on January 24, 1770, he reported to Serra that he had followed Vizcaíno's maps and taken into account his descriptions but, unfortunately, had not found Monterey. Yet, Serra and others in San Diego were certain that he had indeed reached it when Portolá described the marvelous peninsula north of San Simeon. Using his gift for logic and persuasion, Serra convinced Portolá that the beautiful bay of his travels could only have been Monterey.

In spite of the renewed optimism, Portolá's expedition was nearly out of provisions. He reluctantly decided that if the supply ship *San José* did not arrive by March 19, they would have to return to Loreto. On the afternoon of that day, a ship was indeed sighted on the distant horizon, but it continued north, without stopping in San Diego. They had no way of knowing that it was the *San Antonio*, which had been directed to bypass San Diego Bay and proceed directly to meet Portolá in Monterey.

Preparations had been made to return to Loreto when the *San Antonio* unexpectedly put into port in San Diego on March 23. On her way to Monterey, the *San Antonio* had lost an anchor and had put ashore for repairs and fresh water. At that time, they learned from friendly Indians that the Portolá expedition had passed their village on their way back to San Diego.

Freshly re-supplied, Portolá ordered the *San Antonio*, on April 16, 1770, to set sail for Monterey while he set out again, taking with him all 16 of the remaining able-bodied soldiers. On June 1, the *San Antonio*, with Fathers Junípero Serra and Juan Crespí aboard, finally reached Monterey. Sailing north along the coast into the prevailing winds, it had taken the ship longer to reach Monterey than the party traveling on foot.

In Monterey, Serra inspected the mission site selected by Portolá. It was on the shore of the bay, near the spot where Vizcaíno had landed in 1602, and where the Carmelite friars said mass "in the shadow of a large oak tree, some of whose branches reached the water." On June 3, 1770, Father Serra dedicated the new mission. In a letter, Serra described it as follows:

> *On the holy day of Pentecost, the 3rd of June, after having gathered together all the officers of sea and land and all the rest of the people by the side of the little ravine and oak where the [Carmelite] Fathers of that other expedition [Vizcaíno's] had held their celebration, an altar was erected, the bells were hung up and rung, the hymn "Veni Creator" was sung and the water blessed, and finally a large cross was erected and the royal standard set up....After the service had been concluded, the officers performed the ceremony of taking formal possession of the land in the name of the King, our lord. We afterwards ate our dinner together under a shade on the beach. The whole service had been accompanied with much thunder of powder both on land and from the ship.*

An altar was enclosed in a structure made of branches and trees. This served as a temporary church. Besides the "church," the original mission consisted of a small chapel, living quarters for the priests and workers and a small workshop area. The whole complex was constructed within the presidio stockade. The Carmel Mission became Serra's home mission and indeed the headquarters for the entire Alta California mission chain.

On that same day, June 3, Portolá hoisted the Spanish flag and dedicated the Monterey Presidio. Portolá then supervised the construction of a group of temporary buildings within the stockade that would serve as the headquarters of the presidio. At the same time, housing was built for his soldiers. The presidio garrison consisted of a troop of colonial leather-jackets, led by Captain Rivera, and a detachment of elite Catalonian Volunteers, under the command of Lt. Fages.

With that, on July 9, 1770, Gaspar de Portolá, one of the most capable and resourceful persons in the history of California, turned over military command of the presidio to his assistant, Fages, and returned to Mexico, never to set foot in California again.

TOP: R.B. Beechey, The Mission of San Carlos *(original name for Carmel Mission), 1827, watercolor, Autry Museum of Western Heritage, Los Angeles;*
BOTTOM:
Charles Rollo Peters, Starlit Mission, Carmel, *oil on canvas, 16 x 24 in., The Irvine Museum*

Mission of San Carlos, Monterey County
(Carmel), c. 1830, etching, Private Collection

Not long after the founding of the mission, Father Serra became dissatisfied with its location. He realized that there were too few Indians in the area and furthermore, the soil was too rocky for agriculture. Also, there is reason to believe that for the protection of the neophytes, he intended to distance the mission from the soldiers at the presidio. He selected a site in the Carmel River valley, about five miles south of the presidio, and petitioned the authorities in Mexico for permission to move the mission.

In June 1771, the Viceroy of Mexico sent his approval for the new mission site. With the basic work of clearing the land underway, Serra left briefly to establish the next mission in his plan, at San Antonio de Padua, which was dedicated on July 14, 1771. In August, Serra returned and had a huge wooden cross erected at the new Carmel River site. To speed up the pace, he decided to move immediately into a small hut where he could supervise the work. Father Francisco Palóu, Serra's friend and biographer, who assisted in the project, wrote of the task of moving the mission:

> *As soon as the Mission of San Antonio had been founded, the reverent padre [Serra] proceeded to the Royal Presidio of Monterey, and although he eagerly desired to go, and found another mission, San Luis Obispo, it was not possible on account of a lack of soldiers for the guard, and so he assisted in [moving] the mission.*
>
> *The three sailors and four California Indians, assisted by the soldiers, had already cut timbers. Work was begun, and soon a small chapel was erected together with living quarters of four rooms, a large room for a granary, and also a house to be used as a dwelling and kitchen for the boys [unmarried male Indians]. All were of wood and had flat roofs and were enclosed in a good stockade. In the corner of the square, there was a house, also with a flat roof, for the soldiers, and near, some corrals for the cattle and stock. As the workers were few…work was not finished and the move was not completed until the last day of December of the year 1771.*

TOP: *Alexander Harmer,* Mission San Juan Capistrano, *Elisabeth Waldo-Dentzel Multicultural Arts Studio, Northridge, CA;* BOTTOM: *Edwin Deakin,* Santa Barbara Mission, *oil on canvas, 12 x 18 in., Dr. & Mrs. Edward H. Boseker*

With the missions in San Diego and Carmel in operation, the system of missions along El Camino Real was expanded by establishing a new mission halfway between existing ones, until each was connected to another by roughly the distance of one day's travel. After San Antonio de Padua, established in 1771, the series of missions continued with San Gabriel Arcángel (1771), San Luis Obispo de Tolosa (1772), San Francisco de Asís (Mission Dolores) (1776), San Juan Capistrano (1776), Santa Clara de Asís (1777) and San Buenaventura (1782).

After Serra's death in 1784, Father Fermín Francisco de Lasuén became Father President of the missions. Lasuén continued building the chain of missions by adding Santa Barbara (1786), La Purísima Concepción (founded in 1787 near Lompoc and commonly called "Purísima"), Santa Cruz (1791), Nuestra Señora de la Soledád (1791), San José de Guadalupe (1797), San Juan Bautista (1797), San Miguel Arcángel (1797), San Fernando Rey de España (1797) and San Luis Rey de Francia (1798). After Lasuén's death in 1803, missions were built in Santa Inés (1804), San Rafael Arcángel (1817) and San Francisco Solano (Sonoma) (1823).

In addition to the 21 missions along El Camino Real, the Franciscans opened several *asistencias*, or branch missions, such as the Mission San Antonio de Pala, founded in 1816. There were also a number of churches and chapels in Indian villages, such as the presidio church at Monterey and the pueblo church in Los Angeles,

TOP: *Albert Marshall,* Mission La Purísima, *1903, oil on canvas, 12 x 28 in., Private Collection, courtesy of The Irvine Museum;* BOTTOM: *Fannie Duvall,* San Fernando, *1891, oil on canvas, 13¾ x 22½ in., Private Collection, courtesy of The Irvine Museum*

which grew in importance but are not usually termed "missions." Likewise, the chapel at Santa Margarita became an *asistencia* of Mission San Luis Obispo; the chapel at San Bernardino became an *asistencia* of Mission San Gabriel; San Pedro, or Las Flores Chapel, a *ranchería* (Indian village) church, became an *asistencia* of Mission San Luis Rey; and Santa Ysabel, in San Diego County, also a *ranchería* chapel, later became an *asistencia*.

All of these missions and related outposts were founded by the Franciscans of the College of San Fernando, in Mexico City. Little known is the fact that another group of Franciscans, albeit from the College of Queretaro in northern Mexico, also established two missions on the Colorado River in 1780. These were the Missions San Pedro y San Pablo de Bicuner, and La Purísima Concepción (commonly called "Concepción"). San Pedro y San Pablo was located at the merging of the Gila and Colorado Rivers, and Concepcíon was built a few miles south, on the California side of the Colorado near Yuma. Both were destroyed in the Yuma Indian uprising of 1781 and never rebuilt.

In 1783, Father Juan Crespí, who had been Serra's student in Spain as well as his faithful friend and companion, died at the Carmel mission. He received the last rites from Father Serra and was buried in the sanctuary. On August 28, 1784, Father Junípero Serra died at the Mission San Carlos Borroméo, at the age of 70. At his request, he was buried in the sanctuary, next to his old friend Father Crespí.

Each California mission was to have two friars, one to manage religious affairs, usually the elder or senior padre, and the other to manage the agricultural activities at the mission. The senior padre was in charge of discipline among the Indian neophytes. With the exception of capital punishment, he had the authority to order any punishment, including flogging, to correct unacceptable behavior among the Indians. All padres were responsible to the Father President at the Carmel Mission, who was in overall charge of the missions in Alta California. He, in turn, took orders from the College of San Fernando, the headquarters of the Franciscan Order, in Mexico City.

The padres were assigned the responsibility of gathering Indians into settlements and teaching them to be self-sufficient according to European standards. In order to tell the Indians of the benefits of becoming part of the mission community, the padres enticed them into the mission with gifts of food and glass beads. If an Indian chose to stay, he or she was instructed in an abbreviated form of the catechism before being baptized and converted to Christianity. Although this was to be voluntary, once converted, the Indian was bound to the mission for life. The padres controlled all aspects of his existence. He was told where to live, where to work and what to eat. If he misbehaved, he was punished. If he ran away, he was brought back. This rigid level of control was deemed necessary by Serra, who believed that the daily life of California Indians was changing, and that they needed to learn skills in order to survive.

Founding missions was only one aspect of the coordinated and well-tested process used by Spanish colonizers for centuries. Concurrent with the

establishment of missions was the founding of pueblos (towns) and presidios, or military installations.

An additional facet of the Spanish colonial process was that the enormous amount of land attached to the missions was to be held in trust for the Indians who, when ready, would take ownership. The entire process of civilizing the Indians was supposed to take ten years. In a typical mission, two padres were supposed to teach Christianity, farming and a number of trades to as many as 2,000 Indians. Moreover, Indians who had lived in a particular pattern for thousands of years were supposed to cast off their old culture and live in a way that was completely alien to them, one that was often hard to understand.

The culture shock was too great for the Indians and the transition too difficult. They did not assimilate and instead, their right to live according to an age-old cultural pattern was forfeited as the dominant Spanish culture took its place. According to Monsignor Francis Day Weber, noted Californian historian, the Franciscans had often opposed premature colonization, fearing the Indians were not prepared and would be in jeopardy. The missions, they had hoped, would be allowed enough time to teach the Indians to survive in a Spanish culture. But ten years was not enough time, nor would 50 be.

Presidios were originally intended to protect Spain's colonies from foreign attack and protect the missions from native uprisings. They were usually located at a strategic port or on a hill overlooking the sea. Although they were armed with cannons, there was rarely sufficient gunpowder to fire them. In the late 1700s, Spain was an international power, and that fact alone served as sufficient deterrent to keep her small and relatively unimportant colonies in California safe.

Almost from the beginning, the presidios could not have withstood any organized attack by a foreign power. Most historians agree that the most daunting enemies the California presidios ever faced were the natural elements, geographical isolation, political neglect and apathy; they were vanquished by all four.

When not keeping order, the soldiers tended flocks and supervised native workers in the fields, but they refused to do any hard labor, leaving tasks such as

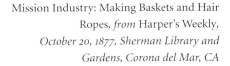
Mission Industry: Making Baskets and Hair Ropes, *from* Harper's Weekly, *October 20, 1877, Sherman Library and Gardens, Corona del Mar, CA*

ABOVE: *Richard Beechey,* Mission of San
Francisco, California, *watercolor on paper,
The North Point Gallery, San Francisco;*
RIGHT: *Anna Hills,* San Fernando Mission,
*oil on canvas, 20 x 24 in.,
George Stern Fine Arts, Los Angeles*

making adobe brick and constructing buildings to the natives. In short time, the padres grew to resent the presence of the soldiers, as they were continually abusive to the Indians and routinely molested their women. In his landmark book on San Juan Capistrano, Father Zephyrin Engelhardt stated that the soldiers in California were *"recruited from the scum of society in Mexico, frequently convicts and jailbirds, it is not surprising that the mission guards...should be guilty of such and similar crimes at nearly all the missions. In truth, the guards counted among the worst obstacles to missionary progress. The wonder is, that the missionaries, nevertheless, succeeded so well in attracting converts."*

The last resort to protect the neophytes was to move the mission itself away from the presidio. For example, since the founding of the first mission in San Diego in 1769, relations between the missionaries and Indians were precarious. Over the first few years, the situation was aggravated as soldiers of the San Diego presidio routinely bullied and beat the Indians and molested their women. The padres' persistent complaints regarding the poor behavior of the soldiers at the San Diego presidio were generally ignored, as the military was reluctant to punish a soldier on the word of an Indian. In 1774, two Indian girls were raped by three soldiers. When nothing was done to punish the offending soldiers, the Indians rebelled and attacked the mission. Even if Spanish indifference did not drive the Indians to violence, the continuation of such events instilled great distrust among the Indians, and it showed the wide gap between the white man's words and his actions.

Unable to resolve this problem, Father Serra was forced in 1774 to move the mission away from the presidio, several miles up the San Diego River valley, to the site where it stands today. Although this move left the mission undefended, it was necessary to protect the Indians from the soldiers. Later, the problem of molestation was resolved by requiring that all soldiers and settlers assigned to the frontier be married and accompanied by their wives. ✦

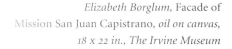

Elizabeth Borglum, Facade of Mission San Juan Capistrano, *oil on canvas, 18 x 22 in., The Irvine Museum*

Alson Clark, San Diego Mission, *1924,*
oil on board, 16 x 20 in., The Irvine Museum

Arthur G. Rider, Mission Garden, San Juan
Capistrano, *c. 1929, oil on canvas, 22 x 20 in.,*
The Irvine Museum

CHAPTER 7

SAN JUAN CAPISTRANO: THE JEWEL OF THE MISSIONS

Father Serra had wanted to proceed with the plan that called for establishing the next mission at San Buenaventura, but unrest with the Indians there postponed the mission in what is now the city of Ventura in favor of the southern site in present-day Orange County. In late 1775, Serra appointed Fathers Fermín Francisco de Lasuén and Gregorio Amurrio to build the seventh in the chain of missions, to be named for an Italian saint, Saint John of Capistrano, a member of the Franciscan Order who had been canonized after fighting in the siege of Belgrade in June 1456. On October 30, the padres, accompanied by Ortega and a few soldiers, returned to the Valley of Santa Maria Magdalena and renamed the site San Juan Capistrano. With the help of friendly Indians and the grudging assistance of some of the soldiers, they erected a wooden cross, hung some bells and began constructing the mission. Lasuén later wrote, *"Ours was a good location, near the stream 'La Quema' [The Fire] and three quarters of a league from El Camino Real in the direction of the coast."*

After only seven days, word came to Capistrano of an Indian uprising at the San Diego Mission. Upon getting news of the attack, a runner was sent to ask Ortega to come to their rescue. Fearing that a general Indian uprising had broken out, Ortega ordered the padres to pack their belongings, bury the bells and return at once to San Diego. While Ortega and his soldiers were in San Juan Capistrano, the situation in San Diego reached a crisis: the Indians killed two Spanish civilians and a priest, Father Luis Jayme, and burned the mission to the ground.

A year later, Father Amurrio and Father Pablo Mugartegui and a detachment of ten soldiers went back to Capistrano. They were relieved to find the cross still standing. They dug up the bells and held a service. Over the next few weeks, a chapel and a few simple buildings of adobe brick were hastily erected.

On November 1, 1776, Father Serra came and personally dedicated the Mission San Juan Capistrano. In order to get supplies to start the new mission, Serra traveled to the Mission San Gabriel, the nearest mission to San Juan Capistrano. On the way, Serra and several of his companions, who were riding ahead of the pack train, were suddenly confronted by a group of hostile Indians. Their lives were spared only because a neophyte Indian told the marauders that a troop of soldiers was just a short distance behind them.

When the caravan returned from San Gabriel, it brought nine milk cows, a breed bull, a team of oxen, three saddle mules, three broken horses, two mares, one colt, a male and female pig, a few chickens, saddles and bridles, 12 hoes, two axes, six large machetes, six new knives, a branding iron, articles for the church and

José de Paez, Saint John of Capistrano, *c. 1775, Mission San Juan Capistrano Museum*

some food for the workers, to get Capistrano started. As was to be the case for all future missions, the first animals, grain, seed and cuttings came from the neighboring missions.

Founded in 1771, Mission San Gabriel was a large and fully self-supporting institution. The earliest recorded use of local water supplies in southern California was at the Mission San Gabriel in 1771. Located in the San Gabriel Basin, the Mission got its water from groundwater springs and *cienegas* (marshes). As the mission had full jurisdiction over the San Gabriel and Santa Ana rivers, the mission fathers and their converts diverted these waters to cultivate food for the settlement. Water conduits were made from tile manufactured at the mission. Large tracts of moist land along streams and rivers were cultivated, while other lands were used for dry farming. Eventually, the local water supplies irrigated as many as 6,000 acres of mission land.

The Mission San Juan Capistrano had a relatively easy time attracting Indians for conversion, while other missions experienced more difficulty. According to Father Palóu, *"Unlike the Indians at other missions, who would molest the missionaries by begging for eatables and other presents, these of San Juan Capistrano molested the missionaries with petitions for baptism."* By 1786, ten years after the mission's founding, there were 544 Indian neophytes; ten years after that, there were 1,649 baptized Indians residing at Capistrano.

As the San Juan Capistrano Mission grew and prospered, it experienced a growing list of problems. In her book entitled *California Missions and Their Romances*, published in 1915, Mrs. Fremont Older detailed the troubles brought about in the mission's relations with an outlying Indian *ranchería* called Aloucuachomi in June 1777. The problems included harassment of mission neophytes by Indians from that settlement, which resulted in the deaths of three and the wounding of another offender by a mission soldier named Corporal Mariano Carrillo. Additionally, the

Acagchemem Indian Village, *Mission San Juan Capistrano*

Colin Campbell Cooper, Near San Juan Capistrano, *mixed media, 5 x 7 in., Private Collection, courtesy of The Irvine Museum*

chief of Aloucuachomi had to be punished for furnishing Indian women to the mission soldiers.

On October 4, 1778, all work was abandoned, as the Capistrano Mission was moved to ensure a constant supply of fresh water for the growing community. In the Annual Report of the Mission San Juan Capistrano for the year 1782, the move was explained as follows: *"This mission was founded Nov. 1, 1776, but because of water failure at the place where it was first founded, the site was transferred to that which it occupies today, where we have the advantage of secure water. It is located about three-fourths of a league [about two miles] distant from the original site. This transfer was made on October 4, 1778."*

The new site was located between two streams, now called San Juan Creek and Trabuco Creek. In a letter to Serra, Father Mugartegui states that among the first structures built at the new mission site was a small church, which was located outside the quadrangle. This little church was used until the adobe structure now called the Serra Chapel could be completed, sometime around 1782. In addition, living quarters and a shelter for the calves were also erected. The first crops planted at the new site were vineyards and a vegetable garden.

According to historian Don Meadows, the original mission site was in San Juan Canyon, on the old Lacouague Ranch, about two miles up San Juan Creek. Father Palóu, who never visited the original site, quotes Serra as saying, *"The site of the Mission is very pleasant and it has a good view. From the buildings, the ocean can be seen and the ships when they cruise there; for the beach is only about half a league distant. There is good anchorage for the frigates, and during the season when the barks come, there is good shelter; but during the season of the southwinds, the vessels would not be secure, because in that direction the harbor is open and exposed. Toward the north, however, and on the other side, the ships are secure owing to the high point of land which runs far out, and forms a roadstead [anchorage] named in honor of San Juan Capistrano by the mariners. This had a moderate inlet into which empties the little stream of fresh water that runs down by the Mission buildings."*

ABOVE: *Henry Chapman Ford,*
San Juan Capistrano, *Mission Inn Foundation
and Museum, Riverside, CA;*
RIGHT: *Charles Percy Austin,*
San Juan Capistrano, *1924, oil on canvas,
30 x 60 in., Private Collection, courtesy of
The Irvine Museum*

Periodically, a mission supply ship would arrive from San Diego at the cove in Capistrano Bay. Although the trip covered a distance of only 50 miles, the voyage was against continuous headwinds and often took ten days to complete.

Mission Indians met the ship and unloaded the cargo of manufactured goods. As the anchorage at Capistrano Bay served as the official *embarcadero*, or port, for both Mission San Juan Capistrano and Mission San Gabriel, supplies were hauled on wooden oxcarts about three miles to Capistrano and more than 50 miles on El Camino Real to San Gabriel.

According to historian Leland L. Estes, the new mission took in some 300,000 acres, and extended from the Santa Ana River south to San Mateo Creek, just below present-day San Clemente, and from the Pacific Ocean inland to the top of the Santa Ana Mountains. Most of the acreage was grazing land.

The padres, working with local Indians, built a new church and a cluster of buildings around a large square courtyard. The herds were relocated to the new site, and field crops, vineyards and orchards were planted. When all these things were done, a series of small adobe houses were built outside the mission quadrangle to house the Indian neophytes.

Materials for construction were obtained from various nearby locales. Adobe bricks were made on-site, using local mud and grasses. Wood was cut from large trees in El Toro. Large boulders, which served as foundations for adobe walls, were gathered from the beach at Dana Cove. They were loaded onto *carretas*, two-wheeled wooden oxcarts, and hauled to the mission. Mortar was made with lye, made by burning ground-up abalone shells collected along the shore.

The mission complex became vast in design, including granaries, a winery and brandy distillery, tallow vats, hide tanning pits, harness- and shoe-making, weaving, dyeing, candle- and soap-making shops, and 40 adobes, where the neophytes were housed. Moreover, the Mission San Juan Capistrano had the only known foundry and iron forge in Alta California.

Eventually, the mission maintained vast herds of cattle and sheep, which covered the bluff tops of Capistrano Bay, on its open-range grazing lands that stretched for miles along the coast. It was the Indian converts' job to tend the mission

LEFT: J. Whytock, Smelting Furnaces, Mission San Juan Capistrano, *Mission San Juan Capistrano; RIGHT: Ruins of San Juan Capistrano smelting furnaces, photo courtesy of Mission San Juan Capistrano*

Lloyd Harting;
LEFT: Loading the Carreta;
RIGHT: Processing Hides at the Mission;
Mission San Juan Capistrano

herds. The Spanish rule that neophytes must not learn to ride was ignored, and the Indians, who had never seen horses or cattle, were taught to be cowboys. The Indians were also taught to scrape and tan hides and to fashion leather into harnesses and shoes. They learned to render fat into tallow, which they used to make soap and candles. They were taught to shear sheep from the mission flocks, process the wool and then dye and weave the yarn into rough cloth. Much of the instruction was done outside the mission quadrangle.

Mission historian Monsignor Weber described what seems to be an ideal work schedule for mission Indians, suggesting that the neophytes' daily activities were far from arduous. They were awakened at sunrise with the ringing of the first bell. A second bell summoned them to mass, after which they had breakfast and assembled in the courtyard for their daily tasks. From 9 a.m. to 11:15 a.m., they worked at their chores. After a break of an hour and a half for lunch, they returned to work for two more hours. After dinner, there were games, music and fun. The last bell was rung at 8 p.m., and 45 minutes later, the mission gates were closed for the night. Field and cattle hands followed a different schedule, and work hours varied, depending on the tasks.

Benjamin C. Brown,
Corridors of San Juan Capistrano, *watercolor,*
Mr. & Mrs. David Lassen

In 1797, the cornerstone was laid for the greatest and most ambitious building at the Mission San Juan Capistrano, the Great Stone Church. This edifice, made of sandstone quarried from a local site, became the largest structure in California. The plan called for a Spanish-style cruciform church, with the main doors facing south, a central aisle, a large dome over the crossing, six smaller domes and a tall bell tower. The large labor force needed for the construction was composed of Juaneño Indians, as the soldiers found any type of heavy labor unacceptable. A master stonemason named Isidro Aguilar was brought in from Mexico to supervise construction.

During construction of the church, religious services continued as before, in the small adobe chapel now called the Serra Chapel. In 1803, Aguilar died; without his guiding hand, construction took more than eight years, much longer than expected.

Finally, in 1806, the Great Stone Church was completed and personally dedicated by Father Serra. Many dignitaries attended the ceremony. Governor José Arrillaga arrived accompanied by soldiers in glittering uniforms, from San Diego and Santa Barbara. The cathedral-like church was crowded with neophytes from distant *rancherías*. The rows of magical, flickering tapers, made of tallow mixed with native beeswax, excited the mystical side of those Indians whose spirits now resided in the Christian community. Many had even agreed to be baptized primarily so they could attend the alluring candlelit ceremonies, not fully understanding the implications of the act. A fiesta followed that became a legend in southern California, with feasting and praying lasting for several days.

For the next six years, the Mission San Juan Capistrano had the largest and grandest church in California. It could be seen along the entire Capistrano Valley and its bells heard at least ten miles out to sea.

Franz A. Bischoff, San Juan Capistrano Mission Yard, *c. 1924, oil on canvas, 24 x 30 in., Private Collection, courtesy of The Irvine Museum*

Alexander Harmer, Mission San Juan Capistrano, *1886, oil on canvas, 22 x 32 in.,*
The Irvine Museum

The mission thrived with activity. More than 1,200 people lived and worked there. Because of the mild climate, fertile soil and good water supply, agricultural production flourished. In 1811, the mission records show a harvest of 500,000 pounds of wheat, 190,000 pounds of barley, 202,000 pounds of corn, 20,600 pounds of beans, 14,000 cattle, 16,000 sheep and 740 horses. Thriving vineyards produced wine and brandy, and olives from the orchards were pressed for valuable oil. Pomegranates and figs were also important produce from the mission orchards.

Because of this abundance, ships frequently stopped at Capistrano Bay to conduct trade. Some ships came to purchase supplies for their voyages, such as grain, wine, olive oil and hemp rope, while others came bearing manufactured goods and exotic items to trade for mission hides and tallow. Among the most desirable items these ships offered to the mission were books, bells, special utensils and ornaments for the church, and long awaited news from the rest of the world.

Tragically, on a summer-like morning of December 8, 1812, a severe earthquake shook the region, just as Indian converts were in the church celebrating mass. Walls swayed, the domes fell in and the bell tower collapsed on the main part of the church, killing 40 people. Adequate resources were never again gathered to rebuild the church. What had been the most imposing edifice of its time had become California's most beautiful ruin. Religious services were once again held in the old adobe church known as the Serra Chapel.

The earthquake and destruction of the Great Stone Church gave rise to one of California's enduring legends, the story of a mestizo girl named Magdalena and an Indian artist named Teofilo. Magdalena was a beautiful young Juaneño girl, and Teofilo was in love with her. However, Magdalena's parents objected to the relationship, and any hope of their marriage was forbidden. Still, they met in secret until she was caught by her father. On the morning of December 8, 1812, Magdalena was compelled to walk into the church holding a penitent's candle for all to see. When the earthquake struck, Teofilo ran into the church to rescue Magdalena. Both were killed when the church collapsed. The legend says that on certain nights, one can see Magdalena in the upstairs window of the ruins of the Great Stone Church, still holding the penitent's candle, which illuminates her beautiful face.

Although the Great Stone Church was destroyed, the mission survived. Like a small city, it was self-contained and self-sufficient. People grew their own food, made their own clothes and worked at many trades.

Sydney Laurence, The Evening Star, San Juan Capistrano, *oil on canvas, 20 x 16 in., The Irvine Museum*

Bouchard the Pirate

Starting in 1808, a number of Spanish colonies in the New World began revolutionary movements that would eventually lead to the breakup of the Spanish Empire. Revolutionists in Chile, Ecuador and Argentina were boldly staging sporadic attacks on Spanish assets in the colonies. Although distant and isolated, California felt these stirrings indirectly when in 1808, the regular supply ships from San Blas failed to arrive in sufficient numbers to meet the needs of California. Resources were redirected to more urgent problem areas; Spain was being stretched to the breaking point.

In 1810, Mexico started the long process that would eventually gain it its independence. The Spanish Empire took quick action. All ship traffic that routinely supplied Alta California from Mexico was stopped, and all resources and supplies were consolidated in the effort to keep the rich province of Mexico within the Spanish fold. In fact, after 1810, soldiers in California were no longer being paid by Spain, and Alta California was all but abandoned. With no military support from Spain, the settlements along the California coast were poorly prepared to defend themselves against any outside attack.

Russell A. Ruiz, Hippolyte Bouchard, *oil on canvasboard, 16 x 12 in., Santa Barbara Historical Society*

Thus, in November 1818, California was "invaded" in a series of raids, first at Monterey, then at Santa Barbara and finally at San Juan Capistrano. The invader was Hippolyte de Bouchard, a French captain operating as a privateer under authorization from the revolutionary government of the Republic of Buenos Aires (Argentina), which had only recently gained independence from Spain. His commission authorized him to raid Spanish ports in the Pacific. Although he flew the flag of the insurgent Republic of Buenos Aires and claimed to be fighting for Argentina against the Spanish Empire, Bouchard took delight in looting homes and churches, and his actions were in reality none other than those of a pirate.

Setting out on his ship, the *Argentina*, Bouchard raided Spanish ships and settlements in Madagascar, Indonesia and the Philippines. The ship was so heavy with plunder—which his detractors said included crucifixes and chalices from churches—that he stopped in Hawaii to sell it. He was also in Hawaii to reclaim an American ship that had been an Argentine privateer before it was impounded by King Kamehameha. When Bouchard demanded the return of the vessel, the Hawaiian king quickly agreed, and the ship, now called the *Santa Rosa*, became the second half of Bouchard's fleet, with Peter Corney, an English soldier of fortune, as captain.

Bouchard's officers were mostly Americans fighting for the liberation of Spain's colonies. His crew, however, was an assortment of 350 men, made up of adventurers, criminals and revolutionists, all interested in getting rich by looting Spanish outposts. Most were Hawaiians, who went about naked and fought with long pikes instead of swords and pistols. The rest were from Spain, Portugal, England and Australia. Bouchard was notorious for the harsh and strict discipline he imposed on his crew, who feared him more than any enemy.

Bouchard was equally notorious to his enemies. He counted on his reputation for cruelty and ruthlessness to instill fear in his intended victims. In spite of the preposterous aspect of his crew, Bouchard's ships were a serious fighting force and posed a deadly threat to the lightly defended settlements of California. The *Argentina*, the larger of the two vessels, had a crew of 266 and boasted 38 heavy cannons. The *Santa Rosa* carried 100 men and 26 cannons.

When word reached Alta California that Bouchard was on his way, Governor Pablo Vicente de Solá ordered that all sacred objects and vestments be taken from the missions and hidden inland. Women and children were warned to be ready

J. Cardero, Presidio of Monterey, *The Bancroft Library, University of California, Berkeley*

to evacuate at a moment's notice. Even though they were usually short of gunpowder, the presidios did the best they could to prepare for attack.

Bouchard entered Monterey Bay and immediately opened fire on the presidio with the mistaken notion that the small, dilapidated fort was in no shape to defend itself. To his surprise, the Californios, under the command of Governor Solá, returned fire and showed no inclination to surrender. The *Santa Rosa* was hit several times. Three of the *Santa Rosa*'s men landed to discuss a truce but were immediately taken prisoner. Thereafter, Bouchard moved in with the *Argentina*, landed men and cannon and proceeded inland. Seeing that they were greatly outnumbered, Solá ordered a retreat inland toward present-day Salinas.

Bouchard and his crew landed in Monterey and burned the presidio. The pirates went from house to house, taking what they wanted and burning the rest. He stayed in Monterey for about a week to bury the dead, care for the wounded and make repairs to the *Santa Rosa*. After taking several Spanish prisoners, Bouchard left Monterey.

Sailing south, he attacked and looted several settlements. In Refugio Bay, Bouchard stopped to loot the rancho of the wealthy Ortega family. He was met by a group of 30 vaqueros led by Sergeant Antonio Carrillo. Although the pirate force overwhelmed the local defenders, the vaqueros nevertheless managed to capture three pirates by lassoing them in true Californio style.

Bouchard's next stop was Santa Barbara. He did not attack the town, but managed to exchange his prisoners for the pirates taken in Monterey. News of Bouchard's attack in Monterey and his landing in Santa Barbara reached Los Angeles, and a small detachment of men was sent to Capistrano to help defend the mission.

On December 14, 1818, Bouchard put into Port San Juan, now called Dana Point Harbor. He marched inland to the town of San Juan Capistrano under a flag of truce. In need of supplies, he sent a note stating that if he were given aid, he would not attack the town. The town fathers were aware of his previous stops in California and the destruction he had caused. They reasoned that they were Spanish, and Bouchard was an enemy of Spain, and therefore he was refused supplies.

The next day, Bouchard and 140 of his men raided San Juan Capistrano. The defenders fired a few shots and ran into the hills to hide. Bouchard's men looted the town, took what they needed and burned several buildings. The raid lasted well into the night. Many of the crew got drunk on wine and liquor. Peter Corney, captain of the *Santa Rosa*, noted, "*We found the town well stocked with everything but money, and destroyed much wine and spirits and all the public property, set fire to the King's stores, barracks and Governor's house, and at about two o'clock, we marched back though not in the order that we went in, many of the men being intoxicated.*"

When he heard news of an approaching army from Los Angeles, Bouchard set sail, leaving six men behind. It is thought that they either took the opportunity to jump ship or simply were too drunk to find their way back.

After Bouchard's departure, the residents returned to the hills to retrieve their buried possessions. It was thought that many people could not remember just

Edward Borein, Mission San Juan Capistrano,
etching, 9 x 12½ in.,
DeRu's Fine Arts, Laguna Beach, CA

exactly where they had buried their valuables, thus giving rise to stories of buried treasure in the hills around the mission. While it is highly unlikely that either the padres, who had taken vows of poverty, or the Indians, who were poor, had anything of value to hide, the stories of fantastic buried treasure still persist.

Fearing that they would be next, the citizens of San Diego evacuated all women and children. At the presidio, soldiers prepared for battle. But Bouchard never landed in San Diego; instead he sailed south where he attacked a ship near San Blas, Mexico.

Bouchard returned to South America and ended up fighting in the Peruvian navy. He was awarded a cocoa plantation for his services, but his treatment of the native workers was so harsh that they rebelled and killed him in 1837. In November 1962, Bouchard was recognized by the Government of Argentina as a hero of the War for Independence. They sent a special ship to Peru to take his remains back to Buenos Aires, where he was given a state funeral.

After Bouchard, life in San Juan Capistrano returned to normal. Yet, the years leading to Mexican Independence in 1821 were marked by neglect and gradual decline. From 1810 to 1821, no supply ship was sent from Mexico to any settlement in Alta California. The Mission San Juan Capistrano experienced repeated periods of poor harvests and declining Indian conversions. The years after Mexican Independence were even more discouraging, as it was official Mexican policy to reduce the power of the missions and eventually secularize and close them altogether. In 1829, Alfred Robinson, an American traveler, visited Capistrano and wrote, *"Though in its early years, it was the largest [mission] in the country, yet it is now in a dilapidated state and the Indians are much neglected."*

Although Mexico's official policy was to secularize the missions throughout its realm, enforcement of laws was generally left to local officials, and in Alta

California, none of the governors were willing to take this drastic step until 1825, when José Maria Echeandía, the first Mexican-born Governor of California, came into office.

In 1831, Governor Echeandía passed the Declaration of Emancipation, stating that from that point on, Indians would receive Mexican citizenship and be free from mission control. The law, however, was never carried out. In 1833, Mexico passed a general secularization law, which was approved by the Californio Diputación a year later. All mission lands, livestock, tools and supplies were confiscated and divided, half to resident Indians and the other half to be administered "for the public good." By law, the missions were to become Indian pueblos, but in reality, the most desirable tracts of former mission lands ended up in the hands of Californio administrators and their families. By 1834, all friars were reduced to be simply curates, and the civic power that they had once exercised was stripped away.

In San Juan Capistrano, the lands and buildings were valued at $56,456. The 861 Indian neophytes who were attached to the mission were given the choice of staying in a newly organized pueblo or simply returning to Indian life in the hills. Either way, it would be a life of poverty and uncertainty.

By 1841, the Indian pueblo was declared a failure and terminated. In its place, Governor Juan Bautista Alvarado, on July 29, 1841, created a new pueblo by granting a small plot of land to any citizen willing to cultivate and maintain it. The plan was a success and the town of San Juan Capistrano was born. The old mission, however, continued to decline. It had been stripped of all its lands, fields and orchards, the resident priest had vacated and the buildings were left to decay. ❧

ABOVE:
Main Street, San Juan Capistrano, c. 1890;
Yorba Adobes, c. 1910;
San Juan Capistrano Historical Society;
RIGHT:
Joseph Kleitsch, San Juan Capistrano, 1924,
oil on canvas, 36 x 40 in., Private Collection,
courtesy of The Irvine Museum

John Frost, Mount San Jacinto, *1926,*
oil on canvas, 24 x 28 in., Private Collection,
courtesy of The Irvine Museum

CHAPTER 8

DE ANZA AND THE COLONIZATION OF CALIFORNIA

*U*ntil the missions could develop their own food production, Alta California had to be supplied by ship from the port of San Blas, about 50 miles north of present-day Puerto Vallarta, in Nayarit, Mexico. The voyage was long and the hazards of the journey—sailors dying of scurvy or ships being lost at sea—made the supply link unreliable. The growing dependence of the newly founded missions on an unreliable maritime supply route resulted in periods of deprivation and hardship that caused many neophytes to leave the missions and return to their native way of life. On one such occasion, a priest who had visited the San Diego Mission in its early days remarked that the missionaries there had only the "bread of affliction and the waters of disaster."

The supply issue was of vital concern to Father Serra, who petitioned Visitador-General José de Gálvez to take steps to establish an inland supply route. To this end, Juan Bautista de Anza (1736–1788) was sent in 1774 to find a passage from the northern part of Mexico, in the present-day state of Sonora, through the desert to Mission San Gabriel.

Captain de Anza was the military commander of Tubac, an important frontier outpost in Sonora. Born in Mexico, he grew up in the small town of Frontera, in Sonora, just south of present-day Douglas, Arizona. Anza was a third-generation Indian fighter whose father had been killed by Apaches.

A capable and determined man, Anza was renowned as a fearless fighter. Under the direction of Gálvez, Anza had earlier led a punitive expedition against the Pima and Seri Indians and had killed a famous Indian chief in hand-to-hand combat. In his dealings with the Indians, he had often heard them talk of other Spaniards, far inland, across the desert. As the only other Spanish settlement in that direction was in California, Anza understood that there was indeed a way from Northern Mexico to California, via the desert.

On January 8, 1774, Anza set out from the presidio of San Ignacio de Tubac, located about 45 miles south of present-day Tucson, Arizona. The expedition counted on Father Francisco Garcés to guide them. Garcés was a courageous frontier missionary who had explored the desert in 1771 and gone across the Colorado River to the foothills of the Sierra Nevada Mountains. Anza also had the services of Juan Bautista Valdés—a veteran of the Portolá expedition and called "de Anza's Kit Carson" by historians—to get them across the desert. If they succeeded in crossing the desert, they would need to find San Gabriel, and for that Anza had the services of an Indian named Sebastián Tarabal, who had run away from the Mission San Gabriel, ending up across the desert in Sonora. The rest of the party included two priests,

20 soldiers and eight Indians. They took along 35 pack-loads of supplies, 65 cattle and 140 horses.

Following the Gila River, Anza kept to a northwest course and reached the Gila-Colorado junction and the region of the war-like Yuma Indians. There, he befriended the natives by distributing small trinkets, crossed the Colorado River and headed into a vast area of sand dunes. Anza reasoned that this would be the most difficult part of the journey.

By the first of March, they had come 591 miles from Tubac. Fortunately, just as they were desperately short of water, they encountered two Indians who directed them to a site where water could be found. On March 8, Anza arrived at a place they named "Santa Rosa de las Lajas" (Santa Rosa of the Flat Rocks), where they found water and good pasturage for the animals. Most important, however, Sebastián Tarabal, the San Gabriel Indian, found the country familiar. This was good news, as Anza wrote in his diary, *"We celebrated our arrival at this place [Santa Rosa de las Lajas] because from it, the California Indian has recognized that he is now near a place where he formerly was, and therefore we now promise ourselves that our expedition will not fail."*

They next arrived at the peninsular ranges, between the San Jacinto and Santa Rosa mountains, and thanks to Sebastián Tarabal, on March 15 they found a pass that Anza named "El Puerto Real de San Carlos" (San Carlos Pass, in Riverside County). Entering the coastal plain, the expedition made quick headway and on March 22, Anza reached the Mission San Gabriel, after a trek of more than 700 miles from Tubac. After a brief stay in San Gabriel, Anza continued to Monterey, mapping potential settlement sites along the way.

In his report to the Viceroy of Mexico, Anza described his route as one that would allow movement of supplies without great difficulty. He also noted that all Indian tribes encountered were either weak or friendly, failing to point out the notable exception of the powerful and belligerent Yuma Indians, who controlled the vital crossing point across the mighty Colorado River.

Cocopah, Colorado River, *lithograph, Sarony, Major & Knapp, 1857, Private Collection*

RIGHT:
Benjamin Brown, *South Fork, San Gabriel,*
oil on canvas, 25 x 30 in., Private Collection,
courtesy of The Irvine Museum;
BELOW:
Paul Grimm, *San Jacinto, oil on canvas,*
30 x 40 in., Jean and Laura Stern

Jack Wilkinson Smith,
Untitled (Landscape with Mountains)
oil on canvas, 24 x 30 in., Private Collection,
courtesy of The Irvine Museum

THE PUEBLOS OF CALIFORNIA

During the Spanish period in Alta California, only four presidios were established: San Diego (1769), Monterey (1770), San Francisco (1776) and Santa Barbara (1782). *"The actual construction of presidios,"* writes W.W. Robinson in his book *Land in California,* *"followed an established pattern. The features of the presidio…were an outer surrounding ditch, the enclosure forming a quadrilateral; a rampart twelve or fifteen feet high and three feet thick; small bastions; an armament of bronze cannon, eight-, twelve-, and sixteen-pounders; within the enclosure, a church, barracks, houses for colonists, storehouses, workshops, stables, wells, and cisterns; outside were some houses and, at greater distance, the King's farm (El Rancho del Rey), which furnished pasturage to horses and cattle."*

In total, Spanish military presence in Alta California numbered no more than 400 men. In time, the protection of the presidios attracted commercial activity, and the small pueblos that developed outside their walls eventually became the large cities of San Diego, Monterey, San Francisco and Santa Barbara. At first, the presidial pueblos were under military rule, but as they grew, they established their own civilian administrations.

Soon after the establishment of the presidios and missions in San Diego and Monterey, Spain began making plans for pueblos in Alta California. The pueblos were the civilian part of Spain's colonization policy. Each pueblo was granted four square leagues (a square league was about 4,440 acres) of land, a little more than 17,000 acres. This would allow for houses, small garden plots and common grazing grounds.

While most missions and presidios developed pueblos around them, only three civil settlements (pueblos) were actually established on their own, one of which failed. Governor Felipe de Neve (in office from 1775–1782) authorized colonists for San José de Guadalupe (the present-day city of San José), founded on November 2, 1777, Nuestra Señora la Reina de Los Ángeles de la Porciúncula (Los Angeles), founded on September 4, 1781, and Branciforte, in 1797, which was later abandoned.

San José was at first just a collection of mud huts on the banks of the Guadalupe River. The Mission San José de Guadalupe was established 20 years later.

Los Angeles began with a group of 44 *pobladores* (settlers), 11 couples and their 22 children. The heads of these 11 founding families included: Antonio Villavicencio and José Fernando Lara, who were Spanish; Antonio Mesa and Luis Quintero, who were black; José Venegas, Pablo Rodriguez, Basilio Rosas and Alejandro Rosas, who were Indian; José Antonio Navarro, a mestizo; and Manuel Camero and José Moreno, who were mulatto. The two Spaniards and three Indians had Indian wives; the remaining six had mulatto wives. These first citizens, recruited from western Mexico, clearly had differing backgrounds, but they were all Catholics and Spanish subjects. None of these settlers could write his own name.

In 1788, Los Angeles elected its first mayor, José Venegas, an Indian. Juan Francisco Reyes, a mulatto settler who arrived later, served as mayor of Los Angeles from 1793–1795. Catarina Moreno, daughter of the mulatto founder José Moreno, married General Andrés Pico, whose illustrious family had both Indian and African ancestors. Her brother-in-law, Pío Pico, was the last Mexican Governor of California. Their sister, Ysidora Pico, married John Forster of San Juan Capistrano.

The third civic pueblo, named "Branciforte" after the Viceroy of Mexico, was established across the river from the Mission Santa Cruz in 1797. It was planned to be a pueblo as well as a small presidio. Its 17 founders were made up of nine soldier-colonists and eight convicts sent to California as part of their prison terms.

From the beginning, the padres at Mission Santa Cruz were opposed to having Branciforte in the vicinity. The unruly settlers quickly encroached on mission pastureland and began to lure away neophytes to work as servants. In 1818, while the pirate Bouchard was attacking Monterey, the citizens of Branciforte crossed the river and looted the Mission Santa Cruz after it had been evacuated as a precaution. Over the years, the growing criminal element in Branciforte drove many of its honest settlers away, and the pueblo became a staging area for smugglers in the hide and tallow trade. By 1841, it was no longer a functioning pueblo and went out of existence.

Each pueblo family was given a piece of land to farm and on which to build a house. In addition, they were furnished with an allowance for clothing and supplies, a horse, mules, cattle, tools to clear and plow the land and free use of public grazing lands. They were expected to clear their land, build a house, dig irrigation ditches and keep their plot under cultivation. For five years, they were exempt from taxes. After that, they would own the land free and clear. In return for all this, the men were to make themselves and their horses available for military service should the need ever arise, and once they owned the land, pay taxes to the Governor in Monterey.

Miguel Cabrera, Castas de Mexico, Mestizos, 1763, Elisabeth Waldo-Dentzel Multicultural Arts Studio, Northridge, CA

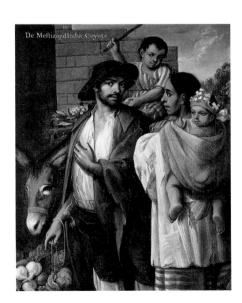

In 1775, Anza was commissioned to establish a presidio in the San Francisco Bay area. At the same time, he would found a "pueblo de Gente de Razón" attached to the presidio. The term "Gente de Razón" (People of Reason) was used by the Spanish authorities to differentiate between Spanish settlers and Indians, who they called "Gente sin Razón" (People without Reason) and whose settlements were termed *rancherías*. One of the stated purposes of the mission system was to bring civilization to the natives by converting them to Christianity. Thus, an Indian neophyte would enter the mission system and after several years of education, become one of the civilized people, or Gente de Razón.

The second Anza expedition brought the very first group of colonists to Alta California. The party of 245 people included several soldiers who brought their families. All soldiers recruited as colonists were to be married men. This was done for two reasons: to rectify the recent troubles caused by unmarried soldiers and their offensive behavior toward Indian women, and also in view of the Indians' general hostility toward any unmarried man, believing him to be a social outcast. Looking to settle the new territory, the colonists also brought along tools, farming implements, seed, horses, mules and cattle.

Anza and the colonists set out from Tubac on October 23, 1775. They passed through Tucson, then west to the Colorado River, and arrived at San Gabriel on January 4, 1776. Having safely completed the most dangerous part of the journey, the expedition continued north on El Camino Real and reached Monterey on March 10. Leaving the colonists in Monterey, Anza led a scouting party to San Francisco Bay and mapped the future sites of the presidio and mission. In June, he returned with the colonists and on September 17, 1776, dedicated the Presidio de San Francisco de Asís. On October 9, Father Palóu founded the Mission San Francisco de Asís (Mission Dolores). The route Anza pioneered is now called the Juan Bautista de Anza National Historic Trail.

The key to the Anza overland route was the settlement of Concepción, guarding the strategic crossing of the Colorado River at Yuma, Arizona. In spite of several reports about the hostile nature of the Yuma Indians, Teodoro de Croix, the Commandante-General of the Interior Provinces, diverted most of his military forces to deal with the Apaches in Arizona, dismissing all California Indian tribes as peaceable and compliant. In fact, of all California Indians, the Yumas proved to be the least amenable to the mission system.

At first, the Spaniards were generous with their gifts to the Yumas, hoping to buy their friendship. At best, relations between the Spaniards and Yuma Indians were always precarious, but as the presents grew fewer, tensions grew hotter. Adding to the pressure, the Yumas complained that the soldiers were abusive to their women. Unwilling to appear weak by addressing grievances, the military responded with force to all Indian demands.

The crisis peaked on July 17, 1781, when irate Indians attacked two missions, La Purísima Concepción (commonly called "Concepción") and San Pedro y San Pablo (St. Peter and St. Paul), which were situated not far from the river crossing. In all, the Yumas killed Father Garcés and three other missionaries, as well as all the adult males they encountered. Word of the raid spread through the entire region, driving many settlers into the garrison for protection. The following day, the Yumas attacked the garrison and killed as many as 50 soldiers, including Captain Rivera y Moncada, the leader of the "leather-jackets" who had accompanied Portolá. Ninety-one others, mostly women and children, were taken prisoner by the Yumas. No Spanish settlement was spared. All buildings and structures were burned to the ground as the Indians retreated into the hills with their captives.

Lloyd Harting;
TOP: Crossing the Colorado,
BOTTOM: Founding the Presidio of
San Francisco,
The James S. Copley Library, La Jolla, CA

In September, Pedro Fages, now a Lieutenant Colonel, led an expedition of 50 of his Catalonian Volunteers and 70 soldiers from the presidio of Hermosillo, in northern Mexico, to rescue the captives and punish the Yumas for the uprising. They faced the Indians in several skirmishes but none was decisive. By October, they had recovered the remains of Father Garcés and the other missionaries and given them a proper burial. They had also rescued 63 people, mostly by ransom, on one occasion negotiating with a Yuma chief who wore Captain Rivera's bloody uniform. Fages pursued the Yumas over the next 12 months but failed to subdue the warlike tribe. In September 1782, Fages was called back to serve as Governor of Alta California, and the campaign against the Yuma Indians was abandoned. The failure to regain the Colorado River crossing effectively closed the Anza route for many years and returned California's missions, presidios and pueblos to the uncertain and irregular lifeline from the sea.

THE FIRST LAND GRANTS

With the coming of colonists soon after the establishment of the first missions in Alta California, Spain began bestowing a small number of land concessions, called "ranchos", to individuals who merited special rewards. In 1784, a few men who had been soldiers under the command of Juan José Fages in 1769 were chosen to receive recognition. These first ranchos included the Rancho Dominguez, about 72,000 acres from the San Gabriel River west to Redondo Beach; the Rancho San Rafael, about 36,000 acres north of Los Angeles, given to José Maria Verdugo; and the most generous of these early grants, the Rancho de Nieto, 300,000 acres to Manuel Nieto,

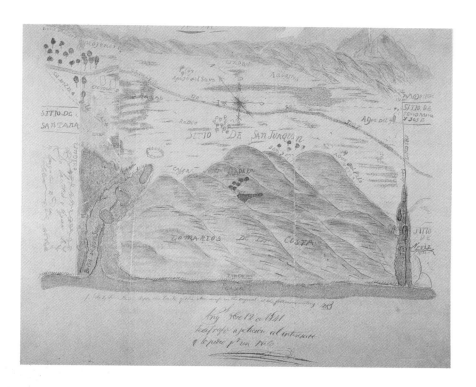

Rancho San Joaquin, *diseño, 1841, Sherman Library and Gardens, Corona del Mar, CA*

including all the land from the San Gabriel River south to the Santa Ana River, and west to the ocean.

The largest rancho in what is now Orange County was the Rancho Santiago de Santa Ana, granted on July 1, 1810. This grant stretched from the east bank of the Santa Ana River south to the ocean and east to the mountains. At about 79,000 acres, the Rancho Santiago was the principal rancho to later be incorporated into the sprawling Irvine Ranch. The grant was made jointly to José Antonio Yorba, who had come to California as a soldier in the Catalonian Volunteers for Portolá's expedition of 1769, and his father-in-law, Juan Pablo Grijalva, a colonist who had arrived with Anza in 1776.

These early ranchos were granted at a time when no other property claims existed. As such, they were recorded on a simple map, called a *diseño*, surveyed with crude measuring devices and described with landmarks such as streams, rocks, trees or roads, which may or may not have remained after a few years. It was inevitable that boundaries would overlap when new claims were recorded, and grants would be contested many years later as more accurate maps were plotted. ◈

CHAPTER 9

SECULARIZATION OF THE MISSIONS

All California missions were supported by huge tracts of land. The missions were intended to be only temporary, as they were to convert and civilize the natives and then move on to new frontier areas. In fact, the original plan by José de Gálvez in 1769 projected no more than ten years before a mission would complete its work and proceed to a new area. As such, their lands were granted by Royal Charter with usufructuary rights, meaning that the grantees were allowed free use of the land and could derive benefit from it, but the grants could be canceled at any time. Indeed, the ten-year plan did not work out and by the 1820s, the missions were permanent fixtures in California.

In time, the missions became large agricultural systems that depended on Indians as an unpaid labor force. To ensure that the missions had all they needed for their important tasks, the king granted them very generous amounts of land. The first mission in the chain, San Diego de Alcalá, had lands that stretched about 34 miles to the south, 44 miles to the east and 18 miles to the north. The Mission San Fernando was granted more than 220,000 acres, or 50 square leagues. Larger yet was the grant to the Mission San Juan Capistrano. The largest of all, however, was the Mission San Gabriel, which held land that stretched some 15 miles south to San Pedro, and 52 miles to the east and southeast. In addition to all this open land, used primarily for grazing, Mission San Gabriel held 6,000 acres of irrigated land for various crops to support its large neophyte population.

OPPOSITE:
Manuel Valencia, Inside the Ruins of Carmel Mission, *oil on canvas, 30 x 20 in., DeRu's Fine Arts, Laguna Beach, CA*
RIGHT:
Ferdinand Deppe, Mission San Gabriel, *1832, Santa Barbara Mission Archive Library*

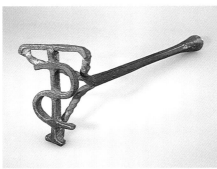

LEFT: *Branding iron of the Mission San Juan Capistrano, History Collections, Los Angeles County Museum of Natural History;* RIGHT: Cattle Drive at the Mission San Gabriel, *pen and ink, Mission San Juan Capistrano Museum*

By the early 1830s, the peak period of the missions, just prior to secularization, the 21 missions in Alta California, situated along the 700 miles of El Camino Real, housed more than 30,000 Indian neophytes. Moreover, as a group, the missions kept more than 400,000 cattle, 60,000 horses and 300,000 sheep, goats and pigs. Their combined annual agricultural production totaled 120,000 bushels of wheat, corn and beans. As for manufacturing, the mission system turned out substantial quantities of wine and brandy; hides for saddles and other leather goods; tallow, which was made into soap and candles; olives and olive oil; wool for rough cloth; as well as cotton, hemp, linen, brick, tiles, tobacco and salt.

The variety of industries and occupations at the Mission San Gabriel was noted in great detail by Hugo Reid, a Scotsman who lived in San Gabriel in the 1840s:

Thus the people were divided into various classes and stations. There were vaqueros, soap makers, tanners, shoemakers, carpenters, blacksmiths, bakers, cooks, general servants, pages, fishermen,

Virgil Williams; LEFT: Opposite the Church, San Gabriel, *oil on board, 4½ x 10⅝ in.;* RIGHT: House of the Padre's Housekeeper, San Gabriel, *oil on board, 10⅝ x 13⅝ in.; North Point Gallery, San Francisco*

agriculturists, horticulturists, brick and tile makers, musicians, singers, tallow melters, vignerons, cart makers, shepherds, poultry keepers, pigeon tenders, weavers, spinners, saddle makers, store and key keepers, deer hunters, deer and sheepskin dress makers, people of all work, and in fact everything but coopers, who were foreign; all the balance, masons, plasterers, etc., were natives. Large soap works were erected; tanning yards established; tallow works, bakery, cooper, blacksmith, carpenter, and other shops; large spinning rooms where might be seen 50 or 60 women turning their spindles merrily; and looms for weaving wool, flax and cotton. Then large storerooms were allotted to the various articles which were kept separate. For instance, wheat, barley, peas, beans, lentils, chickpeas, butter and cheese, soap, candles, wool, leather, flour, lime salt, horsehair, wine and spirits, fruit, stores, etc., etc.

Louis Choris;
TOP: *Danse des Californiens, 1816, watercolor, The Bancroft Library, University of California, Berkeley, Robert B. Honeyman, Jr. Collection;* BOTTOM: *Jeu des Habitants de Californie, colored lithograph, 7 x 10 in., Santa Barbara Museum of Art, Gift of Carol Valentine*

Padre's Garden in San Juan Capistrano
Mission, *c. 1880, photograph,
San Juan Capistrano Historical Society*

In 1821, Mexico won its independence from Spain. The provinces of California (Alta and Baja) and New Mexico (made up of the present-day states of Arizona and New Mexico) were claimed by the new nation of Mexico. The Spanish Royal laws that had always protected the missions were now replaced by Mexican laws, which had a decidedly anti-church character. In distant California, Mexican authority was generally slack, and enforcement of Mexican laws was an entirely local matter, the purview of the small group of wealthy families that virtually ran the government in California.

The California mission system, which had flourished under Spanish rule, deteriorated quickly in the Mexican period. The missions lost their special protection, and moves were made to break up their large landholdings. In one of the first steps toward secularization of the missions, California Governor José María de Echeandía passed the 1831 Declaration of Emancipation, and even though it was never carried out, it set the tone of things to come by stating that Indians would receive Mexican citizenship and be free from mission control. As the friars were the only ones who could induce the Indian neophytes to work, it was feared that complete and immediate secularization would cause a severe labor loss. Furthermore, the missionized Indians were generally peaceful and posed no threat of rebellion, whereas non-mission Indians were becoming more hostile, staging raids on isolated ranchos and settlements with greater frequency.

Nevertheless, in 1833, Mexico issued a sweeping law that immediately secularized all remaining mission property in California. Under this measure, all mission lands were immediately confiscated, leaving the Catholic Church only the buildings, which were to be turned into parish churches.

According to the secularization laws of 1833, the vast tracts of former mission land were to be divided equally, half going to the local Indians and half to the public domain to be granted as ranchos. However, within a few years, the portions of land that were set aside for mission Indians also ended up in the public domain, under the jurisdiction of the governor and local government officials who had the authority to issue grants. In the end, most of the best pieces of former mission land ended up going to wealthy Californios, usually friends or relatives of the governor.

As an institution of the frontier, the mission system was unable to withstand the assault of legislated civic envy. Within a few years, most missions were completely abandoned, with just a few enduring as small parish churches, catering to only a pale shadow of their former constituents. The only mission that was continually active and remained in the control of the Franciscan Order was the Mission Santa Barbara, although, like all other missions, it had lost its expansive holdings of land. Because it was near a busy port and served a prosperous population that included merchants and Yankee settlers, it successfully made the transition from a mission serving Indians to a parish church for local residents. Of the others, many were completely abandoned, and the only traces of the former glory of the California missions were occasionally a small group of Indians and one or two monks occupying the decaying remains of an old adobe building that once formed the mission church.

According to historian Robert Glass Cleland, the Secularization Act was *"designed to benefit the Indians and make them a self-sustaining people. Actually, it led to the rapid disintegration of the mission-controlled communities, scattered the partly civilized neophytes like sheep without a shepherd, ushered in a half century's tragic aftermath of wretchedness and poverty, brought about the virtual extinction of the mission system in California, and by throwing open millions of acres to private*

TOP: Mission Nuestra Señora de la Soledad, *c. 1885;*
BOTTOM: Mission San Luis Obispo, *c. 1890;*
vintage postcards, Private Collection

Towards the last few years of the 19th century, several of the larger, more accessible missions underwent various attempts at restoration. For many years, the Mission San Luis Obispo bore a Victorian-style tower and pointed-roof cupola, having no stylistic resemblance to its original Spanish Colonial architecture. The mission has since been restored again, to look much as it did when it was founded.

Charles Harmon, San Luis Rey,
oil on board, 30 x 46 in., Private Collection,
courtesy of The Irvine Museum

denouncement, revolutionized the departmental land system and made the rancho the
dominant economic and social institution of California."

THE LAND GRANTS

The period between 1833, when the missions were secularized, and 1848, when America took territorial possession, marks the peak of the rancho era, called the Golden Age of California. During the more than 50 years of Spanish Colonial rule, from 1769 to 1821, only about 25 land grants were awarded. Of these, most of the important ones were in southern California, situated within 100 miles of Los Angeles. Yet, from 1821 to 1848, under Mexican rule, between 500 and 700 grants were made. In 1840, a survey by William Heath Davis, Jr., an American resident of California, counted more than 1,000 ranchos of various sizes in the province.

The ranchos were the outcome of governmental grants of land. The Colonization Act of 1824 specified that land grants be no smaller than one square league (about 4,500 acres) to a maximum of 11 square leagues, or about 50,000 acres. The maximum size was arrived at by allowing one square league for irrigated land, four for farming and six for pasture. All previous "grants" made during the Spanish Period—which in reality were no more than provisional concessions or cattle-grazing permits to military veterans—were officially recorded and reissued as true grants. The law of 1824 also prohibited grants within ten leagues (about 25 miles) of the coast or 20 leagues (50 miles) from a national boundary, unless specially approved by the government in Mexico.

A subsequent Mexican land law, the Reglamento of 1828, gave provincial governors authority to grant vacant lands to *empresarios* (contractors who wished to start colonies) and families or private individuals for the purpose of cultivation or habitation. The two land laws of 1824 and 1828 became the legal basis under which all former mission lands were disposed of as grants by local officials between 1834 and 1846. The rigorously prudent system under which the Spanish administrators distributed land was quickly replaced by a system that favored generous gifts, bestowed without supervision to a multitude of private recipients.

In his book *The Resources of California*, published in 1869, John Hittell states: *"Public land was granted not by the acre, as in the American states, but by the square league (about 4,600 acres). The government granted away its land willingly, and without compensation; no pay was required; the only condition of the grant was that the grantee should occupy the land, build a house on it, and put several hundred head of cattle on it. It was a grand Mexican homestead law; and the chief complaint about it by the government, was that the number of applicants for grants was not greater."*

A grant applicant had to meet certain requirements: he had to be a Mexican citizen, either native-born or naturalized, had to present a description of the desired tract, and had to certify that the land was indeed vacant—that is, not already included in an existing rancho. In addition, applicants had to promise to build a house, plant trees and stock the land with the required number of cattle and horses. Failure to carry out these requirements within a certain time limit would void the grant. Inasmuch as native-born Mexican citizens received preference by law and foreigners were barred from owning land in proximity to the coast, the prime coastal lands that once belonged to the missions were almost always given to the native-born.

The grant request, which required a *diseño* (map) of the land in question, was sent to the governor and if he approved, the request was then sent to the local district official who ordered a "survey" to make certain the tract was in the public domain. This official survey was performed in an almost casual manner, with no serious attempts at accuracy so characteristic of modern land surveying, and liberal use of the Spanish phrase *mas o menos*, meaning "more or less." Since there were no fences and all livestock was allowed free range over the countryside, there was no need for accurate determination of property lines, as it was customary in California to view range lands belonging to various rancheros as common pasture.

Henry Chapman Ford, San Carlos Borromeo de Carmelo Ruins, *Mission Inn Foundation and Museum, Riverside, CA*

Two surveyors and an assortment of witnesses went to the site and prepared the *diseño*. The surveyors rode the periphery of the grant and measured the distances by using a long rawhide rope, or *reata*, the ends of which were tied to stakes. As one surveyor remained stationary, the other rode at a fast gallop along the proposed boundary line for the full length of the *reata*. He, in turn, would remain still as the first rider galloped past him to the end of his length of line, and so on. As they rode along, the witnesses counted the number of *reata* lengths between recognizable landmarks, such as a hill, a large tree, a boulder, a patch of cactus, a coyote den, or even a pile of rocks, and determined the length of each boundary. Where there were no recognizable landmarks, large wooden posts were driven into the ground and the prospective owner's cattle brand was burned into the posts. The information and measurements were noted and used to make the *diseño*.

According to Cleland, the 45,000-acre Rancho San Juan, or Rancho Cajón de Santa Ana, in present-day Orange County, was officially recorded as *"beginning at the River Santa Ana and running out on to the hills where there is a oak, near the Valley of the Elders, which line is contiguous to the property of Bernardo Yorba, from the oak to a stone which is permanent and another resting upon it. From the stone to the Pillar which is now fallen, from the Pillar to the Sycamore tree, from the Sycamore to the Lake and from there to the river."*

The survey of the Rancho La Bolsa Chica, also in Orange County, describes a line running from a willow tree on the shore to the edge of a marsh. When the mounted surveyors could not find a way across the marsh, a group of experts was called in to estimate the distance across the marsh to a tall hill, and that figure was entered as the official measurement of the boundary line.

When the *diseño* was completed and the grant request approved, the tract was formally presented and the owner walked through his new land. In a time-honored ceremony, he broke off branches, pulled up weeds and planted a fruit tree to show that he had taken legal possession.

While there was a limit to how large a grant could be, there was no limit to the number of grants one could own; a wealthy ranchero family could own several ranchos, some surpassing 100,000 acres in combined total. Furthermore, through marriage between two wealthy families, the total land owned by certain individuals reached immense proportions. The Rancho San Antonio, owned by Luís Peralta and his family, now comprises the cities of Oakland, Alameda, Berkeley and a large part of the East Bay across San Francisco. Perhaps the greatest of the rancheros in the north, Mariano Vallejo owned more than 100 square miles of land north of San Francisco. His rancho was manned by 2,000 Indians, who tended his extensive herds of cattle and horses.

Americans who settled in California and married into Californio families sometimes became owners of large ranchos. Henry Delano Fitch, who married into the Carrillo family, owned the Rancho Sotoyome in Sonoma County, with 50,000 acres, 14,000 head of cattle, 10,000 sheep and 1,000 horses. Abel Stearns, another Yankee-Californio who prospered in the hide and tallow trade, owned several ranchos that supported 30,000 head of cattle.

LEFT: The Old Spanish and Mexican Ranchos of Los Angeles County;
RIGHT: The Old Spanish and Mexican Ranchos of Orange County;
published by Title Insurance and Trust Co., Sherman Library and Gardens, Corona del Mar, CA

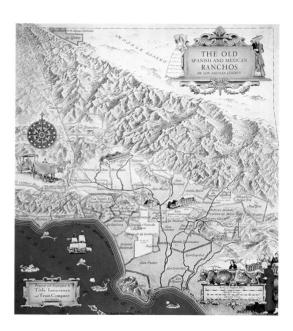

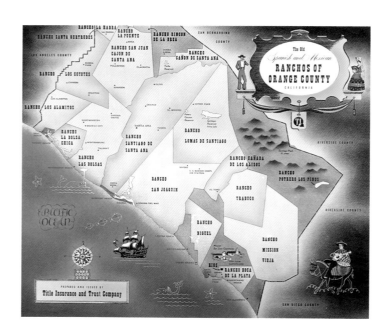

As large as the ranchos were in the north, those in southern California were even larger. The Rancho Los Nietos, given to Manuel Nieto in 1784, totaled more than 300,000 acres in what is now the southern part of Los Angeles County. This remarkable rancho had all the land from the San Gabriel River, south to the Santa Ana River, and west to the ocean, including half of what is today Orange County. The Rancho San Pedro, also called the Rancho Dominguez, was about 72,000 acres. Granted to Juan José Dominguez in 1784, it stretched from the San Gabriel River west to Redondo Beach. The Rancho Santiago de Santa Ana, a portion of which would later form a part of the Irvine Ranch, was granted to José Antonio Yorba and Juan Pablo Grijalva in 1802, and encompassed nearly 79,000 acres of present-day Orange County. The Rancho San Vicente y Santa Monica, granted to Francisco Sepúlveda, measured more than 30,000 acres of what is now the west side of the City of Los Angeles.

After 1821, all new grants in California were given by Mexico, and all previous grants dating from the Spanish period had to be confirmed by the Mexican government. After the Secularization Laws of 1834, all former mission lands were put into the public domain and made available for land grants. Toward the end of the Mexican regime, few governors could resist the temptation of the nearly limitless windfall at their disposal, and it became common practice for governors to give land grants to relatives and friends.

The last Mexican governor of California, the notoriously corrupt Pío Pico, gave out 87 grants in the last six months of his term, and almost all at the maximum size allowed of 11 square leagues (approximately 50,000 acres). However, Pico's role was not just as benefactor to his California friends—he had often been the beneficiary of other governors' largesse and had built his own tremendous fortune. ◈

Edward Vischer, Andrés Pico at Home, Mission San Fernando, *colored lithograph, The Bancroft Library, University of California, Berkeley*

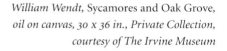

William Wendt, Sycamores and Oak Grove, *oil on canvas, 30 x 36 in., Private Collection, courtesy of The Irvine Museum*

William Hahn, Ranch Scene, Monterey, California, *1875, The Oakland Museum of California, Kahn Collection, Gift of Mr. & Mrs. Sidney L. Schwartz, to honor Dr. & Mrs. John J. Sampson and in memory of Mr. & Mrs. William E. Gump*

CHAPTER 10

CALIFORNIA'S GOLDEN AGE

California's so-called Golden Age, which was created long ago by romantic writers and deeply imbedded in popular tradition, was in reality an existence of extreme contrasts, as life on the ranchos was one of either lavish abundance or almost total deprivation. In a society for which the only occupation was raising cattle, manufactured goods and articles of clothing were always in short supply, and even the wealthiest rancheros and their families were completely cut off from all cultural amenities. Except for the missions, which were used for the indoctrination of the Indians, there were no schools in California, and many landowners signed legal documents, such as wills and petitions, with an "X," for the sign of the cross.

The Golden Age of California began with secularization of the missions in 1834, and lasted until the start of the American Conquest in 1846. *"It was,"* according to historian Robert Glass Cleland, *"the 'Day of the Dons,' the era of the private ranchos, the idyllic interlude during which a people of simple wants, untroubled either by poverty or by the ambition for great wealth, gave themselves over, wholeheartedly and successfully, to 'the grand and primary business of the enjoyment of life.'"*

Other than Native Americans, society in the Golden Age comprised three distinct classes. The most numerous were the cholos, or lower class, who inhabited the pueblos and were always desperately poor and sometimes a dangerous, vicious and lawless bunch. The second group was composed of Americans and other foreigners, some of whom married into families of the Gente de Razón and became large landowners or successful merchants. Among these influential foreigners were such men as Abel Stearns, Thomas O. Larkin, William Heath Davis, John Temple, William Workman, William Wolfskill and John A. Sutter. After the secularization of the missions, the rancheros made up the third and most significant element in California society.

The dependence on cattle ranching has led scholars to call the Californio rancho period one of the largest non-nomadic pastoral societies the world has ever known. Even after the U.S. Land Act of 1851 became law and Americans acquired most of the great ranchos, southern California remained a typical cattle frontier. The daily lives of the people retained the color, customs and traditions of the Mexican era, many of which have been passed on to us even to the present day.

During the Golden Age, the province's sole industry was cattle ranching, and its only exports were hides, horn and tallow. This was the only source of income and became the basis for all international trade. The few animals that came with

Anza's party of colonists and the small herd of 200 cattle brought by Portolá's expedition were the ancestors of the vast herds, numbering in the tens of thousands, that grazed on hillsides in southern California during the rancho period.

"Large quantities of arable and grazing land are held under Mexican or Spanish titles, and occupied by rancheros of the ancient order of shepherds and herdsmen," stated the assessor of San Diego County in 1855. "Many of them are adverse to the changes and innovations brought about by the advent of American rule, and cleave manfully to the time-honored institutions of rawhide ropes, wooden plows and stumpy-wheeled oxcarts…Several thousand cattle, of a fierce and savage breed, infest the valleys of this whole county."

The dominant influence of the Dons was shown by the survival of Spanish as the common language of the newly formed state and the American settlers' common use of such Spanish words as vaquero (cowboy), rodéo (roundup), *reata* (lasso), *fierro* (branding iron), *caballada* (herd of trained horses), *paisano* (friend), *zanja* (water channel), cañon (canyon), arroyo (riverbed) and the like in their vocabulary. Another vestige from the old traditions was the use of rawhide as a general "repair-all" for farm and household purposes, further illustrating the intermingling of the old culture with the new. Rawhide's many uses included, among other things: glue, nails, pegs and mortises, slitting latch string and hinges, lacing shoes, making chair seats, weaving bridle reins and lariats, stretching bedsteads, and even as a substitute for glass window panes. As William Brewer noted in 1861, "Everything was done with rawhide."

The vast herds of cattle and horses that were pastured on rancho lands were tended by vaqueros, who were superb horsemen, having spent most of their lives in the saddle. All vaqueros took great pride in their ability to ride, and nearly every chore of their calling was an opportunity to demonstrate their prowess in the saddle.

The *reata*, from where we get the word "lariat", was the vaquero's favorite tool, both at work and at play. The finest *reatas*, made of woven rawhide, were highly prized objects. They were usually 40 to 80 feet long, although some were as long as 100 feet. They were made of the softest part of the cowhide and were braided from four, six or eight strands. An expert vaquero could rope a horse or cow up to 60 feet away. The use of the *reata* was essentially a Mexican skill, common in California and Texas, but little known in other parts of the United States at that time. Visitors to California ranchos in the 1830s and 1840s often requested a show of the vaquero's ability with the lariat.

Cleland writes: "Life on one of the great ranchos followed, in the main, the ancient customs, laws, and practices brought to Mexico by the early Spanish conquerors, there adapted to the conditions of the country, and thence transferred to California. Stock was grass-fed the year round, and ran almost wild on the open ranges. California cattle had slim legs, short noses, and sharp, widespreading horns. 'The general carriage of the Spanish cow,' said [writer John] Hittell, 'is like that of a wild animal: she is quick, uneasy, restless, frequently on the lookout for danger, snuffing the air, moving

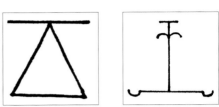

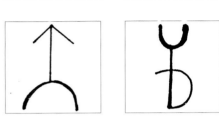

with a high and elastic trot, and excited at the sight of a man, particularly if afoot, when she will often attack him.' The meat of California cattle was nutritious; but it was neither as tender nor as juicy as that of American-bred beef."

THE ANNUAL ROUNDUP, OR RODÉO

Every year, each rancho held at least one roundup, or rodéo, for the purposes of segregating the cattle belonging to different owners and branding the calves. The event sometimes involved thousands of cattle in a swirling mass a half-mile wide or more. As there were no fences, every ranchero was required to have three registered brands to identify his stock: the *fierro*, or branding iron; the *señal*, or earmark; and the *venta*, or sale brand.

According to Cleland, *"Tally sticks, on which each notch represented ten animals, were used to record the number of cattle branded in a rodéo. The size of a herd was roughly estimated at three or four times the number of the branded calves. Mavericks, including calves without mother or brand, were called 'orejanos' by the Californians and became the property of the ranchero holding the rodéo."*

After separating the herds, each ranchero branded his calves, and after all the animals were counted, determined how many cattle could be slaughtered during the coming year. Roundups were always presided over by one or more Jueces del Campo, or Judges of the Plain, who settled disagreements involving the ownership of cattle, interpreted rules and customs, and among other things, had the authority to arrest cattle thieves.

In the days of the great ranchos, the rodéo was always an exciting and colorful event. The occasion called for traditional hospitality. Neighboring landowners and their retainers, as well as friends and relatives of the ranchero, often traveled great distances to participate in the days and nights of dancing, gambling, horse racing, cock fighting and occasional bear and bull baiting.

The following passage from Cleland's *The Cattle on a Thousand Hills: Southern California 1850–1880* catches the color and excitement of a California rodéo in those early days:

LEFT TO RIGHT, FROM TOP:
Brands of Mission San Juan Capistrano, Bernardo Yorba (Santiago de Santa Ana), Abel Stearns (Alamitos), Juan Forster (Trabuco), Juan Forster (Trabuco), Diego Sepulveda (Estancia Costa Mesa);
Casting the Javelin and Riding at the Rings, *from* Harper's Weekly, *October 29, 1877, Sherman Library and Gardens, Corona del Mar, CA;*
RIGHT:
Early Life: Californians Throwing the Lasso, *from Frederick Beechey,* Narrative of a Voyage to the Pacific, *Book Collection, California History Section, California State Library*

To keep the thousands of frightened, bewildered and maddening creatures from stampeding, cowboys or vaqueros rode continually about the herd, seeking to hold it together. Whenever an animal broke from the mass, a rider immediately roped him; seizing him

Branding certificate, cattle tally sheet, History Collections, Los Angeles County Museum of Natural History

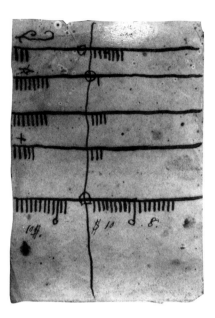

by the tail, with a peculiar twist, requiring both strength and dexterity, threw him heavily to the ground.

Meanwhile, each owner and his vaqueros rode in and out among the cattle, separating such animals as he found marked with his own brand, from the main herd. The question of ownership was seldom a difficult matter because of the brands, and even the unbranded calves followed the cows to which they belonged. As an owner's cattle were cut out from the general herd, they were driven a little distance away, to a place previously chosen, and kept by themselves until the rodéo was ended. Here the rancher branded his calves and determined the number of animals he could profitably slaughter during the coming season.

A round-up of this kind was one of the most picturesque events in early California life. The vast herd of cattle, sometimes half a mile from center to circumference, the thick clouds of dust that rose from thousands of moving feet, the sudden dash after some escaping steer, the surprising feats of horsemanship which were performed continually by the vaqueros, the bellowing of frightened and maddened bulls, the clash of horns striking horns, the wild shouts and laughter of the cowboys, all lent an air of excitement and interest that the printed page cannot begin to reproduce.

James Walker;
RIGHT: California Vaqueros, *oil on canvas,*
31 x 46 in., The Anschutz Collection;
BELOW: Vaqueros in a Horse Corral, *1877,*
oil on canvas, 24¼ x 40 in., Gilcrease Museum

James Walker;
ABOVE: The Judges of the Plains;
RIGHT: Vaqueros at Roundup;
Elisabeth Waldo-Dentzel Mulicultural Arts
Studio, Northridge, CA

In addition to the customary rodéos and the usual routine of ranch activities, some landowners found it necessary at certain seasons of the year to hold a special drive, probably unknown in any other part of the world. In southern California, the growth of wild mustard (*Brassica nigra*, a European species introduced to California by Spanish colonists) has been even more remarkable than that men-

tioned in Christ's striking parable. During the late spring, a sea of yellow mustard bloom flowered over valley, plain and foothills; the thick-set stalks, higher than a man's head, made an ideal hiding place for cattle. Even when the bloom and leaves had died, a forest of dry, rustling stalks furnished ample cover for livestock. In badly infested districts, neighboring rancheros and their vaqueros united for a few days to carry on what was colloquially known as a "run through the mustard."

Cattle were killed for food as needed. However, when the specified time arrived to harvest the hides, horn and tallow, the vaqueros would carry out the *matanza*, or wholesale slaughtering. They would ride, one at a time, through the herd at full speed, select an animal and kill it with a single, well-placed cut of a sharp knife. Then the carcasses were skinned and the tallow rendered.

"At the killing season," states William Heath Davis in his book *Seventy-Five Years in California, "cattle were driven from the rodéo ground to a particular spot on the rancho, near a brook and forest. It was usual to slaughter from fifty to one*

ABOVE, LEFT TO RIGHT:
Iron shears, c. 1770; iron lance points,
c. 1810–20; iron hide scrapers, c. 1810;
fire strikes, c. 1800–25;
Mort and Donna Fleischer Collection
BELOW, LEFT TO RIGHT:
William Hutton;
The Matanza;
Trying out Tallow;
The Huntington Library, Art Collections, and
Botanical Gardens, San Marino, CA

William Hahn, Mexican Cattle Drivers in Southern California, 1883, Dr. & Mrs. Edward H. Boseker

hundred at a time, generally steers three years old and upward; the cows being kept for breeding purposes. The fattest would be selected for slaughter, and about two days would be occupied in killing fifty cattle, trying out the tallow, stretching the hides, and curing the small portion of meat that was preserved."

The fat of the slaughtered animals was rendered in large iron kettles—usually obtained from whaling ships, where they were used to process whale blubber—and poured into rawhide bags, or *botas*, which held more than 1,000 pounds. Some of the beef was cut into strips and dried in the sun to become *carne seca*, which was the most essential article in the provincial diet. The remainder was available at no cost to anyone who wanted it. But as there was no commercial market for the meat, most of the carcasses were left to rot in the field.

Every California rancho kept a herd of carefully trained horses called a *caballada*. In their way, these animals showed as much skill in rounding up, roping or cutting out cattle as the vaqueros themselves. Like the Mexican horses from which they sprang, they were partly of Moorish or Arab blood, small, finely formed, agile, and capable of almost incredible endurance. The *caballada* was acquired from tremendous herds of wild or unbroken horses, which also grazed on the ranchos.

At times, these horses became so numerous that hundreds were slaughtered to save the pasturage for cattle. According to Cleland, in his classification and nomenclature of horses, the Californios employed some 200 names—many of which have no synonyms in English—to indicate precise shades of color and variations in markings.

A roundup of horses was generally called a *recogida*. On December 3, 1859, the *Los Angeles Star* contained the following graphic account of one of William Workman's *recogidas* on the Rancho La Puente:

> *The scene was most exciting. The plain was literally covered with horses; they were driven into the corrals, in bands of from twenty to fifty and there examined and parted. The proceeding [was] conducted under the superintendence of Don Félipe Lugo, a Judge of the Plains, but there were several others present—Messrs. Workman, Temple, Rubottom, etc. There was a very general attendance of the neighboring rancheros, besides framers from the monte and vicinity, to all of whom Mr. Workman dispensed his hospitality in the most liberal and profuse manner. The feats of horsemanship performed by the Californians were astonishing; but the facility and precision with which the "lasso" was thrown could scarcely be credited by those who have [not] witnessed such experts. The animal aimed at was secured whether in the band running at full speed over the plain; and that, too, by the neck or limb at the fancy of his pursuer. The proceeding occupied two days.*

On a visit to Sonoma in 1841, Sir George Simpson of the Hudson's Bay Company called on General Mariano Vallejo and was his guest for several days. To satisfy his curiosity, Simpson asked to see a demonstration of the use of the *reata*. His host arranged to have several vaqueros exhibit their skills.

> *A band of wild horses had been driven into a pen or corral of very strong build. The door being thrown open, Don Salvador [Mariano Vallejo's brother] and one or two others entered on horseback, and the former, having his lasso coiled up in his hand, swung it 'round his head to give it impetus, and then with a dexterous aim secured in the noose the neck of a fiery young steed. After plunging and rearing in vain, the animal was at length thrown down with great violence. Soon, however, it was again on its legs, and its captor, having attached the lasso to his saddle-bow, dragged it tottering out of the*

Charles Christian Nahl,
Vaqueros Roping a Steer, *oil on canvas,*
42 x 51⅝ *in., The Anschutz Collection*

William Henry Jackson,
The Horse Herd at Los Angeles in 1867,
William H. Jackson Collection, Los Angeles
County Museum of Natural History

corral, 'til, with eyes staring from its head and nostrils fearfully distended, it fell panting and groaning to the ground. The lasso being now slackened, the animal regained its breath, and, infuriated with rage, started away at its utmost speed, Don Salvador, of course, following at an equal pace. One of the assistants now spurred forward his steed, and overtaking the victim, seized it by the tail with his hands, and at length, watching for a favorable moment, he threw the animal by a jerk to the earth with such force as threatened to break every bone in its body. This cruel operation was repeated several times, 'til we begged hard that the wretched beast should be released from further torture. A second horse was then caught and thrown down in a manner still more painful. The captor suddenly stopped his horse when at full gallop, which being well trained, threw its weight toward one side in expectation of the impending jerk, while the captive steed was instantaneously pitched head over heels to a distance of several yards. Cruel as the sport was, we could not but admire the skill of the Californians in the management of their horses. One of the people…dropped his lasso, of which the other end was attached to a wild horse in full career, and following 'til he came up with it as it trailed on the ground, he stooped to it from his saddle and picked it up without slackening his pace for a moment.

James Walker, Californios at the Horse Round-up, *oil on canvas, Elisabeth Waldo-Dentzel Multicultural Arts Studio, Northridge, CA; William Tylee Ranney,* Hunting Wild Horses, *oil on canvas, Autry Museum of Western Heritage, Los Angeles*

James Walker, Cowboys Roping a Bear, *1877,*
oil on canvas, 29¾ x 49¾ in.,
Denver Art Museum, Fred E. Gates Collection

When not roping cattle or horses, the vaqueros indulged in the dangerous sport of roping wild animals, such as wolves and grizzly bears. Bears were captured and taken to an arena where they would be pitted against ferocious bulls, much to the delight of cheering crowds. Everyone on the rancho and in the pueblo and surrounding communities would attend these popular events. Men and women of every social class, rich or poor, from the local priests to the highest officials, all attended and often gambled huge sums of money on the outcome of this bloody sport.

The October 19, 1852 issue of the *Stockton Journal* describes in gruesome detail one such spectacle between a grizzly bear and a bull:

> *The bear [named General Scott] made his appearance before the public in a very bearish manner. His cage…was dragged out of the ring, when, as his chain only allowed him to come within a foot or two of the fence, the General was rolled upon the ground in a heap…He was a grizzly bear of pretty large size, weighing about twelve hundred pounds.*
>
> *The next thing to be done was to introduce the bull. The bars between his pen and the arena were removed…But he did not seem to like the prospect, and was not disposed to move till pretty sharply poked from behind, when, making a furious dash at the red flag which was being waved in front of the gate, he found himself in the ring face to face with General Scott.*
>
> *The bull was a very beautiful animal, of dark purple color marked with white. His horns were regular and sharp, and his coat was as smooth and glossy as a racer's.*

Bull and Bear Fight, *from*
Overland Monthly, *November 1895, California*
History Section, California State Library

The battle between the grizzly bear and the bull raged for several minutes, with the bull charging and the bear biting and clawing. Near the end, the bull was seriously wounded and had little will to continue fighting.

> *The conductor of the performance then mounted the barrier, and*

Californio saddle, c. 1845;
Mexican saddle, c. 1860;
Mort and Donna Fleischer Collection

*addressing the crowd, asked if the bull had not had fair play, which
was unanimously allowed. He then stated that for two hundred dollars he would let in the other bull, and the three should fight it out
till one or all were killed.*

*This proposal was received with loud cheers, and two or
three young men going around with hats soon collected the required
amount. The people were intensely excited and delighted with the
sport. A man sitting next to me, who was a connoisseur in bear
fights, and passionately fond of the amusement, informed me that
this was the finest fight ever fit in the country.*

During the Golden Age, the sport of horse racing was unmatched in the
huge amounts of money that wealthy rancheros bet on special races. No figure in

California history approached José Andrés Sepúlveda in his love and daring of the sport.

José Andrés Sepúlveda was the son of Francisco Sepúlveda, owner of the Rancho San Vicente, which occupied what is now most of the western part of the city of Los Angeles. In 1837, young José Andrés was granted a large tract of former Mission San Juan Capistrano land called "Cerrito de las Ranas" (Hill of the Frogs), which included the coastline from the present-day city of Newport Beach to the city of Laguna Beach, and inland to the foothills of the Santa Ana Mountains.

In 1842, Governor Alvarado granted Sepúlveda a second, adjoining tract of land known as the "Bolsa de San Joaquin." Sepúlveda combined the new grant with his existing one, the Cerrito de las Ranas, and formed the Rancho San Joaquin, which he made into his home rancho. The Rancho San Joaquin was one of the three ranchos that eventually made up the Irvine Ranch.

Sepúlveda built a large adobe house for his family, developed a large part of the tract into fields and gardens and used the remainder for grazing his horses and cattle. In time, he became one of the most picturesque figures in southern California, known for his great landholdings, fast racehorses, reckless wagers, open-handed hospitality and elegant costumes.

The most famous horse race in early California history occurred in Los Angeles in March 1852. In a wager between Sepúlveda and the Pico brothers, Pío and Andrés—who were as renowned for their passionate devotion to horse racing as Sepúlveda was—each side put up $25,000 in cash, 500 horses, 500 mares, 500 heifers, 500 calves and 500 sheep. The wager was ventured by Pío Pico, who offered to race his horse Sarco against any horse in California for a distance of three leagues, or nine miles.

Taking up the challenge, Sepúlveda arranged to have an Australian-bred mare named Black Swan—which had set several records in races in northern California—brought to Los Angeles to race against Sarco.

According to Thomas D. Mott, who witnessed the event, very little of the actual race could be seen except the start and finish as *"mustard on both sides of the road was ten feet high. Everybody in the country was present and the whole country as far north as San Luis Obispo and south to San Diego was depopulated. They all came to see the great race."*

The race ended with Black Swan winning by 75 yards. Flushed with victory, as well as the Pico brothers' tremendous wager, Sepúlveda purchased Black

Henry Chapman Ford,
TOP: Rancho San Marcos,
BOTTOM: Rancho Santa Margarita,
Mission Inn Foundation and Museum,
Riverside, CA

Swan and took her home to Rancho San Joaquin. Unfortunately, the mare died within a year after contracting lockjaw from stepping on a rusty nail.

Through it all, life was conducted with respect and honor. Each rancho was a self-sustaining unit, almost completely isolated from the outside world. The patriarch of the family, the father or grandfather, was in complete control. Families were large, with 15 or 20 members, and bonds were strong and close. Discipline was strict and always administered by the patriarch.

According to Cleland,

From an economic and social standpoint, the great ranches of the period had much in common with the medieval English manor. Except for a few luxuries obtained from trading vessels on the coast, each estate was virtually self-sustaining. In return for simple but

Rancho Cahuenga (*built by Don Thomas Feliz*), 1844, Southwest Museum, Los Angeles

abundant food, primitive shelter, and a scant supply of clothing, scores of Indians, recruited chiefly from the fast-decaying mission communities, served as vaqueros. Many of these native families lived in the Indiada, *a cluster of primitive huts near the main adobe or casa, while others dwelled in small villages called* rancherías, *widely scattered over the estate.*

The deference shown to a Californio ranchero by members of his own family, as well as by his retainers, was like the homage rendered by his vassals to a feudal lord. The members of a typical California household were numbered by the score. The ranchero provided a home for a host of poor relatives, entertained strangers, as well as friends, with unwarying hospitality and begot...many sons and daughters.

Henri Penelon, José Antonio Yorba, *oil on canvas, Bowers Museum of Cultural Art, Santa Ana, CA*

Nellie Van de Grift Sánchez describes the domestic staff needed to maintain the large rancho of Mariano Vallejo (quoting Señora Vallejo): "*Each child [of whom there were sixteen] has a personal attendant while I have two for my own needs; four or five are occupied in grinding corn for tortillas, for so many visitors come here that three grinders do not suffice; six or seven serve in the kitchen, and five or six are always washing clothes for the children and other servants; and finally, nearly a dozen are employed at sewing and spinning.*"

Don Bernardo Yorba, one of the most distinguished figures of the romantic rancho era, was patriarchal head of the large and influential Yorba family at the time of California's annexation by the United States. His "home place" was the Rancho Cañon de Santa Ana, located in what is now Orange County, just north of the Santa Ana River, where he lived like a lord of a medieval manor.

Historian Don Meadows writes:

By 1850, the Hacienda de las Yorbas was the social and business center of the Santa Ana Valley. The master's house became a two-story structure of about thirty rooms, not including the school, harness shop, shoe maker's room, and other places occupied by dependents. In all, there were more than fifty rooms arranged about a court or patio in the rear of the main residence...

According to a descendent of Bernardo Yorba, the tradesmen and people employed about the house were: Four wool combers, two tanners, one butter and cheese man, who directed every day the milking of from fifty to sixty cows, one harness maker, two shoe makers, one jeweler, one plasterer, one carpenter, one majordomo, two errand boys, one sheepherder, one cook, one baker, two washer women, one woman to iron, four sewing women, one dressmaker, two gardeners, a schoolmaster, and a man to make the wine...More than a hundred lesser employees were maintained on the ranch. The Indian peons lived in a little village of their own...

The rancho had two orchards, where various types of fruit were grown, and some wheat was raised...Ten steers a month were slaughtered to supply the hacienda.

Brand Registration by José Antonio Yorba,
History Collections, Los Angeles County Museum of Natural History

At the time of his death, Yorba was one of the richest men in southern California. He had been married three times and had 16 children. His estate consisted of 37,000 acres of land and additional assets worth more than $100,000.

Rancheros took great pride in their generous hospitality. Visitors to California wrote of the extraordinary welcome accorded them by rancheros and their families. It was said that a person could travel from one end of California to the other without having to pay for food or lodging, thanks to the celebrated hospitality of the ranchos. Crime was rare among the Californios, and murder was almost unheard of.

The Bernardo Yorba Adobe, *c. 1900, photograph, Launer Local History Room, Fullerton Public Library, Fullerton, CA*

As there were no fences on the ranchos, horses that did not belong to the vaqueros were tied around the neck with a trailing *reata* and set to run free. As such, any traveler could catch a horse, ride it to his destination and simply release the horse after he arrived. Likewise, parties traveling across rancho lands were free to pick out a steer, slaughter it and consume the meat. The only condition was that they leave the hide.

Rancho guests were accorded full access to the *hacienda* (ranch house), with the same privileges enjoyed by family members. There was never any expectation of being asked to pay for anything. Rancho guests recounted that the host would even make arrangements to convey the visitor to the next rancho in his journey, and if the guest appeared needy, to discreetly provide funds.

Even though one rancho might border on another, their ranch houses could be many miles apart. Most of the early adobe houses were neither comfortable nor inviting. They had a few large rooms with earthen floors and very little furniture, which was usually very crude. Later, these rambling haciendas became more comfortable and very attractive.

Nellie Van de Grift Sánchez writes in her 1929 book *Spanish Arcadia*:

Adobe was the material generally employed for the walls, which were sometimes two or three feet thick, making a deep embrasure for the rather small window openings. The poorer houses were thatched with straw or tulles smeared with mud or asphalt, while the better ones had roofs of overlapping tiles. As a rule, the rooms were few but quite large, and the houses were comfortable, roomy, warm in winter and cool in summer, as is coming to be recognized in our day.

At first, there was no glass in the windows, and sometimes the doors were made of rawhide stretched over sticks, while the more ambitious had painted wooden doors. None of these doors had locks, for there was little fear of thieves where there was nothing to be stolen. The rafters were made of straight young trees, with the bark stripped off. Often, no nails were used, but the rafters were tied to the cross-beams with thongs made of ox hide...

After 1834, when a large number of colonists came in, some of them from the better class in the City of Mexico, material changes took place in California. A more luxurious mode of living was adopted, and some of the wealthiest residents constructed commodious and even handsome houses after the Spanish fashion, built around an inner court filled with luxuriant plants, watered by a fountain in the center. All around the court ran a corridor, upon which opened the large, dimly lighted rooms, with low ceilings, furnished sparsely, after the manner of the abstemious Spaniards.

Much of everyday life and festive entertainment was done in the courtyard, under the veranda. Beef was the staple food of the ranchos and was usually included in all three meals of the day. Sir George Simpson, a houseguest at Mariano Vallejo's rancho in Sonoma in 1841, wrote in his journal,

After spending about half an hour with our host, we left him to partake of a second breakfast...In front of Mr. Leese [another one of the 20 guests] who sat at the head table as master of ceremonies, was placed an array of five dishes—two kinds of stewed beef, rice, fowl and beans. As all the cooking is done in out-houses—for the dwellings, by reason of the mildness of the climate, have no chimneys or fireplaces—the dishes were by no means too hot when put on the table. Everything had literally been seethed into chips, the beans or frijoles in particular having first been boiled and lastly fried...Then every mouthful was poisoned with the everlasting compound of pepper and garlic, and this repast, be it observed, was quite an aristocratic specimen of the kind, for elsewhere we more than once saw, in one and the same dish, beef and tongue, and pumpkin and garlic, and potatoes in their jackets, and cabbage and onions, and tomatoes and peppers, and heaven knows what besides—this last indefinite ingredient being something more than a figure

LEFT: Vallejo's House, Petaluma, vintage postcard, Private Collection; RIGHT: Henry Chapman Ford, Rear of the de la Guerra House, 1886, etching, 4 x 8 in., Santa Barbara Historical Society, Gift of Mary Marwick Bard

of speech, considering that all the cookery…is the work of native drudges, unwashed and uncombed. When to the foregoing sketch are added bad tea and worse wine, the reader has picked up a perfect idea of a California breakfast, a California dinner and a California supper.

In the evening, the family and rancho guests—there were almost always guests—enjoyed a meal of *carne asada* (roasted beef) as well as roasted chicken, *enchiladas*, *tamales* and *tortillas*, and later, all would join in dancing the *fandango* or *jarabe*.

In the Golden Age, the Gente de Razón, the people of means in California, wore colorful, and often sumptuous, fashions. According to Don Antonio Francisco Coronel, as translated by Nellie Van de Grift Sánchez:

The dress worn by ladies of some means in 1834 and 1835, consisted of a narrow skirt made of muslin or silk, a high, tight waist, trimmed with ribbon or flowers, or in any way that the caprice of the lady dictated, and an underskirt of red or any other color according to the taste of the person…The manner of dressing the hair was to draw it

RIGHT, FROM TOP:
Frank H. Myers, Fiesta in Old Monterey, *oil
on board, 22 x 30 in., The Irvine Museum;
Charles Christian Nahl,* The Fandango, *1873,
oil on canvas, 72 x 108 in., E.B. Crocker
Collection, Crocker Art Museum, Sacramento*
BELOW:
W.H.D. Koerner, A Welcome to the Casa,
*1932, oil on canvas, 36 x 30 in.,
Santa Barbara Historical Society*

smoothly back into a braid, and tie it together with a silk ribbon or
cord, with a small knot of ribbon at the lower end of the braid, gracefully arranged. A small silk shawl was worn around the neck, the points
crossed on the breast. Some of the women wore a comorra, which
consisted of a black silk handkerchief tied gracefully around the head.

The dress of men consisted of short breeches reaching a little above the knee, open for about six inches on the outside seams
of the legs, where they were trimmed with ribbon or braid and some
four or six buttons of silver or other metal, according to the means
of the individual…A vest of cloth, velvet, silk, or cotton (according
to the resources of the man) coming down over the abdomen and
fancifully trimmed.

Pineapple Pattern Spanish Shawl, *China,*
silk with silk embroidery,
Santa Barbara Historical Society

CLOCKWISE, FROM TOP LEFT:
Gold and tortoise shell wedding combs, c. 1836,
Santa Barbara Historical Society;
tortoise shell combs, c. 1820;
cinch buckles with silver in-lay, c. 1825;
silver combs, c. 1820;
Mort and Donna Fleischer Collection

LEFT: California Family Reunion, Casa de la Guerra, *1924, Santa Barbara Historical Society;* *RIGHT:* Edward Vischer, Cattle-Drive Santa Barbara, *1865, colored lithograph, The Bancroft Library, University of California, Berkeley*

The jacket was of the same materials but a little longer than the vest…The leggings were made of a single piece of deerskin, tanned, black or red, embroidered in parts with silk, according to the means of the wearers…The shoes were made of cowhide or deerskin, of four or six pieces, each piece in two colors, red and black, embroidered on the toe-piece with agave thread or silk…The hat had a broad brim and round crown; it was made of wool and was very strong; it was held on by a chin strap of ribbon about two inches wide, tied in the shape of a large flower under the chin. Nearly all of the men wore a kerchief tied around the head.

For the ranchos in southern California, the Gold Rush had a significant indirect effect. While only a few native-born Californios participated in the Gold Rush, they instead became wealthy by driving their vast cattle herds north to meet the demands of hungry forty-niners. The cattle were fattened on the lush grasslands along the way, and by the time they reached the gold fields, the rancheros got as much as $75 a head for beef they would have otherwise left to rot in order to get $1 or $2 per hide in southern California.

While many of the northern California ranchos were overrun by thousands of squatters and broken up, the southern ranchos were saved from this threat, and landholdings remained unaffected. However, the sudden rise in population in the north would eventually shift political influence away from the south.

For the Californios, rancho life was full of charm and contentment. If Californio culture lacked some of the amenities of a more sophisticated, advanced society, it nevertheless had the greater virtues of simplicity, sincerity and unaffected

happiness. Hospitality was spontaneous and genuine. The whole tenor of life was leisurely and gracious. California was indeed "the land of the large and charitable air."

Cleland offers the following descriptive narrative:

The rancho lay beyond the mountain range and extended over rolling hills and little valleys. A creek flowed through it, and on the banks were many sycamores. Shaded by oaks was the long, low adobe house, with its red tiled roof and wide veranda. Behind the fence of chaparral was the orchard and the melon patch, and beyond the orchard was the meadow, golden with buttercups in the early spring. In the open fields, dotted with oaks, the rich alfilerilla [filaree, or storksbill] grew, and on the hillsides were the wild grasses which waved like billows as the breezes from the distant ocean blew across them. The sameness of recurring events from each succeeding year never seemed monotonous, but brought repose, contentment and peace. When the dew was still on the grass, we would mount our horses and herd the cattle if any had strayed beyond the pasture. In the wooded cañons where the cool brooks flowed, and where the wild blackberries grew, we ate our noon day meal and rested. And as the hills began to glow with the light of the setting sun, we journeyed homeward. When the long days of summer came, we ate our evening meal beneath the oaks, and in the twilight we listened to the guitar and the songs of our people. In the autumn, we harvested the corn and gathered the olives and grapes.

Those were the days of long ago. Now all is changed by modern progress; but in the simple ranch life of the older time there was a contented happiness which an alien race with different temperament can never understand.

With the closing of the missions, the Indian population in or near the towns dropped drastically as their forced conversion and acceptance of European culture proved extremely destructive. Prior to Spanish occupation, California's natives were estimated to number around 300,000. By 1845, that figure had dwindled to half, or about 150,000, with most dying of diseases brought in by Europeans, diseases to which the natives had no resistance.

Most Indians returned to their former ways of life. Those who remained became the labor force for the ranchos, herding cattle, slaughtering, tanning hides, rendering tallow and performing all other petty tasks as servants and housekeepers.

With the missions, there had been a sort of communal relationship with the Indian workers, but in the ranchos, all the profits of Indian labor went to the rancheros. The Indians were supposedly free subjects of Mexico and were free to leave their employer as long as they were not in debt to him. In reality, the Indians were always in debt and were forced to remain until they paid it off, an eventuality that was never allowed to occur. ❧

William Keith, St. Michael's Cathedral, Sitka,
1886, *oil on board, 16 x 24 in., Jo & Len Braarud*

CHAPTER 11

FOREIGNERS IN CALIFORNIA

During the last 20 years of the 18th century, foreigners began to take great interest in the North Pacific, looking to exploit its wealth of natural resources in the fur trade and whaling industry. As a result, California experienced a series of visits by American, English, Russian and French trading and exploration parties before the end of the century.

The first foreign vessel to harbor in California since Sir Francis Drake's *Golden Hind* visited the coast in 1579 was the ship that brought the French Comte de la Pérouse in 1786. It docked in Monterey for ten days, from September 14 to 24, as part of a round-the-world reconnaissance for the King of France. La Pérouse was entertained by Governor Fages and was accompanied by Father Lasuén on a tour of the Mission San Carlos in Carmel.

This occasion would prove to be the only French contact with Spanish California. In his journals, published posthumously, La Pérouse concluded that the Spanish would not develop the province adequately, and that the missions were making only slight progress in their task of civilizing the natives.

THE RUSSIAN EMPIRE IN ALASKA

The first permanent Russian settlement in Alaska was on Kodiak Island in 1784. At first, Russian fur-trading activity in Alaska was uncontrolled. Aggressive trapping by Russian fur traders led to the near-extinction of many species of animals, especially the sea otter. Likewise, native occupants were often cheated, abused and sometimes massacred by fur traders. In 1799, Czar Paul I put the Alaskan fur trade under the strict control of the newly formed Russian-American Company. New Archangel (now called Sitka) became the headquarters of the company.

Constantly looking to enlarge its operations, the Russian-American Company began to expand south along the west coast of North America. With a virtual monopoly on the fur trade, Russia accumulated large and valuable storehouses of various furs in Sitka, but the harsh climate made it nearly impossible to support the settlement through agriculture.

In 1805, Nikolai Petrovich Rezanov, a high official in the Russian court, made an inspection tour of all the outposts in Alaska. He repeatedly found severe shortages of food and colonists close to the point of starvation. In one settlement, he found people reduced to eating crows. As these settlements generated a great amount of money for the Russian Czar, there was no thought of terminating them. With little alternative, Rezanov decided to sail to Spanish California to purchase supplies.

TOP: Whaling Scene, *from* Harper's Monthly, *March 1856, Sherman Library and Gardens, Corona del Mar, CA;*
BOTTOM: T. Suria, La Pérouse at Carmel, *drawing, The Bancroft Library, University of California, Berkeley*

Cleveland Rockwell, Sitka, *c. 1884, watercolor, 14½ x 20½ in., Braarud Fine Art*

In 1806, Rezanov, in the Russian ship *Juno*, entered San Francisco harbor looking for a ship-load of food for his men in Alaska. Official Spanish policy forbade any trade with foreigners, but by happenstance, Rezanov fell in love with the daughter of the port commandant, 15-year-old Concepción Arguello. In short order, Rezanov was allowed to buy his supplies, and the *Juno* was loaded with wheat, barley, peas and dried beef. He left San Francisco with his solemn promise to return and marry Concepción. She waited for years, but he never returned. Finally, in 1850, Concepción, who by then had become a nun, found out that Rezanov had died in Siberia a few years after leaving San Francisco.

In time, the Russians realized that without a reliable source of food, they would not be able to maintain their fur-trading outpost in the Pacific Northwest. To that end, in 1809, Ivan Kuskov, an officer in the Russian-American Fur Company, surveyed several sites along the coast of California, north of San Francisco

LEFT TO RIGHT: Fort Ross Chapel, Block House, vintage postcards, Private Collection

Bay. Knowing full well that he was in territory claimed by Spain, Kuskov neverthe-less obtained land on Bodega Bay from the local Indians in exchange for three blan-kets, three hoes, two axes, several strands of beads and three pairs of pants. There, the Russians erected a settlement consisting of several wooden buildings.

In 1812, Kuskov returned and selected a second site 18 miles north of Bodega Bay and again purchased land from the local natives in exchange for various trin-kets. Over the next few months, he built a wooden stockade and several buildings, which he named Fort Rossiya (Fort Russia), now called Fort Ross.

Fort Ross was built on a bluff between two ravines that ran down to the ocean. It was surrounded by a 12-foot-high redwood palisade topped with pointed stakes. Two fortified bastions and several sentry boxes were built at strategic points along the palisade. The north bastion had five cannons and the south bastion, seven. Finally, all approaches to the fort were difficult due to the ravines, and entry was possible only by crossing over three bridges above the ravines.

Harry Cassie Best, Redwoods, *oil on canvas, 36 x 20 in., Jean and Laura Stern*

Although well-protected, Fort Ross was not intended as a fort, but rather as an assembly point for transporting supplies to Alaska. Ship-building was one of the most important activities at Fort Ross, in keeping with its role as supplier for the Alaskan colonies. To produce sufficient food for these colonies, various vegeta-bles and fruits were grown in nearby fields and orchards. Meat for the settlements was supplied by a flock of about 200 sheep, which grazed nearby. The abundance of seals and otter along the California coast kept the warehouses at Fort Ross full and profitable.

The presence of Fort Ross was in clear violation of Spanish territorial claims. Yet, the Californios were not at all threatened by this incursion—quite the opposite, as Governor José Joaquín de Arrillaga actually granted permission for local merchants to conduct trade with the Russians. Indeed, a good part of the trade conducted at Fort Ross was to supply the local missions with provisions and build-ing materials.

Word of Fort Ross finally reached the Viceroy in Mexico City, and Arril-laga was ordered to force the closing of the settlement. However, the governor lacked both the desire and the military power to expel the Russians. Spanish soldiers would periodically march to Fort Ross and issue an order to vacate the fort. They would be well-received, but the Russians routinely ignored the order.

Gideon Jacques Denny, Fort Ross, *1866, Oakland Museum of California, on loan from the collection of C. Albert Shumate, M.D.*

Although Fort Ross was the southernmost limit of Russian territory in the Pacific Northwest, many small Russian settlements were established in northern California. Evidence of this can be found in the 15 or so California place names that bear the word "Russian." The best known of these is the Russian River (Rio Ruso, on later Spanish maps) in Sonoma County.

AMERICANS IN CALIFORNIA

In spite of restrictive travel and immigration measures initiated by the Mexican government in 1821, the Americanization of California accelerated. In 1835, Texas declared itself independent from Mexico. The following year, Mexican General Santa Anna laid siege to the Alamo, and in a pointed demonstration of his resolve to thwart American aspirations, killed every single defender. Nevertheless, Texas gained its independence. Thereafter, resolved not to repeat the Texas experience in California, Mexico passed even stricter measures to keep Americans out. These efforts met with some success, and during the 1840s, most American immigration was directed at Oregon, not California.

Charles Gildenmeister, Harbor and City of Monterey, *1842, Oakland Museum of California, Gift of Mrs. Emil Hagstrom*

From the start of Spanish colonization, Monterey had been the only legal port of entry into California. When Mexico gained its independence, the nearly total ban on trade with foreign countries imposed by Spain was lifted. According to Mexican law, each ship now had to stop at Monterey and pay a duty on its entire cargo before continuing to various ports in California. To that end, the Monterey Custom House was built in 1827 to collect tariffs and enforce the few trade laws that remained. Clearly, this was done to satisfy the Californios' great demand for imported goods, a demand that bordered on total dependence.

With independence, Mexico's interests turned internally, and California, a distant province that had long been a drain on state finances, was left to raise its own funds for local administrations. As there was no property tax on the large ranchos, and cattle, the principal product of California, was barely taxed, the tariffs on foreign trade collected by the Monterey Custom House became the principal source of government funds.

RIGHT:
Manuel Valencia, Old Custom House, *DeRu's Fine Arts, Laguna Beach, CA*
BELOW:
LEFT: Frederick Shafer, On the Russian River;
RIGHT: Manuel Valencia, Moonlight on the Ocean; *DeRu's Fine Arts, Laguna Beach, CA*

Neglected as they were, the Californios were nevertheless Mexican citizens and were governed by Mexican laws. The task of enforcing these laws fell to the independent-minded Californios, who were largely unconcerned. At this time, the 1820s and 1830s, there were only a few Americans entering California, and the American trade, almost exclusively in hides and tallow, was vital to the rancho way of life.

The end of Spanish trade restrictions also allowed the hide and tallow trade to come into being and quickly characterize California's economy. In the spring of 1822, soon after Mexican authorities opened California's ports to foreign vessels, the ship *John Begg* visited Monterey. One of the passengers was William P. Hartnell; he and his partner, Hugh McCulloch, were British merchants interested in developing trade with California. The firm of McCulloch and Hartnell, or as they were known in California, "Macala y Arnel," signed a three-year contract to handle all the hides the missions could produce at the value of $1 each.

Not to be outdone, Yankee trader William A. Gale arrived on the ship *Sachem* from Boston a few weeks later, with a ship-load of goods belonging to the firm of Bryant and Sturgis. Learning of the British agreement with the mission fathers, Gale offered to trade his highly desirable merchandise at the rate of $2 per hide, a figure that still paid him a handsome profit. Several of the missions accepted Gale's terms and quietly ignored the agreement they had previously made with Hartnell. Over the next few years, Bryant and Sturgis had a virtual monopoly on California hides and tallow.

All trade in California was done by bartering. The Californios provided hides, tallow and horn, and the Americans supplied a large variety of manufactured goods. The value of one hide varied between one and three dollars. Tallow was traded by weight, at $2 per *arroba* (a unit of 25 pounds). A *bota* (leather bag) of tallow could easily weigh eight *arrobas*, or 200 pounds, and would be valued at $16. But no money was exchanged; instead hides, called "California bank notes," were used in all transactions.

The best description of the hide and tallow trade in Mexican California is provided by Richard Henry Dana's book *Two Years Before the Mast*, published in

1840. Dana (1815–1882), who was born in Cambridge, Massachusetts into a family of prominent jurists, was a student at Harvard University when a serious case of measles affected his eyesight and forced him to take a leave from his studies. Wanting to go to sea, he declined the chance to travel as a passenger and instead chose to sign on as an ordinary seaman on the *Pilgrim*, which sailed from Boston in August 1834, destined for California by way of Cape Horn, around the southern tip of South America. He spent nearly two years on the voyage, loading a full cargo of hides and tallow, and returned to Boston on the *Alert*, again as an ordinary seaman, arriving in Boston in September 1836. He re-entered Harvard, graduated in 1837 and went on to earn a law degree. In his career as a lawyer, Dana specialized in cases brought by seamen against cruel and oppressive treatment on board merchant ships.

Hernando Villa, Helene J., *oil on canvas, 20 x 16 in., The Irvine Museum*

Using the diaries he kept on his voyage, Dana wrote *Two Years Before the Mast* "to present the life of a common sailor at sea as it really is." The book gained wide popularity and led to long-needed reforms in the shipping industry. In 1841, Dana published *The Seaman's Friend*, a book that included a summary of laws pertaining to ships and seamen.

To announce the long-awaited arrival of a merchant ship along the California coast, a messenger-agent visited all the ranchos, pueblos and missions in the area to spread the news. When a ship was due in Capistrano Bay, notice was given as far away as the San Gabriel and San Fernando missions, and entire families from those distant areas would journey to Capistrano to partake of trading.

The arrival of a trading ship was cause for feasting and celebration. After waiting on the shore, groups of eager Californios, including wives and children of wealthy rancheros, would be rowed out to the ship. Once on board, they proceeded down below deck, where they found row upon row of merchandise. For the ladies, there was fine cotton fabric, silk, lace, shawls from the Orient, jewelry, perfume, shoes and porcelain dishes. The men could handle guns, knives, iron tools, boots and saddles made from the very same leather secured on previous voyages. The "floating department stores" also stocked furniture, musical instruments, books, toys, window glass, and as Dana related, they had "*everything under the sun, in fact everything that can be imagined, from Chinese fireworks to English cart wheels, of which we had a dozen pairs with their iron tires on.*"

Prices for these highly desirable goods were all marked in hides. A pair of shoes might be priced at two hides; a fancy dress at three hides; a bolt of silk imported from China could cost 15 hides; a fine saddle perhaps as much as 150 hides.

All transactions were noted down, and when the client finished shopping, the goods were off-loaded and a bill was presented. If the buyer had brought hides, the exchange was made on shore and the hides were taken on board. If hides were not available, credit was extended to the buyer.

In every aspect of Californio life—and business was no exception—honor was paramount. As cattle were killed only during the slaughtering season, long-term credit was an essential element of the hide and tallow trade. William Heath Davis, a resident merchant in California, wrote, "*Merchants sold to rancheros what-*

ever goods they wanted…and gave them credit from one killing season to another. I have never known of a single instance in which a note or other written obligation was required of them. At the time of purchase, they were furnished with bills of the goods, which were charged in the account books, and in all my intercourse and experience in trade with them, extending over many years, I never knew of a case of dishonesty on their part. They always kept their business engagements [and] paid their bills promptly at the proper time in hides and tallow. They regarded their verbal promise as binding and sacred, relied upon their honor, and were always faithful."

Carreta, History Collections, Los Angeles County Museum of Natural History

Leaving the port of Boston, the *Pilgrim* traveled south along the coast of South America, around Cape Horn and north into the Pacific Ocean. Her destination was California, and the objective was to obtain hides, horn and tallow, which would be brought back to Boston and made into shoes and other manufactured goods. Of the long and dangerous voyage, Dana wrote: *"Here we were, in a little vessel, with a small crew, on a half-civilized coast at the ends of the earth, and with a prospect of remaining an indefinite period, two or three years at the least…We were in the remote parts of the earth, on an almost desert coast, in a country where there is neither law nor gospel, and where sailors are at their captain's mercy."*

According to Dana, after slaughtering the cattle, the hides were prepared for sale by stretching them on stakes and drying them in the sun. After that, they were scraped to remove any traces of fat and meat and then beaten with sticks to shake off insects and dust. Then the hides, which had the weight and consistency of flat, wooden boards, were stacked for storage, either at the mission or rancho, or if near a port city, taken to a central warehouse for storage until the arrival of a merchant ship.

Once the merchant ship arrived, the hides and tallow were taken from the warehouses to the docks and loaded onto the ship. To pick up cargo from outlying missions and ranchos, ships would frequently stop in small bays along the coast.

Duncan Gleason, Hides being Loaded into the Hold of a Trading Ship, *Courtesy of the Estate of the Artist*

Dana told how the Americans droghers picked up hides in San Juan Capistrano, a place that had no docks. At the mission, the dried cattle hides were loaded by Indian labor on *carretas*, oxcarts with solid wooden wheels made from log slices, and taken to a cliff just above the harbor at Port San Juan (now called Dana Point). There, the droghers unloaded the *carretas* and tossed the hides like Frisbees from the cliff to the beach below, where they were gathered, put in small boats and rowed to the ship. Inevitably, some hides would not reach the beach and instead landed partway down the cliff. Then, Dana explained, the American sailors would have the hazardous task of dangling by ropes down the sides of the cliffs to retrieve the stranded hides. Of the perils of this assignment, Dana recalled, *"I could see nothing below me but the sea and the rocks upon which it broke, and a few gulls flying in mid-air."*

The greatest care was taken to make sure the hides did not get wet. The tallow, which had been melted and poured into *botas*, large leather bags made from hide, was floated out to the waiting ship.

Once on board, the hides were salted to keep them dry and stored in layers upon layers in the hold. When the holds were full, the bulkheads were closed and caulked down. When fully loaded, each ship carried a cargo of approximately 40,000 hides.

The number of hides exported during the rancho period was extremely large, perhaps 1 million or more. The largest number went to Boston, the center of New England shoe manufacturing. As depicted in Dana's book, a typical voyage from Boston might last two years, with frequent stops along the California coast to unload goods and pick up hides.

In addition to the hides, tallow and horn were also valuable commodities. Tallow was used in the production of soap and, above all, candles, an important necessity in the days before kerosene lamps and electric lights. Horn was used much like our modern plastics, for shoe buttons and small utensils.

Two Years Before the Mast had an equally important, yet unintended, effect. It brought California, a distant and unknown region, to the attention of a large number of Americans. Dana's descriptions of the land, its people and the romantic way of life they followed, was the only basis for forming any understanding of California for many years to come. Of all the ports and places he visited on the voyage, Dana found San Juan Capistrano the most beautiful: "*[It was] the only romantic spot in California...there was a grandeur in everything around, which gave solemnity to the scene: a silence and solitariness...no sound heard but the pulsations of the great Pacific...as refreshing as a great rock in a weary land.*"

The message Dana proclaimed about California was clear and convincing; it was "*a country embracing four or five hundred miles of sea coast, with several good harbors; with fine forests in the north; the waters filled with fish, and the plains*

Frank L. Heath, Landscape at Dana Point, *1887, 24 x 45 in., Dr. & Mrs. Edward H. Boseker*

covered with thousands of head of cattle; blessed with a climate than which there can be no better in the world; free from all manner of diseases, whether epidemic or endemic; and with a soil in which corn yields from seventy to eighty fold. In the hands of an enterprising people," he wrote, *"what a country this might be!"*

The hide and tallow trade provided the only commercial outlet for the Californios and furnished much of the raw materials for New England's developing leather industry. It was to become a powerful factor in arousing American interest in the province and in California's eventual annexation by the United States.

ABEL STEARNS

Abel Stearns, *The Huntington Library, Art Collections, and Botanical Gardens*

American merchants fed the seemingly endless Californio demand for imported goods from the eastern United States. The rapidly growing economy of the United States, fueled by numerous factories and mills, the result of the Industrial Revolution, meant that American traders could supply virtually all the material needs of the Californios.

In California, enterprising resident Americans were quick to pick up on the potential of this commerce. Men like Thomas Larkin in Monterey, Abel Stearns in San Pedro and Los Angeles, and Henry "Enrique" Fitch in San Diego had come to California early on, and many had married into rancho families. Seeing the reluctance of Californios to conduct commerce, they established thriving businesses in retail goods. Acting as middlemen, they set up trade warehouses in the principal California cities. As American commerce grew, they centralized the import business by purchasing whole ship-loads of goods and exchanging them for hides.

Abel Stearns (1798–1871) was born on February 9, 1798 in Lunenburg, Massachusetts. In 1810, his mother and father both died within the span of three months, and at the age of 12, young Abel went to sea. For several years, he sailed on merchant ships and learned the business of international trade in places like China, the East Indies and various Spanish colonies in America. By 1818, Stearns was back in Massachusetts, married and had two children.

By 1821, Stearns was the master, and possibly owner, of the schooner *American Ranger*, and in 1822, he applied for and was granted a passport allowing him entry to Spanish ports in Mexico and the Caribbean. Soon thereafter, Mexico declared its independence from Spain and claimed California as a province.

In May 1826, Stearns anchored at the port of Veracruz, Mexico, intent on making his fortune in the newly independent nation. He visited other ports in Mexico and traveled through the country for about three years, eventually becoming dissatisfied with economic prospects in Mexico. In his travels, Stearns met George Washington Eayrs, an American merchant who had long experience in clandestine trading off the coast of California. He was eventually caught by the authorities, and as foreign trading in California was illegal during the Spanish period, his ship was confiscated. Fascinated by Eayrs' description of Alta California, Stearns joined him in applying for a land grant in August 1828, in order to start a colony in the Mexican province of Alta California. The request was approved, and pursuant to the requirements of land ownership, Stearns renounced his American citizenship, converted to Catholicism and became a Mexican citizen on December 24, 1828.

In the summer of 1829, Stearns landed in Monterey, the capital and only port in California that was open to foreign merchants. He and Eayrs immediately presented their documents to Governor José María Echeandía, but as the grant was in a special category called *empresario*—for the purpose of establishing a colony of many families—the approval process was quite lengthy. While he awaited the final approval, Stearns went to work for John Cooper, an American merchant based in Santa Barbara. Stearns handled the business with the San Juan Bautista and Santa Clara missions, collecting hides, tallow, salt and otter skins for Cooper. For these, he paid cash or bartered manufactured goods.

Complicating matters even more, Governor Echeandía had to deal with a minor revolt staged by a group of disgruntled and long-unpaid soldiers of the Monterey presidio, under the leadership of Joaquín Solís and José María Herrera. The revolt drew the support of soldiers from the presidio of San Francisco, who were likewise serving without pay, and eventually involved most of northern California.

By January 1830, Echeandía and a unit of loyal troops from Santa Barbara were able to re-take Monterey and end the first of many of California's home-grown revolutions. In a letter to John Cooper in Santa Barbara, Stearns commented: *"We have this moment rec'd notice that Monterey is again in the hands of the proper authorities, which I was well satisfied would be the case on your receiving notice of the retreat of Solís. I am pleased to think that…we can proceed to business with some confidence."*

In late February 1830, the approval came from Mexico to give Stearns and Eayrs a grant of 20 square leagues of land (about 90,000 acres) on the San Joaquin River, not the Sacramento River as had been requested. Finally, on October 30, 1830, the approval was signed by Governor Echeandía, and all that remained in this seemingly endless battle with governmental red tape was for the California Diputación (Congress) to meet and endorse the grant.

However, before this last step could happen, a new governor arrived in California. In March 1830, Mexico had recalled Echeandía and appointed in his place Manuel Victoria, who arrived to take office in Monterey on January 31, 1831. Fearful of future military revolts in California, Mexico had appointed Victoria, a professional soldier from Loreto, who applied military logic to any problem that came his way. Immediately suspicious of any demands for political reforms, Victoria was perhaps the worst in a series of poor administrators that Mexico sent to rule over the increasingly rebellious Californios.

As soon as he arrived in Monterey, Victoria expressed contempt for the unruly Californios and refused to convene the California Diputación because he thought that many of its members had been illegally elected. Furthermore, Governor Victoria regarded Stearns as a foreigner who could not be trusted. Stearns, he

Clark Hobart, Monterey Bay *(detail), oil on canvas, 20½ x 30¼ in., The Irvine Museum*

believed, would eventually use the land to develop a colony of American settlers who would prove hostile to Mexican rule. Unwilling to proceed with the grant, Governor Victoria ordered Stearns to leave California and return to Mexico. In September 1831, Stearns reluctantly boarded a ship that took him into exile.

After a brief stop in San Blas, Baja California, Stearns' ship continued for Mexico without him, as he had decided to return to California. Unwittingly, Stearns had become a Californio revolutionary. Meanwhile, Victoria exiled several other prominent Californios, including the wealthy and politically popular José Antonio Carrillo of Los Angeles. Sensing a growing resentment to his iron-handed administration, Victoria sent a request to the Mexican government to change the status of California to be a purely military administration. This prompted a group of influential Californios to send petitions of protest to Mexico, asking for the recall of the governor. Before long, open revolt broke out in San Diego and Los Angeles, and an army was raised to forcibly remove the governor. Among the leaders of the revolt were Pío Pico, Juan Bandini, Carrillo and Stearns.

The revolt was brief (see Chapter 13 on Politics in California) and Governor Victoria was removed from office. The Diputación met and on January 10, 1832, Echeandía was asked to return to office until a permanent replacement could be sent from Mexico. In the end, nothing further happened with Stearns and Eayrs' land grant, as the paperwork was lost somewhere between Monterey and Mexico City, and any hopes of establishing a colony in California were put aside.

Undaunted, Stearns decided to build his fortune as a retail merchant. At this time, merchant ships would cruise the waters off California, making several stops at various ports and settlements to pick up small consignments of hides and tallow in exchange for manufactured goods. The merchants would only stay in a specific area long enough to do business and then move on. Stearns' plan was to be a middleman in the hide and tallow trade. He would buy the entire cargo of a merchant vessel and pay on the spot with hides and tallow, enabling the ships to make only one stop on their voyage and thus increase their profits. He would retail the goods on a year-round basis to Californios in exchange for hides and tallow.

Sometime in late 1832, Stearns opened his store in Los Angeles. Business was good from the very beginning. One of Stearns' merchants, John Coffin Jones from Honolulu, who came to California every year for hides, wrote: "*Hides are plenty in the Pueblo [Los Angeles] and [there] are no goods on the market, if you get there before any vessel, you can sell your cargo off immediately. Calicoes and cottons will bring any price asked."*

Realizing that he needed a depot to store his hides in between merchant ships, Stearns built a compound that included his home, store and warehouse in San Pedro, about 20 miles south of the Pueblo of Los Angeles. That way, he could deal immediately with visiting ships, as the hides and tallow that he accepted as payment from his customers would be ready to load upon arrival.

This gave Stearns a tremendous advantage over the previous way of doing business in California, as one merchant from Boston expressed: *"The greatest drawback to a California voyage is the length of time required to collect the cargo of hides with a valuable ship, and a large crew, and it makes all the difference between a good voyage and a poor one if you are able to save the better part of a year or more in the length of the voyage."*

Stearns' decision to establish his trade business in San Pedro was also the original impetus for providing Los Angeles with a seaport. In any event, Stearns did all his cargo loading and unloading from the beach with the ship anchored in the bay, as there was no port or wharf at the time. *"This anchorage should not be termed a port,"* wrote Eugene Duflot de Mofras, a visitor to the area, *"for it is merely a large bay with a mouth that measures about 15 miles from point to point....The anchorage is good only in the summer season, for the bay is open to the prevailing north-westerly winds. However, if the sea is rough, anchor must be cast a mile or two offshore."*

In *Two Years Before the Mast*, Dana described San Pedro as *"the worst place we had seen yet, especially for getting hides,"* as the sailors were forced to transport tons of merchandise from the ship over a beach covered with rocks and stones, to

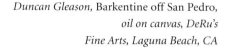

Duncan Gleason, Barkentine off San Pedro, *oil on canvas, DeRu's Fine Arts, Laguna Beach, CA*

the top of a steep hill, where they took possession of the hides that had to be taken back and loaded on the ship. *"I also learned, to my surprise, that the desolate-looking place we were in was the best place on the whole west coast for hides,"* Dana continued. *"It was the only port for a distance of eighty miles, and about thirty miles in the interior was a fine plain country, filled with herds of cattle, in the center of which was the Pueblo de los Angeles—the largest town in California—and several of the wealthiest missions; to all of which San Pedro was the sea-port."*

Stearns had originally planned to go into business with José Antonio Carrillo, who had been exiled with him by Governor Victoria and participated in the subsequent revolt. However, less than a month after they obtained permission to build in San Pedro, Carrillo backed out of the arrangement. To save time, Stearns offered to buy the Casa de San Pedro, the old adobe house used by the Mission San Gabriel to store hides. Knowing that secularization was coming, the mission set a price and Stearns agreed. He added several rooms to the old structure, and by 1837, it functioned efficiently as his headquarters.

By 1841, Abel Stearns was a successful merchant with property in Los Angeles and San Pedro. He had served as *síndico procurador*, or attorney for the city council, and as a member of the Committee for Public Order. More importantly, he had decided to take a wife, the 14-year-old Arcadia Bandini, daughter of Juan Bandini, one of the richest men in southern California. Arcadia's mother was the former Dolores Estudillo, a member of the most prominent family in San Diego.

On June 22, 1841, Stearns and Arcadia were married at the Mission San Gabriel. They moved into Stearns' house at the corner of Main and Arcadia Streets, called "El Palacio de Don Abel." Arcadia, who apparently had never done any work in her life, turned over the duties of house manager to her younger sister, Ysidora, who took charge of the large staff of servants in the Stearns household. They gave a public ball every year, a fiesta that became the premier social event of Los Angeles.

The financial benefits of having married into the Bandini family were soon realized by Stearns. He purchased the Rancho Los Alamitos, roughly 27,000 acres. The rancho was on the Pacific coast, just south of present-day Long Beach. In 1846, Governor Pío Pico granted him the Rancho Los Vallecitos, various plots in the San Francisco area and the Rancho Valle de San Rafael, near Ensenada, in Baja California. In the 1860s, southern California was hit by a series of severe droughts, ending the Golden Age of the cattle industry and nearly ruining Stearns and his company, which had large interests in cattle ranching. Unable to pay taxes, Stearns and his partners began selling off their landholdings. In 1868, more than 200 square miles of his land, from Los Angeles south to the Santa Ana Mountains of present-day Orange County, were put on the market as small farms. The venture was successful, and Stearns was able to recoup much of his losses.

Stearns died in August 1871 in San Francisco. Don Abel and Doña Arcadia had no children. Arcadia lived to the age of 85; at the time of her death in 1912, her estate was valued at more than $15 million, a remarkably huge sum at the time.

Benjamin Brown, Poppy Fields near Pasadena *(detail), oil on canvas, 16 x 22 in., Private Collection, courtesy of The Irvine Museum*

JOHN AUGUSTUS SUTTER

Many American newcomers opened stores and built comfortable fortunes. One of the most famous immigrants to California during this period was Johann Augustus Sutter (1803–1880), a German-Swiss who left his homeland, as well as his wife and children, to avoid going to debtor's prison. He worked at various jobs in the United States before joining an American Fur Company party to the Rocky Mountains in the spring of 1838. Wishing to reach California, he continued north to Vancouver, where he boarded a Hudson's Bay Company ship for Hawaii. From Hawaii, he took a merchant ship to California, arriving in Monterey on July 3, 1839.

Passing himself off as a captain in the Swiss Guards, Sutter petitioned Governor Alvarado for a grant of 50,000 acres. The land, which stretched from what is today the city of Sacramento to as far north as present-day Marysville and beyond, came with the stipulation that he build a fort for the specific purpose of protecting California from raids by hostile Indians and controlling "American criminal elements," specifically trappers who were illegally entering California. The fort was situated at a strategic point where the Sacramento and American rivers came together, the site that is now occupied by the city of Sacramento.

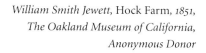

Interior of Sutter's Fort, Sacramento, California, c. 1915, vintage postcard, Private Collection

Sutter called his settlement "Nova Helvetia" (New Switzerland), but most people called it simply "Sutter's Fort." It took two years to build, from 1842 to 1844, and eventually controlled immigration routes from Oregon to the north, and the plains and mountains to the east. To present an organized, militaristic image to visitors, Sutter hired a German military drill instructor to train his Miwok Indian scouts, who were often seen marching in goose-step around the parade grounds.

Even though Sutter was commissioned by the Mexican authorities to stem the flow of immigrants into California, he actually encouraged it, as he was interested in recruiting people to take part in his plans for New Helvetia, the farming and manufacturing empire he envisioned on his property. Captain Sutter, as he called himself, personally welcomed all visitors and immigrants. He kept several

William Smith Jewett, Hock Farm, *1851, The Oakland Museum of California, Anonymous Donor*

Thaddeus Welch, Bolinas Bay, *1896,*
oil on canvas, 14 x 36 in., The Irvine Museum

cannons—purchased when the Russians closed Fort Ross—which were ceremoniously fired to announce passing boats or arriving wagon trains.

As the terminus of the emigrant trails from Kansas City and Omaha, Sutter's Fort became an important frontier outpost. It was a place where weary immigrants, who had just made the perilous crossing over the Sierra Nevada mountains, would stop and make repairs to their wagons and re-stock supplies, such as food, wool blankets, candles, soap, rope and other necessities. Sutter's renowned guides were critical to the safety and welfare of large numbers of travelers, due to their expertise and familiarity with the terrain. In 1847, Sutter's guides rescued the 45 survivors of the ill-fated Donner Party, which had become trapped in the deep snows of the Sierra.

Always looking for ways to expand his empire, Sutter took great interest in news that the Russians, who had colonized parts of northern California, were looking to sell all of their settlements. Although Russia had shown interest in California from as early as the 1770s, by the end of the 1830s, Russia's colonial interests lay elsewhere, and it began abandoning many of its outposts. Moreover, with the opening of new settlements on the Columbia River (the border between present-day Oregon and Washington), the Russians were no longer dependent on California for agricultural supplies. In 1841, the Russians decided to close Fort Ross and their settlement on Bodega Bay.

After some negotiations, Sutter bought the two settlements for $30,000, with $2,000 down and the rest to be paid in installments of produce and cash over five years. The agreement covered all buildings, about 40 structures, and all livestock, including 1,700 head of oxen, 340 horses and mules and 900 sheep. Sutter also received several boats, plows, rakes, harnesses, carts, a winnowing machine and some brass cannons. The sale did not include title to the land, which Sutter acquired from the Russians in a separate deal.

After Sutter took possession of Fort Ross, he made no further payments to the Russians, claiming poor harvests. After American annexation in 1848, the Russians feared that they would never be able to force Sutter to pay his debts. In the hope of somehow recovering what was owed, the Russians renewed the mortgage and continued to press Sutter, who was facing local creditors as well. In an effort to protect his property, Sutter transferred title of all his holdings to his son. Yet the Russians persisted and instructed their consul in Monterey, a non-Russian named Colonel Steward, to collect from Sutter. Finally, Sutter sold several of his lots in the Sacramento Valley and paid Steward in full. Steward quickly converted the assets to cash and left Monterey for parts unknown. Since Sutter had signed receipts from the official consul, the Russians were powerless to pursue the matter, and in the end, never recovered the rest of their money from the sale of Fort Ross.

The southern boundary of Russian Alaska, which had been set by treaty in 1825 at 54° 40', also set the boundary for the Oregon Territory, which lay just south of that parallel. By the 1840s, both England and the United States laid claim to the Oregon Territory. England considered the Oregon Territory to be a part of Canada, and the United States wanted to continue its expansion westward, all the way to the Pacific Ocean.

In 1844, President James K. Polk and the Democrats campaigned with the famous slogan "54° 40' or Fight!" Yet Polk knew that the boundary should be set farther south and offered the compromise position of the 49th parallel. At first, the British refused the offer, claiming instead the entire territory north of California. With the threat of war over the issue, the British finally accepted the compromise. The boundary between present-day Canada and the United States was settled in 1846 by the Oregon Treaty and set at the 49th parallel. With the annexation of the Oregon Territory, the United States now looked south, toward California. ❧

Norton Bush, Sutter's Fort as It Appeared in 1846, *oil on canvas, 30 x 50 in., Private Collection*

Charles Deas, Long Jakes, the Rocky
Mountain Man, *1844, Denver Art Museum,
Funds from Collector's Choice, 1999, and
T. Edward and Tullah Hanley Collection*

CHAPTER 12

TRAPPERS AND MOUNTAIN MEN

*F*rom the beginning of colonization, Spain had intended to supply California only until the province became self-sufficient. The principal means of supply was by sea from the Mexican port of San Blas. Unfortunately, the regularity and reliability of these shipments depended greatly on Spain's political and military situation in other parts of its vast empire. Because California was relatively isolated and far removed from the politics of Europe, it was not of critical importance to Spain. When other, more pressing issues required it, military and financial resources destined for California were diverted. In time, California grew to be self-reliant and maintained extensive trade contacts with other countries, even though this was illegal under Spanish law.

New England merchants were among the first traders to visit California, starting in the late 1700s. The lure was the fur trade, and more importantly, the highly lucrative Chinese demand for sea otter fur. It is estimated that a pelt of fur from a mature sea otter about five feet long fetched the very large sum of $300 or more in China.

The best places to hunt these playful and harmless creatures were along the Pacific Northwest, extending south from the Aleutian Islands along the California coast. Although it was illegal for foreign merchants to trap otters in California, Spain could do little to prevent such activities by ship. By the late 1700s, American trappers were regularly off the coast of California trapping sea otters. While the number of fur trappers was relatively small, by the early part of the 19th century, the otter, as well as the fur seal, which was also an important component of the fur trade, were hunted to near extinction.

The growing unavailability of otter fur and the changing demands of fashion then favored beaver fur, and trade in beaver brought another wave of American trappers and mountain men to California. Unlike sea otters, beavers live inland in streams and rivers, so beaver hunters came by way of the Rocky Mountains, pursuing them from one stream to another.

By appearance, the beaver trapper, or mountain man, as he was more commonly called, made an immediate and lasting impression. According to Rufus Sage, a merchant and mountain man himself, the trapper spent all of his time outdoors, so *"he had skin as dark as that of the Aborigine [Indian]…his hair, through inattention, becomes long, coarse, and bushy, and loosely dangles upon his shoulders. His head is surmounted by a low crowned wool-hat, or a rude substitute of his own making. His clothes are of buckskin, gaily fringed at the seams with strings of the same material, cut and made in a fashion peculiar to himself and associates. The deer and buffalo furnish him the required covering for his feet…his waist is encircled with a belt of leather, holding encased his butcher-knife and pistols—while from his neck is suspended a bullet-pouch…and beneath his right arm hangs a powder-horn transversely from his shoulder. With a…good rifle placed in his hands…the reader will have before him a correct likeness of a genuine mountaineer when fully equipped."*

Because the American frontier was claimed, at various times and places, by the Spanish, French and English, mountain men were a unique blending of these nationalities, with a lot of the American Indian added in. Among the better-known mountain men, Jedediah Smith was an educated Yankee, Jim Bridger was an illiterate blacksmith, Edward Rose was a black man who lived with the Indians, Kit Carson was American, Tom Fitzpatrick was Irish, Manuel Alvarez was Mexican, Bill Sublette was the son of a Missouri Justice of the Peace and Antoine Clément was French-Canadian.

In speech, the mountain men used a language that reflected their multinational origin. In the 1840s, Lt. George F. Ruxton wrote the following passage, recounting how a French-Canadian trapper asked him for some coffee:

> *"Sacré Enfant de Grâce," he would exclaim, mixing English, French, and Spanish…"voyez-vous dat I vas nevare tan pauvre as dis time; mais before I was siempre avec plenty café, plenty sucre; mais now, God dam, I not go à Santa Fé, God dam, and mountain men dey come aquí from autre côté, drink all my café. Sacré Enfant de Grâce, nevare I vas tan pauvre as dis time, God dam. I not comer meat, ni frijole, ni corn, mais widout café, I no live! I hunt maybe two, three days, may be one week, mais I eat nothin; mais sin café, Enfant de Grâce, I no live, parceque me not sacré Espagnol, mais one Frenchman."*

186

Henry Wood Elliot, Seal Drove Crossing, *1872, watercolor, University of Alaska Museum; Alexander Edouart,* Shooting Seals, *oil on canvas, 18¼ x 26¼ in., Private Collection, courtesy of The Irvine Museum*

THE BEAVER TRADE

Although the beaver is an air-breathing mammal, it is fully adapted to life in water. In quiet waters, a beaver will build a house of branches, twigs and mud. This type is called a "lodge beaver." However, in faster streams and rivers, it will build a nest above the water level by digging tunnels into the riverbank. In this case, it is called a "bank beaver."

At one time, the northern part of the Spanish province of Alta California had a thriving beaver population, particularly in the San Joaquin and Sacramento rivers and their tributaries and in the marshy areas of San Francisco Bay. California's beaver population was made up of three varieties: the Shasta beaver, which lived in the interior, in the northern parts of the San Joaquin Valley; the large golden beaver of the Sacramento River and the delta areas of the San Francisco Bay; and the Sonora beaver, from the Colorado River. The farther south the trappers went, the fewer beavers they found, as there were few year-round streams in southern California.

In the Rocky Mountains, trapping season was limited to spring and fall, as snow and ice made trapping impossible. However, in California and other parts of the Southwest, trapping was carried out all year.

Upon finding a promising beaver area, the trapping party—it could vary from one or two persons to a large group working as a "company"—established a base camp, from which they would set their traps for miles around in all directions.

The common way to trap a beaver is described by Hiram M. Chittenden in his 1902 book *The History of the American Fur Trade of the Far West*:

> *The universal mode of taking the beaver was with the steel trap. The trap is a strong one of about five pounds' weight. The chain attached to the trap is about five feet long. The trapper…wades into the stream so that his tracks may not be apparent; plants his trap in three or four inches of water a little way from the bank, and fastens the chain to a strong stick, which he drives into the stream at the full chain length from the trap. Immediately over the trap, a little twig is set…about four inches above the surface of the water. On this is put a peculiar bait, supplied by the animal itself, castor, castoreum or musk, the odor of which has a great attraction for the beaver. To reach the bait…he springs the trap…and is caught.*

After several days, the trapper would return and harvest the traps. Usually, the beaver drowned as a result of a fruitless struggle to escape the trap, but sometimes the trapper would find one that had loosened the chain and gotten entangled in the underbrush near the stream. It was a cruel and miserable death for a gentle and harmless creature.

However, the most limiting and dangerous aspect of fur trapping on the frontier was attacks by Indians. Along with four to six traps and a good skinning knife—the tools of his trade—a trapper would always have at his side a rifle with two locks, a good powder horn and a double shot bag. In camp, he would stock (prior to the invention of self-contained bullets) 100 flints, 25 pounds of powder and 100 pounds of lead to make rifle balls as needed.

Some encounters between mountain men and Indians were grim, and often resulted in the death of one or the other. Captured trappers were subjected to cruel torture and death, and there were numerous instances of trappers killing unarmed Indians and burning defenseless villages. The taking of scalps was practiced by both sides. In an effort to keep the peace and avoid bloodshed, numerous treaties were signed by the United States government and various Indian tribes. Invariably, these treaties were intentionally violated, neglected or simply ignored as the number of whites who encroached on Indian lands rose steadily. Trappers were the vanguard of this invasion, and their attitude was *"The rifle is the only pen with which a treaty could be written."* Generally, however, most trappers tried to keep good relations with the Indians, for whom they accorded the highest respect. A thriving trade developed between trappers and Indians, from which both sides benefited.

The manners and movements of a mountain man were very much like those of an Indian. Many writers of the period noted that, like an Indian, a typical mountain man appeared wild and unsettled, and in casual conversation preferred to use a sign or gesture instead of words. Indeed, nearly all of them had Indian wives, and many were adopted into Indian tribes. It was said that you could not pay a mountain man a greater compliment than to mistake him for an Indian.

The high point of a mountain man's social life came once a year at the rendezvous, the annual trade meeting. The rendezvous, French for "meeting," was where trappers and merchants went to trade pelts for gunpowder, lead, tobacco, and most of all, liquor and women. The most popular rendezvous were held between 1825 and 1840 at a pre-arranged site along the Green River.

JEDEDIAH SMITH

The first Americans to explore the west were trappers and mountain men. Seeking their fortunes in unknown lands, they entered the interior by following established Indian trails that, for countless generations, had existed as ancient trails made by buffalo or other migrating game. When the west was finally opened to settlement, it was the mountain men and former trappers who acted as guides and trail bosses.

Jedediah Strong Smith (1799–1831) was perhaps the greatest of all American mountain men. He was the first recorded white man to enter California by crossing the Rocky Mountains from the east. On August 15, 1826, he organized a group of about 20 fur trappers along with close to 50 horses. They left Bear River Valley in northern Utah and made their way south and west until, on October 4,

Alexander Harmer, Carreta in a Storm, gouache on artist board, 13½ x 24 in., Santa Barbara Historical Society, Gift of Mr. and Mrs. Carl Gray Park

Hernando Villa, Jedediah Smith at Mission
San Gabriel, *1921, oil on canvas, 130 x 139 in.,*
Los Angeles Fine Art Gallery

they crossed the Colorado River near a Mojave Indian village in what is now Nee-
dles, California. With the help of two Indians who had run away from California
missions, Smith and his group made their way over Cajon Pass (near present-day
San Bernardino) and arrived at the Mission San Gabriel in late November. They
stayed at the mission until January 1827, when at the urging of the resident padre,
they left for San Diego to report to Governor Echeandía, as the law required of all
foreigners in California.

When Smith reached San Diego, Echeandía had him arrested as a spy and
thrown in jail while the governor awaited word from Mexico. After recommenda-
tions from several reputable men, including some visiting ship captains from Boston,
Smith was released only on his word that his party would immediately leave California via the same route they had entered and not stop at any settlements. Smith
and his men went back over Cajon Pass, but then turned west into the San Joaquin
Valley and found beaver in nearly every stream. They remained for several weeks
in a semi-permanent camp to trap more beaver. When asked by Spanish authorities why they had not yet left California, Smith replied that the snows were yet too
deep to cross, and that they would leave at their first opportunity.

Leaving most of his men behind to continue trapping, Smith and two
friends left California with seven horses and several mules. They crossed the Sierra
Nevada and made their way back to Utah. On July 13, 1827, he arrived at Bear Lake

with only one companion and, in his words, "one horse and one mule, so feeble and poor that they could scarce carry the little camp equipage which I had along. The balance of my horses [and mules] I was compelled to eat as they gave out."

Smith's long journey proved that California could be reached by crossing the mountains. News of Smith's travels prompted others to do the same, and eventually routes developed by Smith, Kit Carson, Joseph Walker and others would open California to a large number of American immigrants. To the Mexican authorities, however, Smith's exploits were a serious threat, as it proved that California's eastern frontier was no longer impassable.

Soon after arriving at Bear Lake, Smith was ready to return to California to rejoin his trappers. With a group of 18 trappers and two Indian women, Smith retraced his path to the Colorado River. When they attempted to cross the river, they were attacked by Mojave Indians, who killed ten of their party. Smith led the survivors to San Gabriel Mission, where they obtained supplies and continued north to the pueblo of San José de Guadalupe (now the city of San Jose). When he reported to the authorities, he was once more arrested, sent to Monterey and again put in prison. On December 30, 1837, Smith was released after several American ship captains posted bond. In Monterey, Smith rejoined members from his first party and along with the survivors of the second party, headed north toward Oregon.

Elmer Wachtel, Golden Autumn, Cajon Pass, *oil on canvas, 22 x 30 in., Private Collection, courtesy of The Irvine Museum*

From June to July, Smith continued his journey north, finding large numbers of fur-bearing animals to trap. On July 14, while trapping along the Umpqua River in southern Oregon, he and his party were attacked by Indians without warning. Only Smith and three others survived the massacre. They found their way to the Hudson's Bay Company outpost at Fort Vancouver. In spite of all the hardships and dangers, Smith's trip earned him great fame and substantial wealth from the large number of fur pelts he had gathered. Smith continued to serve as a scout and explorer. As fate would have it, he died on May 27, 1831, after being ambushed by Comanches in New Mexico.

Smith's exploits, and his reports of abundant beaver in California streams, opened the way for other trappers. In 1827, James Ohio Pattie and his father, Sylvester Pattie, both experienced trappers, were trapping along the banks of the Gila and Colorado Rivers when they were attacked by a band of Yuma Indians. To escape, the Patties and their companions hastily built crude rafts and floated down toward the Gulf of California. Continuing inland to the west, they nearly died of exposure before encountering a group of docile Indians. The trappers asked for a guide to take them to the nearest settlement, where they were arrested and taken to San Diego. Governor Echeandía accused them of being spies and, just as he had done with Jedediah Smith a year earlier, confiscated their load of fur and threw the Patties in jail. The father, Sylvester, died in jail within a few weeks. James was kept in

Arthur F. Tait, The Check (Keep Your Distance), *oil on canvas, 30 x 44 in., Gilcrease Museum, Tulsa, OK*

jail for about a year before he was released to act as an interpreter for Echeandía. Years later, James Ohio Pattie published a book on his journey, in which he claimed that his release from jail was due to his possession of smallpox vaccine in his supply kit. He claimed that in exchange for his freedom, he had agreed to vaccinate nearly 22,000 whites and civilized Indians in California against smallpox, which at the time was ravaging the region. This statement cannot be substantiated and is generally looked upon as a fabrication by Pattie.

WILLIAM WOLFSKILL

Only known photograph of William Wolfskill, courtesy of Joan Hedding (great-great-granddaughter of William Wolfskill) and Judy Gauntt

One of the early western trappers who would figure in the later history of southern California and Orange County was William Wolfskill (1798–1866). Born near Richmond, Kentucky on March 20, 1798, Wolfskill grew up in Howard County, Missouri, at the time an outpost of the frontier. In 1822, he joined a wagon train to New Mexico led by Captain William Becknell. On the way, he met and formed a partnership with Ewing Young, an experienced mountain man, to trap beavers in various rivers of the Southwest and northern Mexico. On at least two instances over the next few years, Wolfskill's parties were attacked by Indians, who killed several trappers. On one occasion in Mexico, Wolfskill was shot and left for dead by one of his companions, but he limped and crawled more than 20 miles to reach a village and safety.

In 1830, Wolfskill and Young formed a partnership with William Waldo to take a trapping expedition to California. The party of 11 men set out for Los Angeles in the autumn, after which they planned to proceed north to trap in the streams of the San Joaquin Valley. However, they took the wrong trail and ended up in the Wasatch Mountains in Utah, where they were marooned in deep snowdrifts. They survived the bitter cold thanks to their heavy blankets and the beaver pelts they had collected on the way. The party finally came down from the mountains, followed the Colorado River south, crossed the Mojave Desert to the San Bernardino Mountains and came to Los Angeles by way of Cajon Pass, in 1832. The route charted in part by Wolfskill, as well as others who had come before, became known as the Spanish Trail, and later the California Trail, a principal avenue for immigrants and gold seekers.

Disillusioned with the life of the mountain man, Wolfskill decided to remain in southern California the rest of his life. He sold his mules and pelts and used the proceeds to build a boat to hunt otter pelts. At the time, Capistrano Bay had one of southern California's largest sea otter populations, as it was dense in kelp and especially rich in the sea otters' favorite foods: abalone and sea urchins.

Wolfskill's experience as a mountain man was once again put to use. Shortly after arriving in Los Angeles, he displayed his skills as a tracker by leading a posse after a band of Indian horse thieves. Trailed to their hideout in Indian Canyon (now called Black Star Canyon, in the Santa Ana Mountains several miles above present-day Irvine Park), the renegades were surrounded and slaughtered. The incident gave the area—which would later become Orange County—its one claim to an "Indian massacre."

By 1841, having accumulated a modest fortune, Wolfskill pioneered California's fruit-growing industry by planting the first commercial orange grove in Alta California. In 1841, Wolfskill bought out the small orange grove started by Frenchman Louis (Luis) Vignes in 1834. By 1863, half the state's orange trees were in his 70-acre grove, now the site of Union Station on Alameda Street, in downtown Los Angeles. Within a few years, he was joined by his four brothers, and the family began to expand their agricultural concerns.

Wolfskill then turned to growing grapes. In 1856, he received an award at the California State Fair for having the best vineyard in the state. Interestingly, when a group of German winemakers wanted to start the colony of Anaheim in 1857, they planted Wolfskill vines. By 1862, he boasted of having 85,000 vines under cultivation.

As Wolfskill's fortunes began to rise, he started making loans to a half-dozen Mexican rancheros who, because of high-living and mounting gambling debts, were forced to mortgage their cattle and land. In 1851, not long after he started acquiring land, Wolfskill owned 1,100 acres in Los Angeles County (which included what is now Orange County) and was listed as the 14th highest taxpayer. By comparison, José Andrés Sepúlveda, the largest landowner in the county, had 102,000 acres. By 1858, few of the old Californio rancheros had retained their wealth, and Wolfskill was the third highest taxpayer in Los Angeles County. In 1864, he was second only to Phineas Banning, founder of Wilmington and developer of San Pedro Harbor.

Wolfskill was a wise investor and made his fortune through "an enviable reputation as an honest, enterprising, generous, unassuming, intelligent man." In 1859, he loaned $10,000 to Don José Sepúlveda, owner of the sprawling Rancho San Joaquin, for a period of one year at a hefty 2% per month. The note was paid on time. In 1860, due to mounting debt, Teodosio Yorba, whose family had come to California with Portolá in 1769, was forced to sell his Rancho Lomas de Santiago to Wolfskill for $7,000.

The Rancho Lomas was large, more than 47,000 acres, mostly of mountainous land and not suited for agriculture. But its northern boundary was the Santa Ana River, which provided very valuable water rights to the ranchero. Furthermore, the land was ideal for cattle, and Wolfskill had plenty, most received as payment of loans from debt-ridden rancheros.

Soon, however, the Great Drought of 1863–64 ruined the cattle business, and thousands of sick and dying animals were slaughtered only for the value of their hides and horns. Wolfskill converted the Rancho Lomas into a sheep ranch and held it until just before his death in 1866, when he sold it to the Irvine-Flint-Bixby partnership for the same amount he paid, $7,000. ❧

ABOVE: *Anna Hills,* Fall, Orange County Park, *1916, oil on board, 14 x 18 in.*
RIGHT: *Edgar Payne,* Sycamore in Autumn, Orange County Park, *oil on board, 32 x 42 in.;*
Private Collection,
courtesy of The Irvine Museum

Pio Pico, *History Collections, Los Angeles
County Museum of Natural History*

CHAPTER 13

POLITICS IN CALIFORNIA 1831–1845

The growing alienation between California and Mexico led to a fomenting resentment of colonial control, which in turn brought about a large measure of autonomy among the independence-minded Californios. Over the years, there had been several small "revolutions" by the Californios, often with little or no bloodshed. Furthermore, the growing discord between the more cosmopolitan merchants of northern California and the large rancheros of southern California provoked conflicts that often threatened open violence. For whatever reasons, between 1831 and 1836, California endured 11 different administrations.

In 1831, Mexico sent Manuel Victoria to be Governor of Alta California. He was perhaps the worst in a series of poor administrators that Mexico sent to rule over the increasingly rebellious Californios. Following his arrival in Monterey, Victoria expressed contempt for the unruly Californios. His rule was marked by a harsh administration of justice, and he handed out the death penalty for even the slightest infraction. When he refused to convene the California Diputación (Congress) because he thought many of its members had been illegally elected, the Californios sent petitions of protest to Mexico, asking for the recall of the governor. When he exiled several prominent Californios to Mexico without trial, open revolt broke out in San Diego and Los Angeles.

Well-respected Yankee-Californio Abel Stearns and José Antonio Carrillo, who had both been sent into exile, conspired with Juan Bandini and Pío Pico to start the rebellion. After taking the presidio in San Diego, a force of about 50 armed rebels stormed the jail in Los Angeles and released a number of their friends, who had been arrested under orders of Governor Victoria. Victoria responded by marching south from Monterey with a detachment of soldiers.

The two factions met outside Los Angeles in Cahuenga Pass. Surprised to see a large troop of his own soldiers accompanying the rebels, Victoria rode out alone to urge them to return to his side. When the rebellious soldiers refused, he ordered his own men to fire a volley over their heads in order to frighten them. In return, the rebels fired off their own volley and then retreated. However, one of the rebels, José María Ávila, well known for his daring horsemanship, leveled his lance and rode straight for Governor Victoria and his assistant, Captain Romualdo Pacheco. When Ávila got near, he took out a pistol and shot Pacheco through the heart. This ignited some of the rebels, who charged into the battle. After a brief exchange of fire, Ávila was killed, some say by Victoria, who himself was seriously injured by a lance wound in the face. In the end, it was a Pyrrhic victory for Governor Victoria, who won the battle but nonetheless was forced to resign and return to Mexico.

William Wendt, San Fernando Valley, Elisabeth Waldo-Dentzel Multicultural Arts Studio, Northridge, CA

After Governor Victoria's departure, the Diputación met, and on January 10, 1832, chose Pío Pico to be Jefe Político (political chief), or temporary governor, until Mexico could send a replacement. However, when José Echeandía, who had been governor before Victoria, heard of this, he refused to recognize Pico, a man he thought to be untrustworthy. To make sure Pico did not take office, Echeandía formed an alliance with Captain Zamorano, the military commander in Monterey, and unseated Pico after only 20 days in office. Together, Echeandía and Zamorano kept order until January 1833, when Mexico sent José Figueroa to be governor.

Figueroa, a mestizo who had been Commandante-General of Sonora and Sinaloa, Mexico, took office on January 14, 1833. His first act was to grant general amnesty to all who had been involved in the revolt against Victoria. This effectively ended the revolt and allowed all Californio factions to swear allegiance to him. His next act was to appoint Mariano Vallejo (1808–1890) as "Commandante Militar del Frontera del Norte," or Commanding General of the Northern Frontier, to secure the region north of San Francisco against further Russian encroachment and open it to Mexican settlement. To accomplish this goal, he commissioned Vallejo to build a presidio in Sonoma.

Mariano Guadalupe Vallejo was born in Monterey, California on July 7, 1808. He started his military career as a cadet of the company of the Monterey Presidio in 1824. He rose quickly through the ranks and made important social and political contacts along the way. In 1831, Vallejo was one of the prominent Californios who staged the rebellion against Governor Victoria. A year later, Vallejo married the beautiful Francisca Benicia Carrillo, a daughter of the rich and influential Joaquín Carrillo. They had 16 children, ten of whom lived into adulthood.

In 1834, he was sent to secularize the Mission San Francisco Solano (Sonoma) and found the pueblo of Sonoma on the former mission lands. In this capacity, his task was to contain Russian presence at Fort Ross and prevent further

Russian colonization in the north. To accomplish this, he was authorized to build a presidio and issue land grants to settlers.

In Sonoma, Vallejo planned the new town and built a magnificent home on one side of the plaza. As military commander, he built his presidio, which came to be known as "Vallejo's Fort," and manned it with a company of soldiers and a group of 50 trained Indians. When the Mexican government stopped sending funds to pay soldiers, Vallejo paid his troops out of his own pocket.

He would become one of the richest men in California. His Rancho Petaluma boasted of more than 10,000 cattle, 6,000 horses and several thousand sheep. His ranch house, called "La Hacienda," hosted all important visitors to the area and was the scene of fabulous fiestas and banquets.

In August 1833, Governor Figueroa reluctantly implemented the most important act of his administration: the extensive Secularization Decree of 1833. Prior to passage of the law, he made a sweeping inspection of all the missions and discussed the proposed secularization with the padres. He came to the conclusion that the Indians were not yet ready for secularization. Figueroa then sent a report to the Mexican government warning of the consequences if the Indians were suddenly released from the structure of the mission system. In spite of his concerns, the law was passed, and all missions in Alta and Baja California were secularized. Figueroa was an able administrator and was generally regarded as the best of the Mexican-era governors. He died in office on September 29, 1835.

Virgil Williams, View of Mt. Tamalpais from Sonoma, *Bedford Family Collection*

THE ALVARADO REVOLT

The death of Governor Figueroa was followed by a series of locally appointed interim governors who administered California until Mexico sent Mariano Chico as official governor in 1836. Immediately upon arrival, Governor Chico encountered a wall of resentment, and he was expelled from office after only three months. Mexico then appointed Nicolás Gutiérrez, who also lasted about three months before he, too, was expelled by a rebellion.

Sensing the moment had come for an open act of defiance against Mexican authority, Juan Bautista Alvarado and José Castro moved to make California an independent state. To this end, they organized an army made up of Californios and like-minded Americans.

Alvarado was born in Monterey in 1809, the son of José Francisco Alvarado and María Josefa Vallejo. His grandfather Juan Bautista Alvarado had come to California with Portolá in 1769.

Alvarado found that foreigners, particularly Americans, were interested in supporting any movement toward California's independence from Mexico. Accordingly, Alvarado secured the assistance of Isaac Graham, an American fur trader. Graham, who fully looked the part of a frontiersman, wearing a bushy beard and clad in buckskin, assembled a force of 75 American trappers, sailors and adventurers to help in the revolt.

On November 3, 1836, Alvarado and his men promptly took possession of the Monterey presidio. After the first cannonball hit the Governor's house, Gutiérrez surrendered peacefully, and Alvarado immediately sent him back to Mexico.

On November 6, the Diputación, chaired by José Castro, declared California a free and independent state, with the motto "Federation or Death!" The Diputación called for the reinstatement of the Mexican Federalist Constitution of 1824, which had been countermanded by the Mexican Centralist Constitution, giving more power to the central government. Alvarado was named *presidente* of California.

To ease the growing tensions between north and south, the Diputación passed a law splitting California into two sections, making Monterey the capital in the north and Los Angeles the capital in the south. Alvarado became Jefe Político (Political Chief) in Monterey. He was to select a counterpart in the south, but political unrest there threatened to upset his regime.

Even though they stood firmly united against Mexican authority, the Californios were far from a united lot themselves. No sooner was the Alvarado revolt underway than various factions in California openly moved to grab a share of political power. Alvarado had to make a show of force by leading an army of about 80 men into Los Angeles in January 1837.

PÍO PICO

Meanwhile, in Los Angeles, Pío Pico (1801–1894), who helped bring about the brief "revolution" against Governor Victoria in 1831–32, and had since been the voice of

reform in the south, called for the capital itself to be moved from Monterey to Los Angeles. Pío de Jesús Pico IV was born on May 5, 1801 in a grass hut near the Mission San Gabriel. He was the eldest son and fourth of ten children of José Maria Pico, a soldier who had served in San Gabriel and San Diego, and Maria Estaquia Gutiérrez. Pío's father and mother, as well as his grandfather Santiago Pico, had come to California with the Anza Expedition of 1775. His grandmother was a mulatto, and like many other colonials, the Pico family traced their ancestry through African, Indian and Spanish blood. The ten children who made up the family of José Maria Pico included Andrés Pico, who would also rise to leadership in California, and a daughter Ysidora, who would later marry John Forster of San Juan Capistrano.

The Pico children were educated at home and taught reading and writing by José Antonio Carrillo. Carrillo was an in-law to the Picos, first marrying Pío's sister Maria Estefana, and when she died, marrying another sister, Maria Jacinta Pico.

In 1810, Pico's father, a corporal in the Mission San Gabriel garrison, was accused of conspiring rebellion against Spanish rule and briefly confined to house arrest. When the father died in 1819, the family was left without money or property, and it fell to Pío, as eldest son and head of the family, to support the rest. He opened a store in San Diego and built a thriving business by importing goods from Mexico. In time, Pío Pico established good relationships with some of the most influential families in California and rose to become a rich man.

In 1821, Mexico declared independence from Spain, and California assumed more and more autonomy in administering its own affairs. In 1826, an advisory body was formed, the Diputación, to assist the governor. Pico was elected as one of the deputies. The following year, he served as secretary to the provincial attorney general and figured prominently in the case of Señor Bringas, a Los Angeles merchant who had refused to recognize military authority over civilian administration. For

Pico, this case instilled the notion of the rights of citizens to question or refuse orders of the military commander and made him the champion of ordinary Californios.

In 1832, Pico served as governor for a few weeks after the defeat of Governor Victoria. His brief term came to an end when former governor Echeandía reappointed himself to office. In 1834, Pico married María Ignacia Alvarado. Governor Figueroa served as the best man. In 1835, with secularization of the missions underway, Pico secured an appointment as administrator of the Mission San Luis Rey, with authority over the Indian neophytes and the annual production of hides and tallow and other products of the mission. By the time Governor Alvarado came to office, Pico had become a shrewd and powerful veteran of California politics.

Late in 1837, toward the end of his first year in office, Governor Alvarado was confronted with the pressing problem of an insurrection in San Diego. There, Pico's brother-in-law José Antonio Carrillo, a member of the Diputación, had secretly negotiated with Mexico to have his brother, Carlos Carrillo, appointed as acting governor. On December 1, 1837, Carlos Carrillo was sworn in as governor and selected Los Angeles as his capital. Alvarado refused to recognize Carrillo's appointment and continued to rule California from Monterey. Carrillo formed a small army and appointed Juan Castañeda to march north and take Monterey. In response, Alvarado's forces, commanded by José Castro, moved south. The two sides met in a skirmish outside Ventura on March 27, 1838. As was the case in most Californio encounters, very little blood was shed, but Carrillo's army was forced into a humiliating retreat and Alvarado's forces marched into Los Angeles on April 1. For his role in the revolt against Alvarado, Pico was arrested and briefly jailed in Santa Barbara.

Soon after taking office, Alvarado sent an agent to petition Mexico to appoint him as the official governor. With the failure of the Carrillo appointment, Mexico grudgingly agreed and named Alvarado the new governor of California in August 1838.

The biggest social event of Governor Alvarado's term was his marriage to Martina Castro, daughter of Francisco Castro. The marriage was held at the Mission Santa Clara on August 24, 1839. Every notable social and political figure in California attended the wedding except the governor—the groom—who was in Monterey, too sick to attend. His half-brother, José Antonio Estrada, was his proxy and in a perfectly legal ceremony, stood at the altar with the bride.

Although California remained a part of Mexico, the Alvarado revolt had given its citizens a taste of independence and greatly reduced Mexican authority. In the ensuing years, the bitterness between Mexico and California would show in many ways.

In 1841, a group of Americans including Isaac Graham, a fur trapper, whiskey-maker and political rabble-rouser of unsavory reputation, was accused of instigating revolution in northern California. Alvarado had them arrested and sent into exile in Mexico. Eager to promote any prospect of toppling Alvarado, the Mexican government not only released these foreigners, but gave them free passage by ship back to Monterey.

Late in 1842, Mexico re-asserted her dominion over California by sending Manuel Micheltorena, a military veteran with gracious and gentlemanly manners, as the new governor. Recognizing that his appointment would meet with general disapproval, Micheltorena was accompanied by a force of 300 irregulars, scornfully called *cholos* by the locals.

Upon arriving in Los Angeles, he learned that the state treasury was essentially empty, and thus he had no money to pay his men. Like most soldiers in the far-off colonies, many of the *cholos* were ex-convicts and thugs, who did not take kindly to serving unpaid. At their first opportunity, the *cholos* proceeded to make themselves unwelcome by robbing the populace and molesting young women. To ease the situation and stop the *cholos* from victimizing the public, Mariano Vallejo provided a good part of the money needed to feed and maintain Micheltorena's troops. Even though he saw the *cholos* as a curse on California, Vallejo viewed Micheltorena as a good and fundamentally honest person who needed a fair chance to make his governorship effective. In Micheltorena's defense, the governor accepted responsibility for the actions of his men, and when it was proved that they had robbed or stolen, he repaid the victims from his own pocket.

Even before Governor Micheltorena arrived in Monterey, he was confronted with a remarkable incident, the "invasion" and very brief American occupation of Monterey. In October 1842, Commodore Thomas Ap Catesby Jones and his squadron of warships were patrolling off the coast of South America when he mistakenly heard that the United States had declared war on Mexico. In keeping with the U.S. Navy's plans in case of war with Mexico, Jones proceeded to Monterey, and on October 19, landed the Marines, captured the presidio and raised the American flag.

Los Angeles, 1856, lithograph, Sherman Library and Gardens, Corona del Mar, CA

Jones held Monterey from October 19–21 before learning of his mistake. He then apologized to local authorities, restored the Mexican flag, withdrew the Marines and sailed away. Other than a brief footnote in history, Commodore Jones'

provocative actions reveal that the United States had fully developed contingency plans in anticipation of hostilities with Mexico.

As for domestic hostilities, it was just a matter of time before Governor Micheltorena encountered trouble from the Californios. In November 1844, Alvarado, Pío Pico, Andrés Pico and Castro revolted against Micheltorena and sent an army south to depose him. Vallejo, who had become a friend of the governor, took no part in the rebellion but did, however, notify Micheltorena that he could no longer afford to pay the governor's troops, nor could he continue to pay his own troops in Sonoma and disbanded them. Vallejo did this to avoid being put in the position of sending reinforcements to Micheltorena to fight against his friends.

On February 20, 1845, Micheltorena and his *cholos* clashed with the rebels in Cahuenga Pass, near Los Angeles. Both sides spent two days in a fruitless and ineffective long-range artillery contest, each causing no significant casualties to the other. However, it was enough; Governor Micheltorena capitulated and agreed to return to Mexico with his *cholos*. Thereafter, California was virtually independent from Mexico.

In an effort to heal the north-south animosities, Pío Pico of Los Angeles was designated governor, and José Castro of Monterey was named military commandant. However, Governor Pico alienated Castro and the northerners by moving the capital to Los Angeles. There was no legal obstacle to exercising the office of governor from the south. Micheltorena had spent most of his term in San Diego, but by tradition, the seat of Californio power had been in Monterey. Pico's declaration that he would stay in Los Angeles was a manifestation of southern California's emerging commercial and political power. After a term of two years, 1845–46, Pío Pico would be the last Mexican governor of California.

John "Juan" Forster, c. 1860, photograph, San Juan Capistrano Historical Society

Mrs. Juan Forster, photograph, San Juan Capistrano Historical Society

JOHN FORSTER

John Forster (1814–1882) was born in Liverpool, England and left at the age of 15 to help an uncle who was doing business in Mexico. From 1831 to 1833, he traveled between Mexico and California, selling imported Chinese goods with his uncle. For the next few years, he continued his business in Los Angeles, where he befriended the prominent Pico family. In 1837, Forster converted to Catholicism, married Ysidora Pico, sister of Pío and Andrés Pico, and became a Mexican citizen. Thereafter known as Don Juan Forster, he formed a business association with Abel Stearns, a Californio-Yankee who had extensive business interests in the hide and tallow trade.

In 1843, with the influence of the Pico family, Forster received a land grant from Governor Micheltorena. This was the Rancho Nacional (now National City), called "El Rancho del Rey" prior to 1821, south of San Diego. By 1845, Forster was a rich man. He amicably terminated his business relationship with Stearns in order to concentrate on land acquisition. In this venture, he could count on the considerable prominence of his brother-in-law, Pío Pico, who was now Governor of California.

In 1845, Governor Pico decided to sell the Mission San Juan Capistrano at auction to the highest bidder. The winning bid of $710 was offered by John Forster,

Pico's brother-in-law, and James McKinley, who was later bought out by Forster. Because the mission was still a parish church, Forster's purchase included all the buildings at the mission except the old adobe church, now called the Serra Chapel, and an adjoining room where the resident padre lived.

With Pico's influence, Forster became a land baron. In another grant, Forster received the Potreros de San Juan Capistrano (the pastures of the old mission) and Rancho Trabuco, on Trabuco Creek, which is near the Mission San Juan Capistrano. He moved to San Juan Capistrano and purchased the adjoining Rancho Mission Vieja (now Mission Viejo) and the Rancho Desechos (now part of the city of San Clemente). At only 32 years of age, Forster owned an estate of more than 100,000 acres.

Forster moved into the old mission, walling off a portion of the front building into comfortable living quarters, where he and his family settled into the Californio way of life. The Mission San Juan Capistrano would be Forster's home until 1865, when a Federal Land Patent, issued in the name of President Abraham Lincoln, returned the mission to the Catholic Church.

JUAN FLORES

In January 1857, San Juan Capistrano was the scene of a ruthless and terrifying raid by the outlaw Juan Flores. Flores, a 22-year-old Californio-Mexican from Santa Barbara, was the co-leader (with Pancho Daniel) of a gang of escaped convicts who called themselves the "Manillas" (Handcuffs), after the marks left on a convict's wrists.

In 1855, Flores had been sent to San Quentin prison for stealing a team of horses belonging to Garnet Hardy, an American rancher. In the trial, Hardy's testimony against Flores was persuasive, and the jury found the outlaw guilty.

Two years later, the escaped convict was in San Juan Capistrano with 11 of his gang, looking for Hardy. Flores had learned that Hardy would be in San Juan Capistrano on business. When Hardy learned that Flores was in town, he took refuge in the home of his friend Juan Forster, in the old mission. Forster, fearing that Flores would find and kill Hardy, instructed one of his employees to take Hardy to Los Angeles the long way, over the mountains and by way of Lake Elsinore to avoid running into Flores.

Soon after arriving, some of the gang got into an argument with Michael Kraszewski, a storekeeper in San Juan, when one of the outlaws took a pistol without paying for it. When the bandits were confronted, they looted the store and left town.

Later that day, Flores returned to San Juan to visit his sweetheart, a young Mexican woman named Chola Martina. The gang, accompanied by Chola, went to another store, which was owned by George Pflugardt. Pflugardt kept a large stock of guns and ammunition; however, his store was fortified and easily defended. Somehow, Chola got Pflugardt to open his door, whereupon the bandits rushed in and Flores shot the shopkeeper in the head. Then the gang and Chola ransacked the store, found some food, and casually sat down and ate dinner while Pflugardt lied

Alson Clark, Arches, San Juan Capistrano *(detail), oil on board, 14¾ x 17¼ in., Private Collection, courtesy of The Irvine Museum*

Edgar A. Payne, Canyon Mission Viejo, Capistrano, *oil on canvas, 24 x 28 in., Private Collection, courtesy of The Irvine Museum*

William Wendt;
RIGHT: San Juan Creek, *oil on canvas, 18 x 24 in.;*
BELOW: San Juan Capistrano Hot Springs,
O'Neill Ranch, *oil on canvas, 18 x 30 in.;*
Private Collection, courtesy of
The Irvine Museum

dying on the floor. Before the gang finally left at about 2 a.m., they looted several other stores, leaving what they did not take scattered in the streets.

Word of the Flores raid reached Sheriff James Barton in Los Angeles. At the time, Los Angeles County encompassed all of what would become Orange County in 1889. Sheriff Barton quickly organized a posse and encountered Flores and the Manillas the next day in what is now the city of Irvine, near the interchange of the San Diego Freeway and Route 133. A gunfight resulted in which Sheriff Barton, three posse members and three bandits were killed.

Barton's murder caused great consternation throughout the county. After Barton's burial, two posses set out to find Flores, one made up of Americans, the other of Californios. The Californio posse was led by Andrés Pico, hero of the Battle of San Pasqual and brother of former Governor Pío Pico.

The manhunt for Flores and the Manillas took several days, but finally, with the help of local Indians who had volunteered to help Pico, the gang was cornered in Santiago Canyon, near Saddleback Mountain. Pico captured two of the bandits, but Flores escaped over the mountain now called Flores Peak. The American posse followed and caught Flores and two other bandits. At the time of his capture, Flores had Sheriff Barton's gold watch in his pocket. The bandits were taken to the nearby Rancho Santiago de Santa Ana for the night. Somehow, Flores and his companions escaped. When Pico learned of the escape, he immediately hanged his two prisoners and set off after Flores.

The remnants of the gang split up and Flores fled north. He was finally caught by a posse from Los Angeles, alone, in Simi Pass northwest of Los Angeles, and taken to jail. Flores' arrival in Los Angeles stirred the passions of the citizenry, who demanded his immediate execution. On February 14, 1857, Flores was taken out of jail by a vigilante group and hanged. In time, the other members of the Flores-Daniel gang were individually tracked down and hanged on the spot. Chola Martina remained free in San Juan Capistrano, where she resided the rest of her life.

FORSTER VS. PICO BROTHERS

In 1864, a severe drought brought many landowners to bankruptcy. The Pico brothers, Andrés and Pío, were in debt and desperately feared the loss of their vast holdings. Among their many ranches was the 100,000-acre Rancho Santa Margarita y Las Flores, situated along the coast between San Clemente and Oceanside. The property was originally an Indian pueblo called Santa Margarita y San Onofre. Pío Pico maneuvered title to the rancho in 1844, in part through a grant from Governor Alvarado. The Pico ranch house is now the commandant's quarters at the U.S. Marine base Camp Pendleton.

The Pico brothers' debts, the result of years of high living and unrestrained gambling, threatened to ruin them. In February, Pío Pico convinced his brother-in-law Juan Forster to take the Rancho Santa Margarita in exchange for assuming a debt of $37,000. The Picos could not raise this large amount and feared that a foreclosure action against them would bring about the loss of their other proper-

Andrés Pico, daguerrotype, Southwest Museum, Los Angeles, photo by Veronica Tagland

ties. To legalize the transfer, Pío Pico signed a deed, which of course was written in English. Years later, the Pico brothers maintained that the agreement was for only half the ranch, and that Forster had, in Spanish, verbally confirmed this when Pío signed the deed.

To clear his title to the ranch, Forster sued the Pico brothers in 1873. In the trial, the Picos claimed that the ranch was then valued at $75,000 (this appears to be an exaggerated figure, as in 1864, James Irvine and his partners bought the Rancho San Joaquin at about the same price per acre as Forster paid for Rancho Santa Margarita), and that the debt of $37,000 represented half the value of the ranch. Forster, in turn, produced the deed and offered notes that he had paid an additional $24,000 of Pío Pico's ever-increasing debts. He further showed that, as sole owner, he had paid annual taxes on the entire ranch. He also called witnesses who testified that he had conducted business at the ranch as sole owner. According to Cleland, *"The question of who had taken the 'orejanos' [unbranded calves without mothers] in the rodéos on the Rancho Santa Margarita was an important point in determining whether Forster or Pico owned the ranch."* The jury took less than 30 minutes to find in favor of Forster. With clear legal title to Rancho Santa Margarita, Forster's holdings amounted to more than 250,000 acres of land. ❧

William Wendt, Green & Gold, *oil on canvas, 30 x 40 in., Private Collection, courtesy of William A. Karges Fine Art, Los Angeles and Carmel*

M. Nevin.

210

CHAPTER **14**

THE AMERICAN CONQUEST OF CALIFORNIA

*A*s early as the 1830s, the United States saw that California was inevitably growing away from Mexico. Moreover, with the growth of American maritime commerce, the need for an important harbor strategically placed on the Pacific coast became more and more urgent, and the most coveted prize of all anchorages in California was San Francisco Bay. Hoping to gain the region by peaceful means, the United States made more than one serious attempt to buy the territory from Mexico.

In 1835, after Mexico's defeat by Sam Houston and the Texas Republic, President Andrew Jackson offered Mexico $3.5 million for Texas, with the understanding that the western border of Texas would stretch all the way to the Pacific Ocean and include San Francisco. Jackson had in mind that the United States would then annex Texas and get access to the strategic port of San Francisco. Both Texas and Mexico rejected the proposal. Later, in 1845, soon after the acquisition of the Oregon Territory, President James K. Polk offered $40 million for California and the Southwest. The offer was seriously considered by some in the Mexican government who feared that they were about to lose the territory in any event. However, a strong nationalist faction in the Mexican government forced a rejection of the offer.

Spurred by the concept of "Manifest Destiny"—the notion that the United States was destined to expand to its natural frontier, the implication being all the way to the Pacific Ocean—contingency plans were made to invade California if war ever broke out between Mexico and the United States. America's great desire to acquire San Francisco Bay, and indeed all of California, became evident in the bewildering Jones Affair, when the U.S. Navy briefly seized Monterey in 1842. Although it proved embarrassing to the U.S. government, the incident nevertheless illustrated how easily the capital of California could be taken by the U.S. Navy or any other foreign power.

JOHN C. FRÉMONT

In 1844, James Knox Polk was elected President with a platform that advocated expansion and annexation of western territory. Efforts to acquire California were stepped up. In October 1845, Polk sent Lt. John C. Frémont (1813–1890) west, ostensibly to explore the Great Basin and the Pacific coast south of Oregon.

Frémont was born in Savannah, Georgia on January 21, 1813, the son of a French émigré. He was educated at the College of Charleston, South Carolina, but three months before he was to graduate, he was expelled from school for poor attendance. In 1836, he worked as a surveyor for the Charleston and Cincinnati Railroad.

John C. Frémont in his Frontier Costume,
from Harper's Weekly, *July 13, 1861,*
Private Collection

In 1838, he joined the U.S. Army Corps of Topographical Engineers as a second lieutenant. He accompanied French scientist J.N. Nicollet on his survey expedition of Minnesota, where he mapped the Des Moines River. His work for Nicollet allowed him to gain sufficient knowledge and experience to lead his own expeditions. Between 1842 and 1854, Frémont led five expeditions west. In 1843, guided by Kit Carson, Frémont completed a survey of the Oregon Trail, through Wyoming to the mouth of the Columbia River. However, his most notable expedition would be his trip to California in 1845.

In 1841, Frémont met Jessie Benton, the daughter of influential Senator Thomas Hart Benton. In October of that year, the two secretly eloped and were married. Thomas Hart Benton (1782–1858), Frémont's father-in-law, was born in North Carolina but grew up on the frontier in Tennessee. In 1799, he became a lawyer and later served as a colonel under Andrew Jackson in the War of 1812. A headstrong and contentious man, Benton once shot Jackson in an argument and was forced to flee west. He settled in St. Louis, opened a law office and became editor of the *Missouri Enquirer*.

After being elected to political office, Benton served for 30 years (1821–1851) as a Democratic senator from Missouri. As an important senator, he mended his relationship with Andrew Jackson, who was elected President in 1829, and the two became political allies. It is said that when Jackson finally had Benton's bullet removed, many years after he was shot, he offered to return it. Benton declined, claiming that Jackson should keep it, as he had earned it.

Benton's strong opposition to the establishment of a national bank and his support for hard money—that is to say, coinage instead of paper money—earned him the nickname "Old Bullion." In 1832, President Jackson, who also opposed paper money, vetoed a bill that would have renewed the charter of the Bank of the United States, effectively killing it. As a result, the American economy collapsed in 1837. Local banks failed, as people sought vainly to redeem paper money for gold coins. The country's first major depression could have been averted, had there been a national bank.

Benton pursued a moderate position on the slavery issue, a courageous stance in pre-Civil War Missouri, a border state with active Southern sympathies. Eventually, it was his lack of support for slavery that cost him his Senate seat in 1851 and ended his 30-year tenure.

Benton's greatest passion, however, was his belief in Manifest Destiny, the notion that America should expand to the Pacific coast. Correspondingly, he championed the small farmer and maintained that the west, once opened, would generate unlimited, cheap land. Vehemently anti-British, Benton, who was chairman of the Military Preparedness Committee in the late 1840s, felt that the British Empire was moving to acquire Oregon, and that war with Britain was inevitable. He thought that America, in order to properly defend itself, should have the strategic port of San Francisco, even if it meant war with Mexico.

TOP:
John C. Frémont, *1863,*
engraving, 9½ x 6½ in., Private Collection
BOTTOM:
Senator Thomas Hart Benton, *engraving,*
Private Collection

Hugo Wilhelm Nahl and Charles C. Nahl,
The Camp of a Coast Geodetic Survey Party,
1858, oil on panel, 12½ x 18½ in.,
Santa Barbara Historical Society

Christopher "Kit" Carson, c. 1865,
vintage postcard, Private Collection

Echoing his father-in-law's views, Frémont was convinced that war with Mexico was imminent. Unable to get clearance for a military expedition to California, Frémont settled for authorization to form a survey expedition. To man this "survey expedition," Frémont recruited 60 men, all expert riflemen, a strong indication that his intention was not to explore but rather to make a show of American power in the region. Furthermore, the expedition was to be unusually well-supplied. Unlike regular army troops, who were mounted on mules, his men would ride horses. To ensure a steady supply of meat, they would take along a small herd of cattle on the journey. To travel safely across the Rocky Mountains and into California, he recruited the two most experienced American frontiersmen, Joseph R. Walker and Christopher "Kit" Carson (1809–1868), who in 1842 had served as chief scout for Frémont's first western expedition.

One of the most colorful figures of American frontier history, Kit Carson stood about 5'6" and weighed only 135 pounds. He had auburn-red hair and deep blue eyes. Although he was one of America's most famous heroes, he was a plain man, soft-spoken and rarely stood out in a group of people. As he had never attended school, he could not read or write, but was fluent in English and Spanish. As an experienced trapper and guide, he spoke a number of Indian languages, including Apache, Arapaho, Blackfeet, Cheyenne, Comanche, Crow, Navajo, Piute, Shoshone and Ute.

Carson first came to California in 1829 with Ewing Young's fur-trapping company. He developed a reputation as a resourceful "mountain man" and later served as chief hunter for Bent's Fort, the principal American frontier outpost in Colorado. Carson knew Frémont well and considered him a good friend.

At the same time that Frémont and his troops were dispatched, President Polk sent orders to Thomas Larkin (1802–1858), the American Consul in Monterey, instructing him to assure Californios that the United States would not invade

William T. Ranney, Kit Carson,
1854, oil on canvas, 29 x 24½ in., Sotheby's

California or foment revolution, but instead would protect any local group that moved to sever ties with Mexico. An independent California, Polk believed, would subsequently petition the United States for annexation, as Texas had done a year earlier.

Thomas Larkin had been the American Consul in California since his appointment by President Polk on April 2, 1844. He had come to Monterey from Massachusetts in 1832, and within a few years had become the most successful American merchant in Monterey. Unlike other American merchants who settled in California, converted to Catholicism and married into wealthy Californio families, Larkin rejected all offers to become a Mexican citizen and instead married an American woman, Rachel Holmes, the widow of another New Englander. Their children were the first Americans born in California. Even though Larkin and his family remained American citizens, under California law, the children were accepted as Mexican citizens.

From 1832 to 1835, Larkin built a house that served as both his home and the American Consulate. It became the meeting place for many of California's historic confrontations. In this unique and beautiful building, which is now a house museum, Larkin combined architectural elements of the Mexican-Californio style:

Larkin House, Monterey,
c. 1912, vintage postcard, Private Collection

adobe walls, a second-story balcony and enclosed patio-garden, with a slanted roof, central hall and interior stairway of the New England tradition.

Larkin was the ideal choice for this dual role of Consul and secret agent. He was a popular American patriot who was generally accepted as honest and unselfish. Over the years, he had built a sound personal reputation in Monterey and was on friendly terms with the leading citizens of California, both Yankee and Californio.

On maritime matters, he was perhaps the best-informed man in California, with access to fresh information from his shipping contacts. Throughout history, the busy ports of the world, with their multinational sailors and ships, were generally the centers of social and intellectual energy. Moreover, as a successful importer, Larkin knew all the captains who regularly visited Monterey. At any given time, he knew where ships from various countries were, when they would be in Monterey and what they would be bringing to California.

Unlike the contentious Frémont, Larkin dutifully complied with the instructions he had received from Washington. He made it clear to several influential Californios that any movement to declare an independent republic would be looked upon favorably by the United States.

Larkin knew that California would soon be independent, and more importantly, he sensed the desire of many Californios to be a part of the United States. Foremost among sympathetic Californios was General Mariano Vallejo, commander of the military forces in Sonoma. Vallejo believed that it was only natural for the United States to annex California.

Portrait of Thomas O. Larkin,
California Historical Society, San Francisco

"In contemplating this consummation of our destiny, I feel nothing but pleasure, and I ask you to share it," Vallejo said in April 1846. *"When we join our fortunes to hers, we shall not become subjects, but fellow-citizens, possessing all the rights of the United States and choosing our own federal and local rulers. We shall have a stable government and just laws. California will grow strong and flourish, and her people will be prosperous, happy and free."*

Making his way west, Frémont left Bent's Fort in Colorado on August 26, 1845, and entered California sometime around January 15, 1846, at Sutter's Fort, where he received a warm reception from Sutter and a group of American settlers. From there, he continued to Monterey, arriving on January 27. Pursuant to Mexican law, he had to personally appear and request permission to explore the San Joaquin Valley from Colonel José Castro, the military commander of the Monterey presidio. Castro realized that over the past few years, the growing alienation from Mexico had left California practically undefended. He, like the small group of wealthy landowning families who virtually ran California, thought that if California were left to its own determination, local political events would soon facilitate complete independence from Mexico. To Castro as well as Larkin, Frémont's presence in California was a serious threat to that process.

Castro gave his permission with strict qualifications. Concerned that Frémont might be a spy sent to assess the province's defenses, Castro insisted that the Americans keep to their inland route and avoid the coast altogether, thus averting any attempt to send dispatches to American ships that might be waiting offshore. Furthermore, the Americans were to stay away from any settlement and have no contact with local settlers. Frémont agreed to these restrictions, and Castro was happy to see him *"go to the valley of the San Joaquin, where there was game for his men and grass for his horses, and no inhabitants to be molested by his presence."*

However, almost as soon as he left Monterey, Frémont deviated from his route and entered the Salinas Valley. Furious that an uncooperative American officer was freely roaming the countryside with a force of 60 armed men, Castro sent a dispatch rider ordering Frémont to terminate his survey and leave California immediately.

In defiance of Castro's orders, Frémont positioned his forces on a strategic hill overlooking the Salinas Valley, called Gavilán, or Hawk's Peak (now called Frémont's Peak). There, he built a fortified log barricade and on March 5 or 6, defiantly hoisted the American flag. In his characteristic bravado, he stated that they would *"fight to extremity…trusting to our country to avenge our death!"*

Portrait of Mariano G. Vallejo, *Oakland Museum of California, on loan from the Crocker Art Museum, Sacramento*

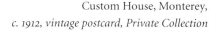

Custom House, Monterey, *c. 1912, vintage postcard, Private Collection*

216

Harvey Otis Young, On the Columbia River, Oregon, *1869, Private Collection, courtesy of Montgomery Gallery, San Francisco*

Larkin, who had been advising Frémont, was completely dumbfounded by these developments. Working to facilitate California's entry into the Union, Larkin had spent months cultivating influential Californios like Vallejo, who were interested in seeing California become part of the United States. His plan, which was made with the full knowledge and approval of influential Californios, called for a declaration of independence from Mexico, followed by the peaceful acquisition of California by the United States.

Frémont's defiant acts threatened open warfare, a serious embarrassment to Larkin, as it rallied his opponents and provoked outrage among his friends. Larkin feared that all his private assurances of non-involvement and peaceful annexation, made on behalf of the President of the United States, would now be seen as a sign of betrayal by the Californios and a ruse to catch them off-guard. Most distressing was his great apprehension that at the first sign of open fighting, Great Britain, which claimed the Oregon Territory just to the north, would land a squadron of warships in Monterey and take the province by force.

Not surprisingly, the Californio authorities took Frémont's flag-raising as a claim on California by the United States, and an angry Colonel Castro threatened to attack if Frémont did not immediately withdraw. Hoping to avert open hostilities, Larkin sent an urgent message to Frémont cautioning him of the gravity of the situation and alerting him that Castro was fully prepared to attack. In addition to rising tensions, rumors—possibly spread by Frémont himself—stated that Castro was using Frémont's presence as a pretense to forcibly expel all Americans from California.

Faced with the choice of staying put and starting a war or giving in to Castro's threats, Frémont abandoned his position on March 9 and slowly marched north toward Sutter's Fort. On March 24, he left Sutter's Fort and proceeded toward Oregon. This came as good news to Larkin, who exclaimed in a letter to his unofficial Vice Consul William A. Leidesdorff in Yerba Buena (later to be called San Francisco), dated March 26, 1846: *"All troubles have passed over. Capt. Frémont is quietly pressing his way to Oregon or elsewhere."*

When Frémont reached the Oregon border, his camp was attacked by Klamath Indians and three of his men were killed. In retaliation, Frémont mistakenly raided a nearby village of Modocs—who had no part in the attack—killing several Indians. Frémont's unfortunate mistake was the first contact that the Modocs had had with Americans, and the attack instilled a bitter hostility among the Modocs. It would be only the first in a series of disastrous Modoc skirmishes with the ever-increasing presence of the white man, leading to the Modoc War of 1872–73 and the eventual destruction of the Modoc tribe.

In mid-April, Lt. Archibald Gillespie, a U.S. Marine officer carrying orders and secret dispatches from Washington, arrived in Monterey and reported to Larkin. Gillespie, who was traveling in disguise, asked Larkin to assist him in finding Frémont. With Larkin's guidance, Gillespie caught up with Frémont on May 9, on the Klamath River, near the Oregon border. In addition to military orders, Gillespie carried letters from Frémont's father-in-law, Senator Benton. According to some historians, these letters, which are lost to history, urged Frémont to instigate all-out war with Mexico. Whatever the case may be, Gillespie's arrival compelled Frémont to turn back to California and re-enter the Sacramento Valley.

Years later, Frémont would write that his return to California was "the first step in the conquest of California," and it was seen by the American settlers as confirmation of impending war with Mexico. To make matters worse, the persistent rumor that the Californios were about to storm Sutter's Fort and initiate a

Col. Charles Waterhouse,
Gillespie and Frémont at Klamath Lake,
courtesy of the Artist

campaign to forcibly expel all Americans from California was more believable than ever. To these frightened settlers, Frémont was, in effect, the full might of the American army sent to protect them and lead them to victory.

THE BEAR FLAG REVOLT, 1846–1848

Sensing the growing disagreement between Governor Pico in Los Angeles and Colonel Castro in Monterey, and counting on an American invasion of California, a group of American settlers, with the knowledge of, if not actual instructions from Frémont, decided to take matters into their own hands. On June 10, acting on reports that Colonel Castro was raising an army to drive out all Americans, a group of armed settlers led by Ezekiel Merritt seized a convoy of 150 Mexican horses. Merritt was a colorful middle-aged mountain man and trapper from Tennessee who had married an Indian woman. Fearless and simple, he was illiterate, of stuttering speech and drank and chewed tobacco to excess. In the belt around his fringed buckskin shirt, he carried a tomahawk, always bragging about the number of Indians he had killed by showing its handle, which bore nearly 100 notches. According to noted historian Hubert H. Bancroft, he was *"well adapted to the use that was made of him in promoting the filibuster's [groups of Americans who, under the guise of being 'liberators', tried to overthrow parts of Mexico and Central America] schemes."* Merritt's men released the Californios they had captured and took the horses to Frémont's camp.

On June 14, perhaps again encouraged by Frémont, that same group of Americans stormed Vallejo's Fort in Sonoma. The action was brief. Mariano Vallejo, probably the richest and most respected person in California, surrendered peacefully. As it happened, Vallejo had disbanded his troops in 1844 during the revolt against Micheltorena, and Sonoma was virtually undefended. Indeed, Vallejo welcomed the intruders and openly declared his support for the American cause. Moreover, he consented to being arrested, as it gave him a pretense to free himself from his responsibilities as a Mexican soldier and military commander of the district.

Barracks, Vallejo's Fort, Sonoma,
vintage postcard, Private Collection

After inviting Merritt and his officers to sit down and eat and drink with him, Vallejo proceeded to discuss the terms of his surrender. However, the rest of Merritt's men, who had been left waiting outside for several hours, became exceedingly impatient. They abruptly held an election and chose one of their own, William B. Ide, to replace Merritt. Ide and his contingent marched into the fort and found

Bear Flag (*flag of the California Republic, modern reproduction*), *Private Collection*

Merritt and his party leisurely drinking brandy and engaged in conversation. Ide, who was a Vermonter and a teetotaler, informed Merritt that he had been removed from leadership and proceeded to place Vallejo, his brother Salvador, his brother-in-law Jacob P. Leese and another man under arrest. The prisoners were then taken to Frémont's camp.

Stealing horses was a hanging offense, except as a military action during a state of war. In the Revolutionary War and the War of 1812, horses were "honorably" stolen to immobilize the enemy. It would appear that Merritt's actions in taking the horses might be considered an act of war, particularly as it was followed by Ide's seizing of the prisoners in Sonoma. Both the horses and prisoners were accepted by Frémont.

Four days later, on June 18, Ide, who had read law and studied the Vermont constitution, issued a formal declaration of intent to establish a republican form of government in California. The rebels then unfurled a flag, said to have been designed by William L. Todd, the nephew of Mrs. Abraham Lincoln, and declared California the "Independent Bear Flag Republic."

The events that followed, and Frémont's perplexing and seemingly independent actions, left Larkin completely dismayed. In a letter to Leidesdorff, dated July 1, 1846, he wrote: *"We are exceedingly in the dark respecting the news from the War party. The Northern affair [in Sonoma] is beyond my comprehension. Another party [of Californios] would like to make me a prisoner…they may yet take me as reprisal or offset for Señor Vallejo.…I have taken an account of my debts and property and am pretty well prepared for anything."*

Bear Flag Monument, Sonoma, *vintage postcard, Private Collection*

By then, Frémont had taken over Sutter's Fort. Although Vallejo once again expressed his support for the American settlers, Frémont, over the objections of John Sutter and other Americans, imprisoned Vallejo and proceeded to Sonoma.

On June 24, a small army of about 50 to 80 Californios, under the command of Joaquín de la Torre, engaged the "Bears", as the rebels called themselves, near San Rafael at the Battle of Olompali. After a brief fight, the Bears, led by Captain Henry L. Ford, beat back the Californios, who suffered four or five killed or wounded.

Henry Lambert Ford (1822–1860) was certainly one of the most fascinating characters in the pageant of California. Born in Vermont on August 24, 1822 as Noah Eastman Ford, he enlisted in the U.S. Army in 1841. He was serving as a Dragoon officer trainee in Pennsylvania when his younger brother Henry Lambert Ford died in 1842. He applied for bereavement leave to attend the funeral but was denied. In a fit of anger, Ford deserted the Army on October 6, 1842 and became a wanted fugitive.

Using his dead brother's name, he made his way by ship to Monterey, where he took an assortment of jobs, including working as a hunter for John Sutter. The rapidly developing events of 1846 drew him into the small group of men who launched the Bear Flag Revolt. As one of the few Bears who had military training, Ford organized a small, but very effective, fighting unit and took the rank of Captain.

LEFT TO RIGHT, FROM TOP:
Alexander Edouart;
Ford with Rifle over His Shoulder,
Ford Looking back at Encampment,
Ford Shooting at a Rider,
Private Collection, courtesy of The Irvine Museum;
Ford Chased by a Californio,
Autry Museum of Western Heritage;
oil on canvas, 18¼ x 26¼ in. each

After the war, Ford settled in northern California, pursued various businesses and served as the first elected Assemblyman for Tehama County. He married Susan Ann Wilson in 1851, but lost her when she and their baby son, John Henry Ford, died in childbirth. He then became an Indian Agent and fathered a child, John Lambert Ford II, by an Indian woman named Martine Higuera. Ford died from an accidental gunshot wound on July 2, 1860, as he was mounting his horse. His pistol, which was in his saddlebags, fired accidentally and hit him in the neck.

On June 25, 1846, the day after the Battle of Olompali, Frémont openly declared his support for the Bear Flag settlers and marched into Sonoma. The Bears immediately declared him their leader, calling him the "Great Bear."

On July 1, Frémont merged the Bears with his own troops. The enlarged force, led by Frémont, crossed the Golden Gate to Yerba Buena (now San Francisco) and entered the sparsely defended presidio of San Francisco. In a typical act of empty bravado, Frémont, with much fanfare, proceeded to disable the presidio's ten antiquated cannons by spiking or punching a hole in each of them. The cannons, which had been made in Lima, Peru in 1625, were in reality no more than elegant museum relics, and after years of neglect by Mexican authorities, the presidio had insufficient powder and shot to load the cannons or even fire ceremonial salutes.

TOP: Raymond D. Yelland, Golden Gate from Angel Island, *1884, oil on canvas, 28 x 48 in., Redfern Gallery, Laguna Beach, CA; BOTTOM: Fortunato Arriola,* View Looking out the Golden Gate, *1868, Private Collection, courtesy of Montgomery Gallery, San Francisco*

The "Golden Gate," the entrance to San Francisco Bay, was named by Frémont in the spring of 1846, 90 years before the famous bridge of the same name. In his *Geographical Memoirs upon Upper California* of 1848, he wrote that he called the entrance, *"Chrysopylae [Golden Gate] on the map, on the same principle that the harbor of Byzantium [Constantinople, now Istanbul, Turkey] was called Chrysoceras [Golden Horn]."* He foresaw that one day, the riches of the Orient would flow through this passage, just as the riches of Asia Minor flowed through the Golden Horn of Byzantium. Frémont was apparently insistent that the Greek form be used; it appears as "Chrysopylae or Golden Gate" on Frémont's maps of 1848, drawn by Charles Preuss, his topographer. However, later maps use only the English form.

On July 5, Frémont resigned his commission in the U.S. Army Topographical Corps, removed Ide as commander of the Bears and formed the "California Battalion" with himself as leader. A moral and honorable man, Ide never forgave Frémont for pushing him aside, later claiming that Frémont had taken glory that others had won. Ide distrusted Frémont and felt that Frémont's actions in provoking war had been done at the expense of the American settlers.

TOP: *Gideon J. Denny,* Ft. Point, San Francisco, *1886, oil on canvas, Dr. Oscar Lemer;* BOTTOM: *Richard Beechey,* Presidio of San Francisco, New California, *1826, watercolor on paper, The North Point Gallery, San Francisco*

Meanwhile, with the Mexican War underway, the U.S. Navy moved to consolidate its position in California. The fleet was in Mazatlán, Mexico in June, when Commodore John D. Sloat, head of the U.S. Navy Pacific Fleet, heard news of the war through unofficial channels. Several months prior, Sloat had been instructed that in the event of war with Mexico, he was to take the fleet to California, occupy its principal ports and make every effort to maintain peaceful relations with the locals. In keeping with his instructions, he immediately headed for California; on July 2, Sloat dropped anchor in Monterey Bay.

Not having official orders and not wanting to repeat the embarrassing Jones Affair of 1842, Sloat did nothing more than offer to fire a ceremonial salute, as any visiting military ship would customarily do. The Mexican authorities declined the honor, as they had no powder to return the salute. Then, Sloat summoned Larkin, hoping for official word from Washington.

Larkin told Sloat that he, too, had not received any dispatches from Washington. He briefed Sloat on the political situation and advised him to wait and allow

William H. Meyers,
TOP: U.S. Squadron, California,
BOTTOM: U.S. Squadron at Monterey,
1847, watercolors,
Franklin D. Roosevelt Library, Hyde Park, N.Y.

RIGHT: *William A. Coulter,* U.S. Warship near San Francisco, *oil on board, 14 x 23⅞ in., George Stern Fine Arts, Los Angeles;* BELOW: *Alson S. Clark,* Commodore Sloat Taking Monterey, *oil on canvas, 48 x 72 in., courtesy of DeRu's Fine Arts, Laguna Beach, CA*

the Californios time to declare a California Republic and request American annexation. For five days, Sloat waited in Monterey Bay, seemingly indecisive about his next step. When Sloat learned that Frémont was stirring up trouble in Sonoma, he feared that the British fleet, which was believed to be on its way to California, would use the occasion of civil strife as a pretense to land in Monterey.

Larkin's Californio contacts remained silent, giving no sign of resolution, and finally, on July 7, Sloat landed 250 Marines and sailors and ordered that the American flag be hoisted over the Custom House. He then issued a proclamation, drafted in part by Larkin, stating that "henceforth, California will be a portion of the United States." A few days later, Captain John B. Montgomery, on the *U.S.S. Portsmouth*, entered San Francisco Bay, anchored at Yerba Buena Cove and hoisted the American flag in what would soon be called San Francisco.

With the formal annexation of California, all administrative acts of the Bears and the California Republic were nullified, and Vallejo was released from Sutter's Fort after two months of imprisonment. The Bear Flag Revolt and the time he spent as a prisoner proved very costly to Vallejo. In a letter to Larkin dated September 15, 1846, Vallejo lamented, *"I left Sacramento [Sutter's Fort] half dead and arrived [in Sonoma] almost without life, but I am now much better. The political change has cost a great deal to my person and mind, and likewise to my property. I have lost more than one thousand live horned cattle, six hundred tame horses, and many other things of value which were taken from my house here in Petaluma."*

In Sonoma, unofficial capital of the California Republic, news of the American annexation of California was greeted with rejoicing. On July 9, the Bear Flag, which had been flying since June 14, came down, and the American flag was hoisted, thus ending the California Republic, which had existed less than a month. Sixty-five years later, on February 3, 1911, the California legislature voted to adopt a slightly modified version of the bear flag, including the words "California Republic," as the official state flag of California.

On July 10, Frémont was ordered to report to Sloat in Monterey. He arrived with 160 men of the newly formed California Battalion. When asked by Sloat, Frémont admitted that he had had no specific orders for what he had done in the past few months. Sloat's reply was to dismiss Frémont and decline his offer to have the California Battalion pressed into U.S. armed service.

Soon thereafter, on July 15, Commodore Sloat, citing ill health, turned over command of California to Commodore Robert F. Stockton. Stockton, in contrast, accepted Frémont and his battalion and gave him the new rank of Major. He also rewarded Archibald Gillespie by promoting him to Captain. As the Military Governor of California, Stockton declared martial law and issued a series of proclamations that were generally protested by the Californios. Furthermore, he divided the state into three parts, with Frémont in charge of the north, Stockton of the middle and Gillespie of the south. With the addition of 80 U.S. Marines, Stockton reorganized Frémont's force of volunteers into service as a unit called the "California

William H. Meyers;
TOP: U.S. Retreat at San Pedro,
MIDDLE: Battle for Los Angeles,
BOTTOM: A Californian Lancer,
1847, watercolors,
Franklin D. Roosevelt Library, Hyde Park, N.Y.

Kuchel & Dresel, Los Angeles, *1857, color lithograph, California Historical Society, San Francisco*

Battalion of Mounted Riflemen." Stockton, together with Frémont and Gillespie, made plans to invade southern California.

Meanwhile, Colonel Castro had retreated to Los Angeles and organized a force of about 500 men with six or seven pieces of artillery. However, the well-organized landing of American forces in San Diego and San Pedro caused panic in Los Angeles. The Californios hastily buried their artillery and fled the city. Castro hid in the San Gabriel Mountains for a time before making his way to Mexico. Governor Pío Pico fled south toward Baja California. On August 13, Stockton and his forces entered Los Angeles and occupied it without resistance. Believing the campaign was over, Stockton returned to Monterey, leaving Gillespie in command of the city with a small force of only about 50 men.

Duncan Gleason, The *U.S.S. Ohio* Leaving San Pedro Harbor in 1849, *Edenhurst Gallery, Los Angeles*

On his way to Mexico, Pico stopped in San Juan Capistrano to seek shelter with John "Juan" Forster, his brother-in-law. In pursuit of Pico, Frémont and his battalion surrounded the old mission and demanded Pico's immediate surrender. Forster had some difficulty convincing Frémont that he, Forster, favored the United States and that Pico was not there. In fact, unbeknownst to Frémont, Pico was hiding at his Rancho Santa Margarita y Las Flores, south of San Clemente, on what is now Camp Pendleton.

Pico and Castro reached Mexico safely in August and petitioned the government for funds, troops and supplies to fight the American invasion of California. The Mexican government was facing its own American invasion and gave the Californios no assistance whatsoever. Pico remained in Mexico until the end of the war.

Meanwhile, Gillespie was administering Los Angeles with an iron hand. One of his many edicts was a curfew from 10 p.m. to dawn for all residents of Los Angeles. This was intolerable to the local citizens, as they customarily had a siesta in the afternoon, ate dinner at 9 p.m. then pursued their social and cultural lives well into the early morning. Gillespie's arbitrary attitude eventually drove the Californios to mutiny. On September 23, an armed mob led by José Maria Flores surrounded Gillespie and his men on a small hill in the center of town. Flores was a Californio officer who, after the initial surrender of the city, had been released by the U.S. Army on his promise not to take up arms against the Americans. With some difficulty, Gillespie was able to send a scout with an urgent message for reinforcements, but before any could arrive, he surrendered. Flores gave Gillespie and his men safe passage out of Los Angeles on the promise that he would take the American troops directly to the port of San Pedro and leave California on a merchant ship.

Safely in San Pedro, Gillespie broke his promise to Flores and stalled his departure until reinforcements finally arrived. On October 7, 1846, the *U.S.S. Savannah* docked with a detachment of Marines. As the Americans regrouped to attack Los Angeles, they were met in the gently rolling hills of Rancho Dominguez, south of the city, by a well-organized force of Californio lancers under the command of José Carrillo. The ensuing skirmish, sometimes called the "Battle of Los Angeles," or the "Battle of the Old Woman's Gun," resulted in six American deaths and proved an embarrassing defeat for their side.

The Californio lancers easily out-maneuvered the Americans, but their most effective weapon was an antique cannon that had been hidden by an old woman when the Americans first entered Los Angeles. This small gun, mounted on a wagon, was continually moved from one firing position to another. The havoc caused by the "Old Woman's Gun" forced the Americans to retreat to the ships, where they remained, waiting for further reinforcements from General Kearny.

The six American soldiers and sailors who were killed in the battle were buried on a small island in the port of San Pedro called "La Isla de Los Muertos," or Dead Man's Island, used as a cemetery as far back as 1769. Later, when the breakwater was built to protect the harbor, Dead Man's Island began to erode from altered wave action. By 1888, erosion had exposed several of the caskets. The remains of the six American servicemen were transferred to San Francisco for re-interment, while all previous graves were relocated to a cemetery in San Pedro. In 1928, Dead Man's Island was completely removed, as it lay in the middle of the new main channel. During blasting, workmen uncovered four additional skeletons in apparently unmarked graves.

After the capture of Los Angeles, Frémont sent Kit Carson east to carry reports to President Polk in Washington. However, when he reached Socorro, New Mexico, Carson encountered the "Army of the West" and General Stephen W. Kearny, who was on his way to California to effect U.S. annexation. Not having a knowledgeable guide, Kearny compelled Carson to turn back and guide his army to California.

Carson's outdated information gave Kearny a false sense of confidence that he would quickly and easily occupy southern California. Thinking Los Angeles had fallen and that there would be no resistance to his march, Kearny sent most of his forces back to consolidate Santa Fe and proceeded for San Diego with only about 120 men, mostly Dragoons and Marines. The Dragoons of the 1840s were the precursors to the cavalry in that they were mounted infantry who rode to a battle and fought either mounted or on foot. They were considered an elite force, made up of only the best soldiers and armed with sabers, heavy pistols and rifles. Unfortunately for Kearny, they were mounted on mules and had not yet adopted the quick and agile techniques of the light cavalry of the 1860s.

THE BATTLE OF SAN PASQUAL

By December 1846, Kearny and his Army of the West had made their way from Santa Fe into San Diego County. News of the troubles in Los Angeles had not yet reached Kearny, as his only information came from Kit Carson, who knew only of the quick surrender in August.

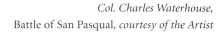

Col. Charles Waterhouse,
Battle of San Pasqual, *courtesy of the Artist*

William H. Meyers, Battle of San Pasqual, 1847, watercolor, Franklin D. Roosevelt Library, Hyde Park, N.Y.

December 6, 1846 was a cold, rainy day, with patches of low, dense fog hanging over the rolling hills. Thirty-five miles north of San Diego, Kearny learned that a group of about 150 Californios were encamped at San Pasqual, a small Indian pueblo near present-day Escondido. Kearny sent a few troopers to investigate. Their sudden appearance startled a group of lancers, who immediately pulled back toward their camp. Acting on the mistaken premise that the Californios had no heart for a good fight, Kearny ordered an immediate attack in the midst of a cold rainstorm. The Californios were ready. They were excellent riders, mounted on well-trained, agile horses. Their leader was General Andrés Pico.

Andrés Pico (1810–1876) was the younger brother of Pío Pico, the last Mexican-era governor of California, and represented one of the most illustrious families in California. A wealthy man himself, Andrés Pico's ranch made up most of the San Fernando Valley. After the lands of the Mission San Fernando were secularized, it fell to local administrators to dispose of them as they saw fit. Andrés Pico had obtained the land from his brother, Pío, at the time an official in Los Angeles. At its height, the entire San Fernando Valley was covered by Pico cattle. In 1845, to raise money to fight the war against the United States, the Pico family sold the ranch for $14,000 to Eulogio de Celis. In preparation for hostilities in the south, Andrés Pico used the funds to form a troop of mounted lancers, drawing on the large number of superb Californio horsemen who worked as vaqueros.

General Andrés Pico in Gala Attire, *photograph, Southwest Museum, Los Angeles*

The Battle of San Pasqual lasted three miserable days. As the rain had thoroughly soaked their supplies, the Americans were caught with damp powder, making their guns unreliable. Moreover, the dense fog that blanketed the battlefield made what little artillery they managed to fire off ineffective.

At first, the Californios appeared to retreat, but they quickly turned and charged into the startled American line. Realizing that the Californios' horses were much faster and more maneuverable than the Army mules, the Dragoons opted to dismount and fight on foot with sabers. The Californios, although a smaller force, had the advantage of being mounted and used their long lances with devastating effects. Finally, after much effort, the Americans were able to fire several volleys of artillery and drive off the Californios. Twenty-two Americans were killed, and 16, including Kearny and Gillespie, were wounded, mostly from lance thrusts. The Californios suffered one dead and 12 wounded.

What followed over the next two days was a slow, bitter, fighting retreat toward San Diego, with the Americans under constant harassment by small groups of Californios. Exhausted, the Americans found themselves surrounded on a small rocky hill that they called "Mule Hill," because of the mule meat they ate to survive. Finally, on the third night of the battle, Carson and a small party crept through Pico's lines and reached San Diego. Anticipating reinforcements from Commodore Stockton, Pico ordered his lancers back toward Los Angeles.

On December 12, Thomas Larkin, the American Consul who had been a party to nearly every historical event of the conquest of California, was captured outside of Los Angeles and taken to prison there. He had been sent by Commodore Stockton to assist Gillespie, who most certainly needed the guidance of someone experienced in dealing with the Californios. Although he was at first threatened with execution, he was well-treated and later, when Los Angeles fell in January 1847, he was released.

Even though the Californios won both major battles in the south—at Los Angeles and San Pasqual—the tide of Americanization was overwhelming. The Californios fought in small, detached units, with no central organization. They had little in the way of heavy armaments and received no assistance from Mexico. In spite of two skirmishes outside Los Angeles, at Rio San Gabriel (near present-day Montebello) and La Mesa (near the Los Angeles stockyards), on January 9, 1847, the Californios were unable to stop Kearny and his reinforced army of 600 men from continuing their march. In the end, General Flores surrendered Los Angeles without resistance on January 10. Wary of Flores' broken agreement after the Gillespie siege, the Americans re-entered the city in battle formation, prepared for any eventuality.

Col. Charles Waterhouse,
ABOVE: U.S. Marine, 1846,
BELOW, LEFT: Lancer Family at Mule Hill,
BELOW, RIGHT: Relief of Mule Hill, 1846,
courtesy of the Artist

William H. Meyers,
LEFT: Battle of San Gabriel,
RIGHT: Stockton at San Gabriel,
1847, watercolors,
Franklin D. Roosevelt Library, Hyde Park, N.Y.

As Kearny was fighting his way north to Los Angeles, Frémont was making his way south from Santa Barbara. Slow to get organized, he arrived too late to do any fighting. However, just north of Los Angeles, he came upon Andrés Pico and his detachment of mounted lancers, the last of the active Californio forces. Not wanting to surrender to Kearny or Stockton, who he feared would have him shot, Pico chose to discuss terms of surrender with Frémont.

On the pretense of acting on behalf of the United States and without waiting for orders from his superiors, Frémont granted Pico generous terms and a full pardon in what has been called the "Cahuenga Capitulation," signed in Cahuenga Pass, just northwest of Los Angeles, on January 13, 1847. Upon news of Frémont's actions, both Kearny and Stockton were outraged, claiming that each in turn, individually, were the only ones authorized to sign a treaty.

On January 30, 1847, the small city of Yerba Buena officially changed its name to San Francisco. Since the name San Francisco was well-known throughout the world, as it was the name of the great harbor, it was ordained that the city and harbor would henceforth have the same name.

Col. Charles Waterhouse,
LEFT: California Lancer,
RIGHT: Lancers at La Mesa on 9 January 1847,
courtesy of the Artist

Across the bay, at the north end near the Carquinez Straits, Mariano Vallejo gave a tract of five square miles to start a new city named "Francisca," in honor of his wife, Francisca Benicia Carrillo de Vallejo. It was to be the most important port in San Francisco Bay, and Vallejo lobbied hard to have it become the state capital. However, when the name of Yerba Buena was changed to San Francisco, it was decided that the name Francisca would be too confusing. The new city took the name of Benicia, Mrs. Vallejo's second name. Benicia never became the capital or the leading port in the bay, as was hoped.

With all of California under United States control, Commodore Stockton prepared to take the fleet to Mexico and resume his role in the Mexican War. Consequently, he designated Frémont to take his place as military governor of California. Kearny, who outranked Frémont, objected vehemently. In response, Frémont stated that he had fought under the auspices of the U.S. Navy and was therefore answerable to Stockton.

Hoping to settle the issue, the three officers met in Los Angeles. Kearny regarded Frémont as no more than a lieutenant colonel in the U.S. Army and therefore clearly inferior in rank. As for Stockton, Kearny pointed out that as a brigadier general, he out-ranked a commodore and was likewise his superior and thus the senior officer in California. Seizing on the disagreement, Frémont stated that until Kearny and Stockton could work out their differences, he would follow Stockton's orders.

Unable to resolve the dispute, Kearny left for San Diego on February 8, 1847 and boarded a ship for Monterey. Commodore Stockton left California, leaving Frémont as Military Governor. Soon after his arrival in Monterey, Commodore William B. Shubrick arrived as Stockton's replacement. He brought dispatches from Washington confirming Kearny as Military Governor and Shubrick as commander of the Pacific Squadron. Kearny forwarded these to Frémont, with the renewed demand that he follow orders.

Frémont, who was in Los Angeles, was still unwilling to relinquish his role as governor, forcing Kearny to go to Los Angeles on March 26. Finally, Frémont renounced all claims as governor and conceded to Kearny's authority. On May 31, 1847, Colonel Richard Mason was sent from Washington to take over as Interim Governor, and together, Kearny and Frémont left California to return east. When they arrived at Fort Leavenworth, Kansas, Kearny placed Frémont under arrest and charged him with insubordination. The court-martial was held in Washington and lasted several weeks. On January 31, 1848, Frémont was found "guilty as charged" and ordered to resign his commission. Even though President Polk commuted his sentence, Frémont announced that he would never accept clemency and resigned from the U.S. Army.

In retrospect, much has been written about Frémont's role in the conquest of California. Larkin's orders from both President Polk and President Buchanan were clear and consistent: he was to do what he could to facilitate a peaceful transition

Vallejo and his Family, *daguerreotype,*
The Bancroft Library,
University of California, Berkeley

Mexican Territory Acquired by the United
States from 1845 to 1854,
from William O. Hendricks, Port Otis, *1971*

Douglass Fraser, Creeping Shadows, Vallejo, *1926, oil on canvas, 26 x 36 in., Jean and Laura Stern*

of California from Mexican to American rule, much like the model of Texas. California would declare independence and thereafter apply for American territorial status. Frémont's orders, on the other hand, are still a mystery. Over the past 150 years, historians have been unable to resolve why Frémont would have been sent to California with orders so different and opposed to Larkin's. The judgment of history has come down to this: Larkin's actions were authorized by the American government, and Frémont's were not.

Similarly, Commodore Sloat was unfairly criticized as being indecisive for waiting five days between his landing in Monterey and his declaration of annexation. While he had been kept fully informed by Larkin's reports, he had no knowledge of Frémont's original orders, nor of the dispatches brought by Lt. Gillespie. ❧

Charles Christian Nahl and August Wenderoth,
Miners in the Sierras, *Smithsonian Institution,*
American Art Museum,
Gift of the Fred Heilbron Collection

CHAPTER 15

THE GOLD RUSH

The end of the Mexican-American War created a surplus of able-bodied men in California, as volunteers who had been released from the U.S. Army were now looking for jobs. Among these were veterans of the Mormon Battalion, men who had served under General Kearny and arrived in San Diego just after the fighting ceased. This unit of Mormon men came from the Midwest and had joined the Army to get to California. They had reasoned that the government would get them there, and when the war ended, it would be easier to get to Utah from the west. Their families had been left in the care of other Mormons, who arranged to have them moved to Utah by wagon train.

The Mormons were discharged from the U.S. Army in Los Angeles on July 15 and 16, 1847. Several small groups organized themselves for the long trip to rejoin their families, by way of Sutter's Fort, then across the Sierra Nevada Mountains, and finally to Utah. One member of the battalion, Henry William Bigler, kept a diary of the events of his service and subsequent travels in California. Of the trip to Utah, Bigler wrote: *"On the twenty-first day of July, we made a move for home, it being just one year since we took up our line of march at Council Bluffs [in Iowa, where the Mormon Battalion was recruited]. Our course was up the San Pedro [Los Angeles River], the pioneers [acting as scouts] leading out. Made that day about ten miles....On the twenty-second, the pioneers led out, leaving the San Pedro, bearing to our right in a northern course over a sandy plain some twelve miles to a Spanish ranch. I think it was called Picoes."* (The ranch, found on the former lands of Mission San Fernando, was also called Pico's Rancho because it was partly owned by Andrés Pico.)

More than a month later, on August 25, after a long, and sometimes aimless, journey, the Mormon party reached Sutter's Fort. Bigler recounts: *"Captain Sutter seemed to have plenty of everything in the shape of cattle, horses and mules, grain, etc. Several of our boys concluded to stop here and go to work for Sutter, as he was wanting to hire and was offering pretty fair wages, as the boys thought, and fit themselves up and come on the next spring."*

Leaving a small number of men behind to work at Sutter's Fort, the main body of Mormons continued toward the Sierra Nevada mountains and on September 5, came upon a camp of the Donner Party, which only a few months prior had been stranded at Truckee Lake, now called Donner Lake.

"Passing down the mountains to the head of the Truckee River...we came to a shanty built last winter, and about this cabin we found the skeletons of several human beings. I discovered a hand...it had been partly burned to a crisp...Some of our company thought that the Indians found them in their starving and helpless condition and

had killed and burned them. Others did not believe it from the fact that we had passed several wagons with trunks and boxes and clothing scattered about...if the Indians had been about, they would have carried off the clothing. I noticed the timber about this shanty had been cut down; the stumps were ten or twelve feet high. This showed how deep the snow was at the time it was cut.

Farther up the mountains, the Mormons came upon another camp of the Donner Party at Prosser Creek and found more gruesome evidence of what had happened there.

"There were men, women and children. Some of them were cut up having their arms and legs cut off, others their ribs sawn from the back bones, while some had their skulls sawed open and the brains taken out!"

On September 6, the Mormon party was met by Sam Brannan, a Mormon elder who had brought a group of about 200 followers by ship "around the Horn" to San Francisco. Brannan, who was part-owner of the general store at Sutter's Fort, was returning from Utah, where he had met and argued with Brigham Young about the eventual location of the Mormon settlement. Brannan had envisioned a settlement called "New Hope," near San Francisco, but Young had decided on Salt Lake City. Disillusioned with Young, Brannan continued his attempts to establish a Mormon settlement in California and collected tithes from his followers. Later, the Mormons would accuse him of pocketing church money and using it for his personal investments. When Young asked him to return the "Lord's money," Brannan is said to have responded that he would do so when he got a receipt signed by the Lord. When Mormon elders finally "disfellowshipped," or expelled, him from the church, Brannan refused to accept their decision.

Sutter's Fort, New Helvetia, from Joseph Warren Revere, A Tour of Duty in California, *1849, California Historical Society, North Baker Research Library, Templeton Crocker Collection, San Francisco*

Early San Francisco Pioneers.
STANDING LEFT TO RIGHT: Samuel J. Hensley
or Talbot H. Greet and Samuel Brannan;
SEATED LEFT TO RIGHT: Jacob P. Leese,
Thomas O. Larkin and William D.H. Howard,
California Historical Society, San Francisco

Brannan had come from Utah with instructions from Young stating that Bigler's party should return to Sutter's Fort, remain there over the winter while they rested and restocked and then set out for Utah in the spring.

Bigler continues in his diary: "*On the fourteenth, at 1:00, we reached our old camp near Mr. Sutter's. After eating a bite of dinner, we sent three men to see Captain Sutter. Late in the evening, they returned reporting they had seen Mr. Sutter, and he was willing to give the whole of us employment. He would either hire us by the month or by the job. He was intending to build a mill and wanted mill timbers got out and a race [spillway] cut about three miles long. He would pay twenty-five dollars per month for working on the race or he would give twelve and one-half cents per yard to be paid in cash. He was to board us, but we were to do our own cooking.*"

Sutter's partner in the saw mill venture was James W. Marshall (1810–1885), an eccentric and somewhat flighty man who was nevertheless an excellent mechanic. Marshall was to organize the work party, which included several Mormons, and supervise construction and eventual operation of the mill. He selected a site about 45 miles northeast of Sutter's Fort, near a rapidly flowing stream and a large stand of timber. As Sutter's partner, Marshall was to build and run the mill. The lumber would be obtained from a wealth of trees in the immediate region. The mill would cut and process the wood, and the lumber would be floated down to Sacramento, where Sutter would take possession of his half. Marshall's half was to continue via various rivers through Suisun and San Pablo bays to San Francisco, where it would fetch a high price. While the scheme looked fine on paper, the wild rivers and canyons along the route would have surely destroyed the sawn lumber along the way.

Construction of the mill proceeded rapidly, but completion of the spillway required additional digging, as the bedrock was shallow. On January 24, 1848, when Marshall inspected the work, he found small flakes of gold in the banks of the river. Bigler was there, and his diary is the only recorded eyewitness account of this historic event: *"This day, some kind of metal was found in the tail of the race that looks like gold."*

For the next two or three days, Marshall and the workers spent some time at the end of each workday collecting little bits of gold. Then, Marshall took a small quantity of the "metal" down to Sutter, and the two of them locked themselves in a room for several hours, testing the gold in various ways. Marshall returned to the mill to tell his men what had happened. *"I and the 'old cap,'"* Bigler quotes Marshall as saying, *"compared it with the encyclopedia and it agreed with it. We applied aqua fortis [acid] but it had nothing to do with it. We then weighed it in water. We took a basin with some water in it, then got our scales and put silver coin in one end and balanced the other with the dust in the air, then let it down gradually until the balances came in contact with the water, and by g____d the gold went down and the silver up…and that told the story what it was."*

Sutter and Marshall tried to keep the discovery secret for several weeks while they acquired as much of the surrounding land as they could. Bigler continues,

> The next move was that all the Indians who owned the land were called in forthwith, and Marshall and Sutter leased a large scope of the surrounding country, some ten or twelve miles square for three years, paying them down some clothing, such as shirts, pants, hats, handkerchiefs, a little flour, peas etc., with the promise to pay them so much every year till the lease ran out. Now it strikes me that Sutter was Indian agent…and any bargain they made with him they considered valid. After this agreement with the Indians, they (Marshall and Sutter) sent…one of the mill hands [on February 8] to Monterey to see Governor Mason and try and have the land secured to them…as it bore strong indications of silver and lead (nothing said about gold). The Governor informed [them] that as affairs were yet in rather an unsettled state between Uncle Sam and the Mexican Government, he could do nothing for them.

TOP: *John H. Dunnel,* Sutter's Mill, *1850, watercolor, The Bancroft Library, University of California, Berkeley;* BOTTOM: Sutter's Mill, *from Frank Soule,* The Annals of San Francisco, *California Historical Society, San Francisco*

For several weeks afterward, mill work continued as usual, and gold panning was restricted to Sundays. Bigler states that each Sunday, the workers readily made three to eight dollars of gold each.

Sutter himself became the first victim of the Gold Rush when his employees quit and took to the hills. *"As soon as the secret was out, my laborers began to leave me, in small parties first, but then all left, from the clerk to the cook, and I was in great distress. The Mormons did not like to leave my mill unfinished, but they got gold fever like everybody else. After they had made their piles [of gold] they left for the Great Salt Lake. So long as these people have been employed by me they have behaved very well, and were industrious and faithful laborers."*

One of the few people Sutter wrote to, telling of the discovery, was former "Vice Consul" Leidesdorff, in a letter dated March 25, 1848, barely two months after the discovery: *"We intend to form a company for working the gold mines, which prove to be very rich. Would you not take a share in it?"*

Always short of cash and over-extended, Sutter was heavily in debt to Leidesdorff. He was hoping to cancel his obligation by offering Leidesdorff a share of the mines. As it turned out, Leidesdorff fell ill and died on May 15, 1848.

The mill was completed and running by the time Sutter wrote to Leidesdorff in March. However, as soon as work on the mill was finished, the Mormons began prospecting in the vicinity of the mill, and by mid-April, were finding substantial amounts of gold. They wrote home, telling of the gold strike, and soon, friends and relatives from Utah were in California, looking for gold on Sutter's land.

By May 1848, the secret was out. Most of the towns in the area were deserted as people took to the hills and valleys of the American River. Brannan, the Mormon leader, had rented a small store in Sutter's Fort. When someone came in to purchase a bottle of brandy using small gold nuggets, Sutter confirmed that it was indeed gold, and that it was found near his saw mill. Immediately, Brannan rented a larger store from Sutter and stocked it with a large supply of merchandise, which he sold to the newly prosperous mill workers. Furthermore, in his capacity as a Mormon official, he requested a "tithing" of 30% on all gold found by any Mormon, to raise money to construct a temple. At first, the Mormons paid the tax, but when it became clear that no temple would be built, they stopped. The matter went all the way to the governor, who gave the opinion that the tax was legal as long as people were foolish enough to pay it.

It was Brannan who first spread the word of the discovery of gold in his newspaper, *The California Star*, in San Francisco. This seems to have been intended as an efficient way to expand his business at Sutter's Fort. He continued to publish news of the gold strike and was responsible for much of the initial rush in the spring of 1848. On June 10, he wrote: *"It is quite unnecessary to remind our readers of the 'prospects of California' at this time, as the effects of this gold washing enthusiasm, upon the country, through every branch of business are unmistakably apparent to every one... Spades, shovels, picks, wooden bowls, Indian baskets [for gold panning] etc., find ready purchase, and are very frequently disposed at extortionate prices...The probable amount taken from these mountains since the first of May last, we are informed is $100,000, and which is at this time principally in the hands of the mechanical, agricultural and laboring classes."*

William Smith Jewett, Portrait of General John A. Sutter, *1856, oil on canvas, 16⅜ x 13¼ in., Oakland Museum of California*

By June, news of the gold strike was confirmed by other San Francisco newspapers and Sutter's property on the Sacramento River was overrun by thousands of people hoping to find a fortune in gold. Squatters and businessmen set up tents and later, cabins, and the city of Sacramento was born. On June 14, Brannan's own paper, *The California Star*, was forced to cease publication, as all its staff had run off to the gold fields. Soon after that, every newspaper in San Francisco was faced with a work stoppage because most of the employees, as well as readers, had done the same.

By summer, news of the discovery began spreading outside California. At first, stories of the gold strike were discounted as merely fantasy and rumors. To confirm wild stories and rumors of fantastic gold finds, on December 7, 1848, in the White House Cabinet Room, President Polk was shown a tea caddy containing 230 ounces of gold nuggets and dust recently sent from California. Not long thereafter, the discovery of gold was mentioned in Polk's annual speech to Congress, and people throughout the country began to leave for California.

It is estimated that only about 6,000 to 10,000 people came looking for gold in 1848. Among the first wave of gold seekers were Mexicans from the mining region of Sonora, Mexico. In 1849, with news of the discovery of gold spreading around the world, that number swelled to more than 100,000, nearly all of whom were adult males.

Almost immediately, Sutter's land on the American River was overrun by thousands of miners who dug pits and shafts along the streams, cut down large numbers of trees for firewood and set up camps without regard for property rights, be they of whites or Indians. As Sutter's Fort was the entry point for overland migration, all of his property in the Sacramento Valley was quickly covered with squatters, and the land in the vicinity of the fort soon became a part of the city of Sacramento.

Sutter's dream of founding a utopian colony evaporated, as he was forced to sell land to keep from going bankrupt. Years later, Sutter wrote an article in the

William Sidney Mount, California News, *1850, The Long Island Museum of American Arts, History, and Carriages, Gift of Mr. and Mrs. Ward Melville, 1955*

LEFT: *Unknown artist,* Mining Scene: Diverting a River, *watercolor, Dr. Oscar Lemer;*
RIGHT: *Nathaniel Currier,* The Way They Go to California, *c. 1849, Oakland Museum of California, Oakland Museum Founders Fund*

Charles A. Fries, The Spirit of Competition,
oil on canvas, 37 x 56 in., The Buck Collection

November 1857 issue of *Hutchings' California Magazine,* lamenting: *"By this sudden discovery of the gold, all my great plans were destroyed. Had I succeeded for a few years before the gold was discovered, I would have been the richest citizen on the Pacific shore; but it had to be different. Instead of being rich, I am ruined."*

THE MINERS

The Gold Rush went through several technical phases: placer mining, hydraulic mining, and shaft or hard rock mining. These methods were determined by how easy or difficult it was to find gold. Each phase required greater and greater numbers of people for the task, from small, one-man operations to large, organized corporations.

In the earliest phase of the Gold Rush, from 1849 to about 1851, gold was largely scattered on the surface. This type of mining, called placer mining or "easy pickings," could be accomplished by a single individual, using a pick, shovel and gold pan. Gold was found in or near stream beds, often in sizeable nuggets. In 1852, the peak year of placer mining and gold production in California, more than $81 million worth of gold was recovered by miners.

In his letter to his family written on March 3, 1850, S. Shufelt, who had previously described his trek through the Isthmus of Panama, wrote from Placerville, in El Dorado County, of the various methods of mining he and his associates used: *"Now I will give you a short history of the mode of getting it [gold], of where it is found and in what quantities so far as my knowledge extends. It is found along the banks of the streams and in the beds of the same, and in almost every little ravine putting into streams. And often from 10 to 50 ft. from the beds up the bank. We sometimes have to dig several feet deep before we find any, in other places all the dirt and clay will pay to*

OPPOSITE:
Martin E. Hall, The Prospector, *1851, oil on canvas, 36 x 25 in., A.R. Phillips, Jr.*
RIGHT:
Ernest Narjot, Placer Operation, Foster's Bar, *1851, oil on canvas, The Bancroft Library, University of California, Berkeley*

French Miners Working the Long Tom,
engraving, Private Collection

wash, but generally the clay pays best. If there is no clay, then it is found down on the rock. All the lumps are found on the rock—and most of the fine gold. We tell when it will pay by trying the dirt with a pan. This is called prospecting here."

Shufelt continues by describing a "long tom" and how it works:

Some wash [the gold-bearing clay or dirt] with cradles, some with what is called a tom and various other fixings. But I like the tom best of any thing that I have seen. It is a box or trough about 8 or 9 feet long, some 18 in. wide and from 5 to 6 in. high, with an iron sieve in one end punched with ½ in. holes. Underneath this is placed a ripple or box with two ripples across it. The tom is then placed in an oblique position, the water is brought in by means of a hose. The dirt, stone, clay and all is then thrown in and stirred with a shovel until the water runs clear, the gold and finer gravel goes through the sieve and falls in the under box and lodges above the ripples. Three men can wash all day without taking this out as the water washes the loose gravel over and all the gold settles to the bottom. One man will wash as fast as two can pick and shovel it in, or as fast as three rockers or cradles.

Ernest Narjot;
LEFT: Miners: A Moment at Rest, *1882, oil on canvas, Autry Museum of Western Heritage;*
RIGHT: The Forty-Niner, *1881, oil on canvas, 40 x 50 in., Santa Barbara Museum of Art, Gift of Marguerite V. West and Charles H. King*

Charles Christian Nahl;
TOP: Saturday Night in the Mines, *1856,
oil on canvas, 10 x 16 ft.,
Iris & B. Gerald Cantor Center for Visual Arts,
Stanford University, Palo Alto, CA;
BOTTOM:* Sunday Morning in the Mines, *oil on
canvas, 1872, 72 x 108 in., Crocker Art Museum,
E.B. Crocker Collection, Sacramento, CA*

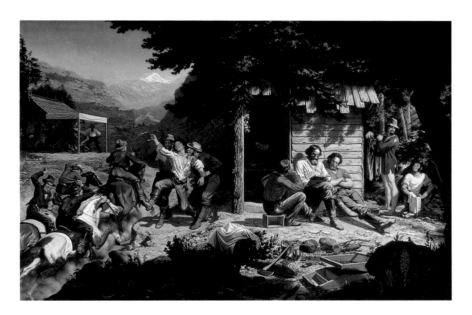

Shufelt then tells his family how successful he was in finding gold:
*The first week I made $82.72 [gold was valued at $20 an ounce in
the United States, but in the California gold fields it traded at $16
per ounce], the next, $42.00, we had to prospect some this week and
fix a new place. The next I made $61.44, we built a dam and dug a
race to turn the water this week and one day it rained and snowed.
The next week $112.81, and one day it stormed so that we did not
work....In the afternoon three of us dug and we made $24.00 apiece.
This was the best half day's work that I have done in the mines.
Pieces [nuggets] have been found that were worth from $1 to $50.
Allerton found one worth $20.00. Some have made [as much as] 4,
5, 6, and 8 oz. per day, and one man last fall made one pound or
$192 in one day...and at Georgetown about 25 miles from here, one
man took out 27½ lb. in one day, and another party found one lump
worth $1,019 and another worth $450.00.*

Stories of fantastic finds and immediate wealth are rare. In truth, very few miners actually got rich, and most miners barely made enough to pay their expenses in the highly inflated economy of the gold fields. Instead, the people who supplied the miners—the merchants and storekeepers—ended up with most of the wealth. On the average, a miner earned $15 to $20 per day working his claim. At the same time, the cost of living in mining camps was so high—flour was more than $3 per pound, eggs were $1 each, blankets were $40, boots were $100 per pair—that nearly all a miner's money was used for everyday expenses. As Shufelt said, "*Some will have to beg their way home, and probably one half that come here will never make enough money to carry them back.*"

In many instances, the miners lost their hard-earned gold nearly as quickly as they found it. "*There is a good deal of sin and wickedness going on here,*" Shufelt wrote, "*stealing, lying, swearing, drinking, gambling and murdering. There is a great deal of gambling carried on here. Almost every public house is a place for gambling, and this appears to be the greatest evil that prevails here. Men make and lose thousands in a night, and…if they lose all, go the next day and dig more.*"

With thousands of gold-seekers crowding the streams and valleys of gold country, it wasn't long before surface gold was depleted, and many miners gave up and either returned home or crowded the larger cities and towns looking for work. A large number of small miners' camps that dotted the countryside, with names such as Lazy Man's Canyon, Ground Hog Glory, Poker Flat and Skunk Bar, were quickly abandoned.

The difficult work, boredom, loneliness and depression drove many miners to give up and either go to work for a large mining company or return home. Disease, accidents and violence also took their grim toll among miners. The pathos

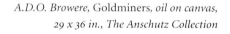

A.D.O. Browere, Goldminers, *oil on canvas, 29 x 36 in., The Anschutz Collection*

of *The Dead Miner*, painted by Charles Christian Nahl after an anonymous poem, found wide circulation and popularity when published as an engraving:

> *Lost! lost, upon the mountain top—*
> *So thickly falls the snow,*
> *In vain he turns—the path is lost—*
> *He knows not where to go.*
> *His faithful dog still follows him—*
> *The miner has one friend,*
> *Who will attend him faithfully,*
> *Unto his journey's end.*
> *And soon it comes, worn out, he falls*
> *Upon the snow drift high,*
> *No friend to hear his mournful calls—*
> *No one to see him die,*
> *Except his dog, which constant still,*
> *Leaves not his master's side,*
> *But bones of both, in future, will*
> *Mark where the wanderers died.*
> (Janice T. Driesbach et al., *Art of the Gold Rush*, 102)

In the mid-1850s, as gold became harder to find, miners started cooperative groups that worked together to move larger and larger amounts of rock and gravel. Instead of the lone miner working a gold pan, large numbers of workers fed dirt and gravel into long, intricate sluice boxes planted in the middle of streams to wash the gold from the soil.

In time, miners who remained in California ended up working for corporations that operated large-scale mines. These companies invested great amounts of money in heavy equipment and employed large labor forces. In "hard rock" mines, workers used dynamite and stream-driven drilling machines to open a network of shafts as they followed veins of gold.

When practical, miners turned to hydraulic mining. In these situations, enormous hoses attached to large nozzles shot tremendous amounts of water against the sides of hills to loosen and expose gold-bearing sediments. Hydraulic mining depended on great amounts of water. Usually, the gold-bearing material was far from any readily accessible source of water, necessitating the diversion of streams across miles of open country. This process conflicted with commonly accepted "riparian rights," which allowed diversion of water only for use on adjacent land, with the excess water returned to its source.

To meet their needs, California miners developed the doctrine of "appropriation and beneficial use" of water, allowing water to be diverted from its normal course for use elsewhere without having to return it to its stream of origin. The doctrine was codified into law with the adoption of the Civil Code in 1872, thus establishing the water system of canals and waterways in use today.

By the late 1870s, there were more than 400 hydraulic mines in California. The millions of tons of mud and sludge that these mines produced flowed into local streams, which were tributaries of the Sacramento River. Over time, the bed of the Sacramento River was built up by mine run-off, causing severe flooding of

Ferdinand Richardt, Lament to the Old Days, *26 x 40 in., Dr. & Mrs. Edward H. Boseker*

Charles Christian Nahl, Joaquin Murieta, *1875, oil on canvas, 18 x 24 in., Museum of Western Art, Denver*

surrounding farms. Levees were built on the riverbanks, but they only served as a temporary solution, as the riverbed kept silting up. Finally, after repeated lawsuits, courts handed down a series of rulings in 1883–84 stating that hydraulic mines had to provide their own catchment areas for the sludge, in an effort to protect the streams that fed into the Sacramento River. This costly measure spelled the end of hydraulic mining in California.

JOAQUIN MURIETA

In the early months of the Gold Rush, many of the gold-seekers who came north from Mexico were experienced miners. Much of the mining terminology associated with the Gold Rush, such as "bonanza" and "placer," are of Mexican origin. The Mexicans' expertise at mining gave them an advantage in locating the best sites and applying the best methods to find gold. This caused resentment among white miners. In reaction, California passed a series of anti-Mexican laws in the early 1850s, aimed at limiting their rights in the gold fields. One such law was the Foreign Miners License Law of 1850, which required a payment of $20 per month to operate a claim. Even though it was intended for all foreign miners, the tax was usually applied only to Mexicans, and the law was enforced by vigilante groups of white Americans.

To protest the restrictions put on foreign miners, bands of Mexican outlaws, most likely dispossessed miners, staged raids throughout the Sacramento and San Joaquin valleys, stealing cattle and horses and robbing travelers. The most notable bandits of these various groups were all named "Joaquin," with last names of Botilleras, Carrillo, Murieta, Ocomorenia and Valenzuela. In time, Murieta would become the most famous of these outlaws, thanks to a series of articles and books that called him the leader of the "gang of robbers commanded by the five Joaquins."

The story of Joaquin Murieta was first told in 1852 in a popular novel entitled *The Life and Adventures of Joaquin Murieta, Celebrated California Bandit*, by John Rollin Ridge. According to the author, Murieta was born in Sonora, northern Mexico, sometime around 1830. In the mid-1840s, he came to California as a horse trainer for a traveling circus. In the spring of 1849, he headed for the gold fields and staked a rich claim in Stanislaus County. Murieta resisted the unfair taxation that was required of Mexican miners by the Foreign Miners License Law, and not long thereafter, the Murietas were victims of vigilante justice. His house was raided, he was whipped, his brother was hanged and his wife and sister were raped, all according to John Rollin Ridge.

Charles Christian Nahl, Joaquin Murieta, *1868, oil on canvas, Gregory Martin*

In retaliation, Murieta, in Ridge's novel, declared that henceforth he would *"live for revenge, and that his path would be marked with blood."* He formed a band of outlaws who robbed mining camps and small towns and held up stagecoaches. He quickly became a hero to the Mexican population of California. Because he fought against unfair laws and represented an oppressed minority, he was called the "Robin Hood of El Dorado."

The story of Joaquin Murieta was elaborated and revised many times in adventure novels and newspaper articles, making any chance of separating fact from fiction nearly impossible. It is generally agreed that there was a man named Joaquin Murieta, but whether or not he truly did all that has been ascribed to him is a subject that is still debated among historians.

In any event, the crimes attributed to Murieta were real enough to have the state legislature pass an act authorizing a former Texas Ranger named Harry Love to form a posse called the "California Rangers" to capture any or all Joaquins. As added incentive, Governor John Bigler of California personally offered $1,000 as reward for the apprehension of "Joaquin," no last name specified, dead or alive. "Wanted" posters were distributed throughout the Sacramento Valley, a move that greatly added to Murieta's notoriety among Americans and prestige among Mexicans.

The hunt for Murieta intensified. Finally, in 1853, the rangers tracked down a group of Mexican renegades near Panoche Pass in San Benito County and killed two of them, one of whom was said to be Joaquin Murieta and the other his accomplice, an outlaw called "Three-Fingered Jack." To prove his claim for the reward, Ranger Love produced the head of the outlaw he claimed was Murieta and the disfigured hand of the other man, who they believed was Three-Fingered Jack. Both of these gruesome items of evidence were preserved in jars of alcohol.

Joaquin Murieta poster, Private Collection

Upon seeing the severed head, several individuals who claimed to have been miners with Murieta confirmed that it was indeed the head of Joaquin Murieta, but his relatives, however, denied it. Even though there was no positive identification available, the governor paid the reward, and not long afterward, all crimes attributed to "Joaquin" ceased.

The two jars with their grisly contents were put on public display at various places for many years afterward. Yet, many people refused to believe that it was indeed the head of Joaquin Murieta. The legend stayed alive with rumors that Murieta had escaped and returned to Mexico, where he lived the rest of his life.

Gutzon Borglum, Runnin' out the Storm,
c. 1896, oil on canvas, 59½ x 108¼ in.,
San Antonio Museum of Art

FREIGHT, STAGE AND MAIL SERVICE

The California Gold Rush of 1848–49, and the Comstock Rush for silver in Nevada a few years later, hastened the development of both freighting and staging in the far west. In the 1850s, there were no good roads, and freight outfits in California were generally slow-moving mule and pack trains, using three loaded wagons per unit, with a hitch of eight mules or oxen. Because of the grueling difficulty of the job, the hard-bitten drivers of the teams, called "mule skinners" and "bull whackers," were known for, among other things, their colorful profanity.

Maurison and Company's service from Stockton to the Stanislaus mines, believed to be the first stage line operating in California, started in May 1849. By the mid-1850s, there were a dozen lines servicing mining centers. Passengers on these early stages were warned that the trip might be a harrowing experience, with treacherous routes and long arid wastes. Rapid streams were crossed on crude ferries, as there were no bridges. Few stages traveled at night, for fear of both Indian attacks and dangerous potholes.

Driving a stage was arduous work, and drivers were well paid. They were expected to manage the large teams of mixed mustangs, hitched to heavily loaded stages, along the rough and stony roads and over the steep grades of the Sierra. To

Concord Stagecoach, History Collections, Los Angeles County Museum of Natural History

keep on schedule, they had to know how to handle nervous teams of animals; a good driver communicated with his mules or horses through gentle movements of the reins. Tough as leather, and well-seasoned to the heat and dust of the trail, these "knights of the rein" raised stage driving to an art.

In 1851, a monthly mail delivery began between Salt Lake City and Sacramento, utilizing mule-drawn relays over a 750-mile route. The following year, Wells, Fargo and Company began carrying much of the local mail service, and in a period of five years, transported $58 million worth of gold to San Francisco alone.

Concord coaches, manufactured by Abbott, Downing and Company in New Hampshire, were the finest available and were used by the best lines. To cushion passengers against buffeting of the road, Concord cabs rode on a leather cradle of "thorough braces." The cost of these carriages was as much as $1,500 and required three spans of good horses costing up to $1,000 a span.

Not until Phineas Banning began to manufacture carriages at Wilmington in southern California were similar coaches built in the West. In 1867, Banning began operation of a stage line between Los Angeles and Wilmington, at Los Angeles harbor, which proved popular because of the quality of his coaches.

In 1858, John Butterfield secured a mail contract from the government to begin carrying the mails across the country. This allowed him to undertake passenger service as well. By using relays of horses, exchanged at ten-mile intervals, his coaches could cover the 2,800 miles between Missouri and San Francisco in 24 days, 18 hours and 26 minutes. The timetable called for fresh horses at a series of wayside stops in order to maintain the scheduled average speed of five miles per hour, day and night.

Perhaps the most exciting and legendary innovation in western mail transportation involved single riders using fast relays of fresh horses to carry mail more quickly between distant points. The Pony Express started its brief existence on April 3, 1860, with the departure of a rider from St. Joseph, Missouri, for California. It consisted of 80 riders, 190 relay stations, 400 station men and 400 fast horses. Young, light riders were selected, armed only with a six-shooter and a knife. Each man changed horses every ten miles, but "Buffalo Bill" (William F. Cody) is credited with one continuous ride of 384 miles.

The westward route of the Pony Express was much the same as that taken by overland wagons. Upon reaching Sacramento, both rider and horse boarded a steamboat down the Sacramento River and across the bay to San Francisco. The run of 1,966 miles was completed in nine days and 23 hours, less than half the time required by the fastest stages to California from Missouri.

The completion of the transcontinental telegraph line in 1861 ended the Pony Express. Though operated for only 16 months and failing to make a financial profit, it had demonstrated the practicality of a central cross-country route, the forerunner of the route of the Transcontinental Railroad, completed in 1869. ❧

Frank Tenney Johnson, Pony Express Station, *1924, Autry Museum of Western Heritage, Gift of George Montgomery*

Within the image: Fording the South Platte River near Julesburg. Sketched July 25, 1866 by W.H. Jackson

William H. Jackson, Fording the South Platte,
Nebraska State Historical Society

CHAPTER **16**

THE JOURNEY TO CALIFORNIA

By far, the greatest number of gold seekers who came to California in 1849 did so by sea. The earliest arrivals came around Cape Horn, the southernmost tip of South America. From New York, the voyage to San Francisco "around the Horn" measured 18,000 miles; normally, the trip took about eight months in a crowded, disease-ridden ship. However, with a fast clipper ship and only a few stops along the way, the voyage could be made in as little as four months.

In addition to sailing vessels, steam-powered ships also made their way to California. In use since the early 1820s, early versions of the steamers were not reliable or efficient and were used only on short trips on rivers and lakes. But by the early 1840s, the steam engine had been greatly refined, and "steamers" were commonly used on long-distance trips, even across the Atlantic Ocean. As reliable as those early steamships might have been, they were nevertheless equipped with sails in the event of mechanical breakdown. By 1847, steamers were carrying a greater and greater percentage of ocean traffic, and although they were not as fast as the large clippers, they could keep moving, even in a calm, windless sea, and frequently made speedier crossings.

Soon, a new, shorter route was developed to meet the growing demand for passage to San Francisco: by way of the Isthmus of Panama. Long before the Panama Canal was completed in 1914, travelers and merchants as far back as the 1500s had used the isthmus as a shortcut to the Pacific Ocean.

One of the earliest American ventures in the isthmus was transportation of mail. The Oregon Territory, annexed in 1846, was the first American possession on the Pacific coast. With the lure of cheap land, it was rapidly attracting American settlers, with the resultant sizeable demand for mail service. In response, the U.S. Congress passed the Mail Steamer Bill of 1847, which provided for delivery of mail from the east coast to the west coast via steamship and across the Isthmus of Panama.

In 1848, just as the Mexican-American War was ending and before hearing of the discovery of gold in California, William Henry Aspinwall founded the Pacific Mail Steamship Company and won a ten-year contract to carry the mail to Oregon by way of Panama. By a fortunate coincidence, Aspinwall's first three side-wheeler steamers, the *California*, the *Oregon* and the *Panama*, began Panama-to-Oregon service in the spring of 1849, just as the Gold Rush got underway.

Hoping to get to California as quickly as possible, and finding the Rocky Mountains still frozen and impassable, the earliest argonauts of 1849 went by ship, and many took advantage of the newly established Panama route. Arriving from the east coast of the United States, ships would dock on the Atlantic Ocean side of

Panama and unload their passengers, who then crossed the isthmus and re-boarded another vessel on the Pacific Ocean side, to continue to San Francisco.

Aspinwall had a virtual monopoly on the Panama-San Francisco route. To meet the ever-growing traffic to the gold fields, he quickly added more steamers to his growing fleet. To keep up his huge business, he placed large numbers of advertisements in nearly every eastern newspaper, offering the traveler a *"pleasant voyage to Panama, stroll across the 50 miles of Isthmus to the Pacific and, after another easy sea voyage, find himself in San Francisco."* It was far from a "stroll". The isthmus route from New York to San Francisco took about eight weeks, and in many other ways it was just as perilous as going "around the Horn."

Upon arriving in Panama, the ships would anchor off the city of Chagres. Long before the Gold Rush, Chagres had seen immense fortunes in gold come in

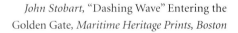

Frank Thompson, Stormy Voyage around the Horn, *Santa Barbara Historical Society*

and out. All the treasure looted by the Conquistadors in South America was sent to Spain from Chagres. To protect the city, Spain had built the venerable fortress of San Lorenzo, situated on a massive rocky outcrop above the port.

After disembarking at Chagres, travelers would have to make their own arrangements for canoe transportation up the river. As demand was high, it took quite a lot of negotiation to reach an agreement with the local canoe providers. Thereafter, the voyagers ventured some 25 strenuous miles up the fever- and alligator-infested Chagres River to reach their next destination.

In a letter home, S. Shufelt, who was on his way to the gold fields, described in unusually pleasant terms his experiences on the Chagres River: *"[We] proceeded up the river in canoes rowed by the natives, and enjoyed the scenery and howling of the monkeys and chattering of parrots very much."* Shufelt's experiences on the Chagres were far from typical. In reality, most travelers who went up the river described the journey as *"miserable…hot…fever-infested."*

A.D.O. Browere, Crossing the Isthmus, *c. 1859, oil on canvas, 33 x 48 in., Crocker Art Museum, Gift of the Crocker Art Museum Association, Sacramento, CA*

Charles Christian Nahl;
TOP: Boaters Rowing to Shore at Chagres, *1855;*
BOTTOM: Chagres River Scene
(Crossing the Chagres);
oil on canvas, Dr. Oscar Lemer

Beyond the Chagres River
Are paths that lead to death
To the fever's deadly breezes
To malaria's poisonous breath!

Beyond the tropic foliage,
Where the alligator waits,
Are the mansions of the Devil
His original estates.

Beyond the Chagres River
Are paths fore'er unknown,
With a spider 'neath each pebble
A scorpion 'neath each stone.

'Tis here the boa-constrictor
His fatal banquet holds,
And to his slimy bosom
His hapless guest enfolds!

Beyond the Chagres River
Lurks the cougar in his lair,
And ten hundred thousand dangers
Hide in the noxious air.

Behind the trembling leaflets,
Beneath the fallen reeds,
Are ever-present perils
Of a million different breeds!

Beyond the Chagres River
'Tis said—the story's old—
Are paths that lead to mountains
Of purest virgin gold!

But 'tis my firm conviction,
Whatever tales they tell,
That beyond the Chagres River,
All paths lead straight to Hell!
(Poet James Stanley Gilbert, author of *Panama Patchwork*)

Having reached the midpoint across the isthmus in canoes, at either Gorgona or Cruces, the travelers would start the bargaining all over again with the mule drivers. Shufelt relates, *"We pitched our tents at Gorgona and most of our party stayed there several weeks. S. Miller and myself went on to Panama [Panama City, on the Pacific coast] to look for a chance to get up to San Francisco. Of our ill success you have probably been informed and consequently of our long stay there, and of the deaths in our party. Yes, here Mr. Crooker, J. Miller and L. Alden yielded up their breath to God who gave it, and as I humbly hope and trust their spirits winged a happy flight upward to that world of bliss and love where sin and sorrow never can come and where parting is not known."*

The trip to Panama City was through the jungle on mule-back. In his journal, Frank Marryat, who made the trek in May 1852, described it as *"stumbling at the rate of a mile and a half per hour…on a narrow, rocky path in the forest, where palm trees and creepers shut the light overhead…splashing through gurgling, muddy streams…stumbling over fallen trees…burying ourselves to the mules' girth in filthy swamps, where on either side dead and putrid mules were lying…amidst lightening, thunder, and incessant rain."*

William H. Meyers;
TOP: U.S. Squadron in Panama, *1847, watercolor, Franklin D. Roosevelt Library, Hyde Park, NY;*
BOTTOM: Aspinwall, Panama Steamer Station, *1855, engraving, Private Collection*

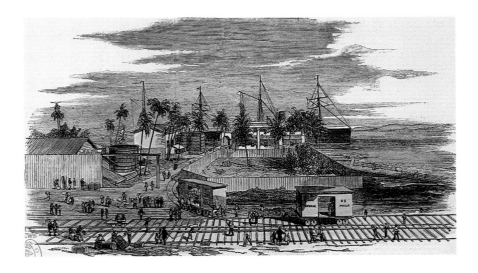

Finally, the mule train arrived on the Pacific side. The continual rain of the tropics made the trip miserable. When the trail was not mired in swamps or deep mud, the overwhelming heat made the trek a living hell. Hundreds of travelers died from malaria and yellow fever. Moreover, gangs of bandits roamed the jungle, attacking travelers at will to rob them of their valuables.

The first travelers to come via the isthmus in 1849 and 1850 did so without assurance of regular steamer service to San Francisco. The wait for an available ship added to the long delays encountered on the hot, miserable voyage. *"After many delays and vexations,"* Shufelt wrote in a letter home, *"we at length took passage on a German ship and set sail again on our journey to the El Dorado of the west. We went south nearly to the Equator, then turned west. The weather was warm, the winds light and contrary to our course. Our ship was a slow sailer and consequently our passage was long and tedious…On the 85th day out we hove in sight of an object that greatly attracted our attention…the green hills of San Francisco."*

With a growing number of people rushing to California, the need for more efficient travel across the Isthmus of Panama was undeniable. In 1850, Aspinwall and his partners, John L. Stephens and Henry M. Chauncey, began construction of the 47-mile-long Panama Railroad. Swamps, muddy terrain and disease made the initial part of construction difficult. In 1852, cholera swept the isthmus, killing large numbers of people. No actual records exist, but it is estimated that between 6,000 and 10,000 workmen died during construction of the railway. The biggest problem was filling in the myriad of swamps that peppered the isthmus. In addition to 47 miles of track, the railroad required 170 bridges of 15 feet or more, as well as 134 bridges shorter than 15 feet.

After the first seven-mile section was finished, the company ran out of funds. But demand for the line was so great that passengers willingly paid $25, an exorbitant fee, to ride the train, or $10 to walk the right-of-way of the short, completed portion. The money raised by fares allowed the company to keep working. Finally, on January 28, 1855, the entire route was completed. The line ran from the Atlantic port of Aspinwall (later called Colón) to the Pacific port of Panama, and reduced a trip that previously could be made in as little as four days—but most often took two weeks or more—to only four hours. With the Panama Railroad, travel from New York to San Francisco could be made in as little as 21 days.

THE OVERLAND ROUTE

People who lived inland or did not have access to a suitable port went to California by stagecoach, wagon, horseback or simply on foot. The fastest way was on horseback, taking two to three months of hard riding. Most immigrants, however, brought along their possessions and thus were compelled to use wagons. An oxen team was the preferred method of pulling the wagon. A fully loaded wagon weighed between 3,000 and 7,000 pounds. For each adult in the party, immigrants were advised to carry 200 pounds of flour, 75 pounds of bacon, 25 pounds of sugar, 10 pounds of salt, 5 pounds of coffee, half a bushel of cornmeal, half a bushel of dried

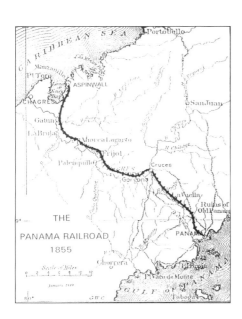

The Panama Railroad, 1855, *Private Collection*

Edwin Deakin, Old Panama, *oil on canvas, 36 x 24 in., Garzoli Gallery, San Rafael, CA*

beans and one bushel of dried fruit. In addition, each wagon carried a water keg, a Dutch oven, a churn, an ax, shovels, a saw, rope and whatever furniture and possessions the family owned.

The most popular route was the California Trail, a five-month-long variant of the Oregon Trail. It was not sufficient to offer simply a useable route through mountains and deserts; it was imperative that the trails provide good availability of water and grass pasturage, and therefore, the best ones followed rivers and streams whenever possible.

The California Trail followed the Oregon Trail to Fort Bridger, Wyoming, then cut off and followed the south bank of the Platte River into Colorado. William Swain, a schoolteacher from Youngstown, New York, left home on April 11, 1849 and was one of a large number of travelers on the Oregon Trail making their way to the gold fields in California. In the first entry of his diary, recounted by J.S. Holliday in his book *The World Rushed In*, Swain was contemplative about his trip.

> *All my things being ready last night, I rose early and commenced packing them in my trunk, preparatory to leaving home on my long journey, leaving for the first time my home and dear friends with the prospect of absence from them for many months and perhaps for years. Among these are an affectionate wife to whom I have been married less than two years, and an infant daughter ten months old, to both of whom I am passionately attached; an aged mother who from her great age—seventy-one years—much probability arises of never seeing again on this side of the grave…and last but not least, an older brother to whom I am deeply attached, not only by the common ties of brotherhood alone, but also by a long course of years of common hardship…Being two years older than myself, he has been my adviser and guardian from youth up, at once a father and a brother.*

To reach the Missouri frontier, either at Independence or St. Joseph, the two most popular jumping-off points for the trails leading west, Swain had to take passage from Buffalo to Detroit, and then by canal boats and river steamers down the Illinois River to St. Louis. As most travelers did, Swain chose to wait until he got to the frontier before purchasing a wagon and all the supplies needed for the trip.

According to Holliday, "*By mid-April some 30,000 gold seekers had reached the outfitting towns along the Missouri River. In meadows and forest groves they camped on the outskirts of these jumping-off points, packing and rearranging their wagon loads and training their teams. Each day, hundreds more pushed ashore at the steamboat landings at Independence, Westport, Weston, St. Joseph and Council Bluffs…At night the campfires looked like those of besieging armies.*"

Ironically, all of these eager and supposedly ready travelers were compelled to remain along the frontier and wait—for the soggy trails, muddied by spring rains, to dry; and for the grass, too sparse yet to provide forage for the thousands of oxen

Handbill for Overland Stage, *History Collections, Los Angeles County Museum of Natural History*

and horses that would soon set out. A few wagon trains went out in mid-April, but most rolled west by the first week of May.

Swain's diary for May 6 reads, in part,

Here I am in camp with arrangements made for my start across the plains…[I] arrived at Independence on the 3rd of May…we were glad to exchange the deck for the fine rolling woodland of this country.

We have spent our time in getting all the information we could, and the result is that we have concluded to cross the plains with ox teams. All those experienced in prairie life think this the best way…And packing on mules is so laborious that we will not think of it. (Mules are so stubborn and will not do what is wanted of them and are more apt to stray off on the prairie, while oxen will stay near where they are turned loose. The Indians will not steal them as they care nothing for an ox, but they will steal a mule whenever they can catch him. Oxen will probably require some fifteen days more on the road, but what is that compared with the safety of an ox team?)

Swain joined a company of fellow travelers who agreed to pool their resources and travel together.

This company was got up last January. We now consist of sixty-three members, Americans, mostly eastern and some western men, but mostly smart and intelligent. There are among them two ministers and two doctors…There are also blacksmiths, carpenters, tailors, shoemakers and many other mechanics…They have had agents here buying their teams and their outfit for the last six weeks. Their outfit has been purchased at the lowest rates. For instance: the wagons were bought and fitted out at Chicago—except for the covers—at $48 apiece. The cost of transporting them here was $6.50 apiece, making $54.50. They would sell here for $115.

There is some cholera here, in fact considerable, there being four deaths among the inhabitants on the 4th, which was wet and rainy.

Cholera was the foremost killer on the frontier. The camps and trails, completely overwhelmed by huge numbers of people, were breeding grounds for the virulent disease, which fostered on the thousands of heaps of rotting trash and food, as well as the fouled and abandoned clothing and blankets of those who had died. The disease was spread by flies, which were ever-present; contaminated water, which sank into putrid puddles throughout; unburied human excrement and, most pathetic of all, the growing number of cholera sufferers who had been abandoned by their terrified companions.

TOP: Otto Sommer, Westward Ho! *oil on canvas, 44 x 74 in., courtesy of Los Angeles Athletic Club; BOTTOM: Charles Christian Nahl,* Crossing the Plains, *1856, oil on canvas, 10 x 16 ft., Iris & B. Gerald Cantor Center for Visual Arts, Stanford University, Palo Alto, CA*

Travelers knew of the epidemic of cholera in advance, but doctors had no idea how the disease spread, and none was adequately prepared to treat patients. Swain writes his brother about the precautions he was taking, *"The physicians of the place appear not to have success in the treatment of the disease. We have but little fear of it, however, and hope to escape it by care and prudence, which we constantly observe...(A doctor with a company from Chicago recommends a dose of laudanum with pepper, camphor, musk, ammonia, peppermint or other stimulant...The medicine is aided by friction, mustard plasters and other external applications.)"* Ignorant of the true causes of the disease, the immigrants hurried out of camp hoping to escape the pestilence that they were, in truth, taking with them. There were more than 1,500 deaths from cholera recorded at Fort Laramie, less than halfway to California.

While travelers were not prepared for cholera, they were more than prepared for Indian attacks, a hazard that rarely befell them. Just past the Missouri frontier settlements, their maps showed a large, generally blank area labeled "Indian Territory." The neighboring tribes, such as the Shawnee and the Potawatomi, had been "civilized" and beaten down into a submissive state by continual contact with

the white man. Peaceful and poor, they were not what the immigrants had expected and feared. However, farther west, along the Kansas River, lived the Pawnee people, who were fierce and warlike, but by 1849, had suffered greatly against their traditional enemy, the Sioux.

Well-armed and prepared to defend themselves against "wild Indians," most immigrants had never even fired a rifle before, in self-defense or hunting, and yet were *"so eager for sport that they will discharge their pieces no matter if they fire in the direction of a whole train."*

By the spring of 1849, there was no significant threat posed by any Indian tribe, as they, too, suffered greatly from cholera, which the immigrants had spread along all trails west. It is believed that by the summer of 1849, more than 1,200 Indians had died from the epidemic. As for the travelers, the number of them wounded or killed by accidental or careless discharge of other immigrants' weapons far outnumbered the few killed by Indians east of the Rocky Mountains.

At first, Swain found the conditions along the trail much to his liking. The initial part of the journey followed the Platte River:

> *June 19—Today fine. The scenery of the river changes to a clear channel, and I think that we are past the mouth of the Forks [the junction of the North and South Forks of the Platte River]. The bluffs change to rolling highlands and the flats descend gradually from the uplands to the shore.*
>
> *June 21—The day is fine. Good roads lined with a variety of gay flowers. Made nineteen and a half miles and encamped. This evening…I bathed in the Platte.*

As strenuous as life on the trail could be, many travelers celebrated the Sabbath, and when situations allowed, Sunday was a day of rest, religious observance and some singing and dancing.

> *June 24—Sabbath. Today the weather is warm and clear. After*

*breakfast...I bathed and washed and spent the leisure time in mend-
ing our clothes. Today, our camp appears more like Sabbath than
any other Sunday before. All things are still, and the scenery around
us partakes of the same stillness. It disposes me to think of home and
the dear ones there; of what they are probably doing now, and of
the appearance of things at their place of worship. It now being
twelve o'clock, they are probably in the meeting house at Youngstown.*

*June 26—We started early this morn and had a good day's
work over sandy roads. I bathed in the North Platte at noon. Elk
are along the road today. Graves are also frequent.*

*June 30—We left camp at six this morning. We filled our
water barrel on leaving the river, as we would not touch it again in
thirty miles...Encamped this evening at a spring spoken of by Frémont. Twenty-one miles today.*

*July 4—[At sunrise a salute of thirteen guns was fired.]
Our celebration of the day was very good, much better than I antic-
ipated. We had previously invited Mr. Sexton...to deliver an
address, and we had appointed Mr. Pratt to read the Declaration
of Independence.*

*At twelve o'clock we formed a procession and walked to
the stand to the tune of "The Star Spangled Banner." The President
of the day called the meeting to order. We listened to a prayer by the
Rev. Mr. Hobart, then remarks and the reading of the Declaration
of Independence by Mr. Pratt, and the address by Mr. Sexton. We
listened to "Hail Columbia." This celebration was very pleasing,
especially the address, which was well delivered and good enough
for any assembly at home. We then marched to the "hall," which
was formed by running the wagons in two rows close enough together
for the wagon covers to reach from one to the other, thus forming a
fine hall roofed by the covers and a comfortable place for the dinner table, which was set down at the center.*

*Dinner consisted of ham, beans, boiled and baked, bis-
cuits, john cake, apple pie, sweet cake, rice pudding, pickles, vine-
gar, pepper sauce and mustard, coffee, sugar, and milk. All enjoyed
it well.*

*After dinner, the toasting commenced. The boys had raked
and scraped together all the brandy they could, and they toasted,
hurrayed, and drank 'till reason was out and brandy was in. I stayed
'till the five regular toasts were drunk; and then, being disgusted
with their conduct, I went to our tent, took my pen, and occupied
the remainder of the day in writing to my wife, in which I enjoyed
myself better than those who were drinking, carousing, and halloo-
ing all around the camp.*

Thomas Moran;
RIGHT: *Plains of the Humboldt, c. 1850;*
BELOW, FROM TOP: *Truckee River,*
c. 1850, c. 1870; engravings, Private Collection

At the Great Salt Lake, the trail went along the Humboldt River to present-day Reno, Nevada, then to Truckee, before crossing the Sierra Nevada Mountains and finally into the Sacramento Valley to Sutter's Fort.

The most strenuous part of this route was the 40-mile segment between the Humboldt River and the Truckee River, in Nevada. This portion of the trail had no water whatsoever, and as wagon teams had to be watered twice a day, most of the devastation occurred here. Along this part of the route, one traveler noted 362 abandoned wagons and countless pieces of furniture and clothing left on the trail. He also counted the skeletal remains of 350 horses, 280 oxen and 120 mules.

Of the Humboldt River, Swain noted:

September 20—We left camp at eight…Such a thing as a tree I have not seen since we struck this Humbug [sic] River, which is nothing more than a ditch with bottoms in the shape of oxbows, through which a good-sized creek runs.

We nooned without feed and traveled across another bluff 'till four o'clock…We have no feed or but little for the teams tonight. I bathed this evening in the river, which is very cold, to try to wash off the alkali dust which eats our skin and makes us itch and scratch dreadfully.

September 22 and 23—We arrived at the Wells at four o'clock. [One of the Rangers wrote of Rabbit Hole Springs or Wells: "I had associated with the name 'wells' a vision of an oasis—verdure, trees, and cooling water. The whole environment as far as the eye could reach was simply an abomination of desolation…ash heaps of hills into which slowly percolated filthy-looking, brackish water. More than half the wells were unavailable as they were filled with carcasses of cattle which had perished in trying to get water. To add to the natural horrors of the scene, about the wells were scattered the bodies of cattle, horses, and mules which had died there from overwork, hunger, and thirst; broken and abandoned wagons,

Colorado Desert (Mojave Desert) and Signal Mountain, *from* Reports of Explorations and Surveys, 1853–54, *U.S. House of Representatives, 1856, lithograph, Sherman Library and Gardens, Corona del Mar, CA*

boxes, bundles of clothing, guns, harness, or yokes, anything and everything that the emigrant had outfitted with…Here and there around the other springs in an area of one tenth of a mile…eighty-two dead oxen, two dead horses, and one mule. Of course, the effluvia was anything but agreeable.]

The most tragic of the early immigrant wagon trains was the ill-fated Donner Party, led by George and Jacob Donner. This group, numbering 87 men, women and children, started out from Springfield, Illinois in the spring of 1846. At Fort Bridger, Wyoming, they opted to take the so-called "Hastings' Cut-Off," which according to the book *Emigrant's Guide to Oregon and California*, by Lansford W. Hastings, would save them 200 miles. Hastings had written the book without having ever seen the terrain, and the "cut-off" turned out to be nearly impassable.

Sierra Nevada Pass, Winter, *c. 1850, engraving, Private Collection*

The month-long delay from taking the wrong trail proved costly, as it put them off their critical timetable. In October, the party was attempting to cross the Sierra Nevada Mountains at Truckee Lake when they were caught in an early snowstorm. Unable to make headway in the deep snow, they were forced to spend the winter stranded at the lake, at an elevation of 7,135 feet. The storms kept coming and eventually 42 of their members died. After three heroic attempts, word finally reached Sutter's Fort. A rescue party arrived on February 19, 1847 and found only 45 survivors.

The story of the disaster, along with details of how the survivors were forced to turn to cannibalism to endure, made national headlines. In memory of the tragedy, Truckee Lake was renamed Donner Lake.

F. Teschmaker, View of the Place of Anchorage at "Yerba Buena" in St. Francisco, *1846, hand-colored lithograph, California Historical Society, San Francisco*

The Gold Rush brought tremendous growth to San Francisco, which in 1848, had fewer than 1,000 people. By the end of 1849, it had more than 30,000. Monterey, which had been the capital and the largest city in California, was immediately surpassed in size and importance.

In 1849, the city of San Francisco spread rapidly over the surrounding hills. Shufelt, the aspiring miner who went west in 1850 via the Isthmus of Panama, wrote of what he saw when his ship first entered San Francisco harbor: *"The city is built on the side [of a] hill south of the bay and commands a fine view of the harbor and shipping and the distant hills that surround it on all sides. The buildings were mostly of cloth, some small frames were covered with it, others covered with shingles and boards, and some few good buildings were up and many more in the course of erection. The hills in all directions were covered with tents and the streets crowded with people from all parts of the world anxious to make their fortunes in a few days in this golden land of promise."*

The port of San Francisco looked like a forest of tall masts. Hundreds of ships entered San Francisco harbor, so many that it became a serious problem. Once in port, most ships were completely abandoned and left to rot as their entire crews ran off to the gold fields. One of these abandoned ships became California's first prison. Ships were pillaged and salvaged of anything that could be used. What was left was eventually burned to the waterline and buried in a landfill to create the modern-day Marina District of San Francisco. Today, pieces and parts of these 49er ships are often found as a result of digging foundations and sewer lines in the Marina District.

San Francisco's population grew so quickly that many services could not keep up. It is said that in the first months of the Gold Rush, laundry was sent to Hawaii, or even China. The deplorable sanitation and crowded conditions became a breeding ground for rats. To combat the infestation, one enterprising merchant imported a cargo of several hundred cats.

The large increases in immigrants to California put tremendous pressure on the Indian population. In the previous century, the Spanish had unwittingly introduced a range of diseases that were common to Europe but unknown in the New World. Nearly half the native population died from lack of resistance to these diseases, and by 1845, it is estimated that California had only about 150,000 Indians. The Gold Rush further devastated Indians' lives to the extent that fewer than 30,000 remained by 1870. Many natives were murdered by whites simply because miners sought to set up claims on Indian lands. Moreover, the great influx of immigrants from all over the world brought a new assortment of deadly diseases to an already-weak native population. In time, many tribes died out entirely. ❧

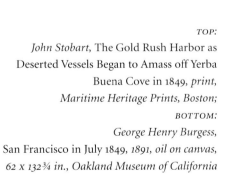

TOP:
John Stobart, The Gold Rush Harbor as Deserted Vessels Began to Amass off Yerba Buena Cove in 1849, *print, Maritime Heritage Prints, Boston;*
BOTTOM:
George Henry Burgess,
San Francisco in July 1849, *1891, oil on canvas, 62 x 132¾ in., Oakland Museum of California*

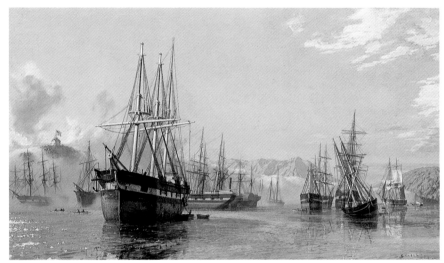

Thaddeus Welch, View of Los Angeles, *oil on canvas,*
20 x 36 in., North Point Gallery, San Francisco

CHAPTER 17

STATEHOOD

T he Mexican War ended with the Treaty of Guadalupe-Hidalgo, signed on February 2, 1848. With the end of the war, California became an American possession under a military government. On June 9, 1848, Pío Pico returned to California and went to his Rancho Santa Margarita y Las Flores to continue his term as governor while the terms of the Treaty of Guadalupe-Hidalgo went into effect. Pico was ordered to report to the American military authorities in Los Angeles, and when he did, he was put under arrest. Several weeks later, he was released as a private citizen and allowed to return to his rancho.

For the next few years, Pico turned to his many businesses and amassed a fortune, principally in the cattle business, by selling beef raised on his rancho to meet the demands of the population boom resulting from the Gold Rush. In 1854, his wife, María Ignacia, died. The floods of 1862–63 devastated his rancho, causing severe financial setbacks. In addition, his lifelong passion for gambling, horseracing and bull-fighting added to his growing debts. In 1873, he built the Pico House in Los Angeles Plaza, at the time the biggest hotel south of San Francisco. That same year, with his brother Andrés, he invested in the Los Angeles Petroleum Refinery Company, the first oil company in Los Angeles. However, his lavish lifestyle and incessant gambling caused him to mortgage his properties in what he thought was a loan of $62,000 from attorney Bernard Cohn. Later, when he tried to repay the loan, Cohn produced a deed of sale, which Pico claimed he had unknowingly signed. Pico went to court and claimed that he did not read English and had relied on an interpreter when he signed the document. The court found in favor of Cohn, and Pico lost all his properties. In 1892, he was evicted from his home for non-payment of debts. He moved into the home of an adopted daughter, where he died, virtually a pauper, on September 11, 1894.

THE CONSTITUTIONAL CONVENTION

Not long after the Treaty of Guadalupe-Hidalgo was signed, news of the discovery of gold began to spread. Within a year, California's population and economy had expanded at a tremendous rate. To deal with all the changes, and to sustain the growth of the previous year, business and civic leaders requested a change from military to civilian government by filing a petition in Congress for annexation of California as a United States Territory.

As part of the annexation process, California was required to hold a convention to produce a formal statement requesting a change from military government to the status of territory. In the long process leading to statehood, California

Colton Hall, Monterey, *c. 1880,*
vintage postcard, Private Collection

895 - Colton Hall - First State Capitol - 1849 - Monterey, Cal.

was to become an American territory and, later, perhaps in several years, apply for statehood. This was the same process that all other territories had followed to be admitted to full statehood.

The Territorial Convention opened at newly built Colton Hall in Monterey on September 3, 1849 with 48 delegates. Of these, only seven were native-born Californios, six of whom understood only a little English and needed a translator. Of the others, one each was born in Spain, Ireland, England and France. The remainder of the delegates were Americans, many of them "Bears" who had taken part in the Bear Flag Revolt. Of the 48 delegates, there were 14 lawyers, 11 farmers and seven merchants. One delegate listed his profession as "elegant leisure." Although they represented many different occupations and lifestyles, most of the delegates had gold-mining interests in one way or another.

Among the more prominent names in the convention were José Antonio Carrillo, Thomas Larkin, Pablo de la Guerra, John Sutter and Mariano Vallejo. The most influential member was William M. Gwin, a Southern politician who would later become one of the first two U.S. Senators from California. The first order of business was to elect a president of the convention. The delegates chose Robert Semple of Sonoma, a former Bear Flag rebel. Although the convention was supposed to produce a territorial constitution, the delegates of the Monterey Convention quickly changed course and agreed instead to draw up a state constitution and immediately apply for statehood.

There were several important debates in the convention. One of the first revived the historic animosity between the northern and southern parts of California. José Antonio Carrillo of Los Angeles proposed dividing the state into two parts. The northern part, which was experiencing the Gold Rush, would continue with the convention and immediately apply for statehood. However, the southern part, the realm of the ranchos, would remain a territory for several more years and perhaps, someday be admitted as a state. The rancheros were particularly fearful that statehood would lead to the imposition of taxes on their vast landholdings, and they preferred to have things remain as they were. The motion brought forth furious argument and was emphatically turned down.

Ultimately, Carrillo's fears would prove prophetic. In the first years of statehood, the southern California landowners, a group that made up less than 4% of the state's population, paid 66% of the real-estate taxes. In an attempt to deal with this predicament, Andrés Pico introduced a joint resolution in the California State Assembly in 1859, once again calling for the separation of the southern counties from the rest of the state. Pico proposed that the southern part of the state, made up of the large counties of Los Angeles, San Diego, Santa Barbara, San Luis Obispo and San Bernardino (Orange, Ventura, Imperial and Riverside counties would be formed later when these vast counties were broken up), revert to territorial status and be called the Territory of Colorado, in recognition of the river that formed the eastern boundary. Flushed with the economic benefits of the Gold Rush, the northern counties had little interest in whether or not the southern, sparsely populated, predominantly rural, cattle-producing counties broke away. The measure was approved by the California Assembly as well as the voters in those five counties. When the measure went to Congress, however, the fear of upsetting the delicate balance between free states and slave states caused the bill to stall, and the outbreak of the Civil War in 1861 killed any chances of its passage.

In Colton Hall, the important question of slavery was likewise decided quickly. Beginning in the 1820s, all new states admitted to the Union had to be designated either as "slave," where slavery was legal, or "free," where it was illegal. Most of the early American residents in California were merchants from New England who had settled and become prosperous and influential. They had a strong anti-slavery tradition, which was well-represented at the Monterey Convention. Yet, a large number of delegates at the convention had come from Southern states. When

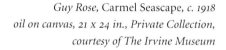

Guy Rose, Carmel Seascape, *c. 1918 oil on canvas, 21 x 24 in., Private Collection, courtesy of The Irvine Museum*

TOP:
Edgar Payne, Mountains at Sunset, Santa Barbara, *oil on canvas, 36 x 44 in.;*
BOTTOM:
Hanson Puthuff, Monarch of the Malibu, *oil on canvas, 32 x 40 in.;*
Private Collection,
courtesy of The Irvine Museum

William Ritschel, The Glorious Pacific,
*oil on canvas, 50 x 60 in., Private Collection,
courtesy of The Irvine Museum*

William Wendt, Grassy Hillsides, *oil on canvas, 18 x 28 in., Private Collection, courtesy of The Irvine Museum*

the issue came up, only a few delegates spoke in favor of slavery, and with no serious movement to make California a slave state, the convention voted to bar slavery from California.

Interestingly, another reason for the anti-slavery stance in California was related to the economics of the Gold Rush and the miners' tradition of equal opportunity, which unfortunately only applied to whites. There had been several instances in which Southern slaveowners had brought slaves into California for the sole purpose of filing fraudulent claims in their names. One such case had received much public attention in July 1848, when a group of Texans filed claims in the names of 15 slaves they had brought to California. The claims were angrily opposed by the miners in that district, and after much furor, the Texans abandoned the claims.

Another difficult problem facing the convention was the question of where to draw the eastern boundary of the state. Due to natural and political circumstances, California had clearly defined boundaries in three directions: the Oregon Territory set the northern boundary, the Pacific Ocean was on the west, and Mexico was on the south. What would be the eastern boundary?

One faction in the convention, the "large state" group, wanted to set the eastern boundary as far east as possible, perhaps to the Rocky Mountains. This would have encompassed the present-day states of Nevada, Arizona, Utah, and most of Colorado and New Mexico. The "large state" group included those who wanted to abolish slavery. By having one huge state, they could ban slavery from the entire Southwest region with one stroke.

The opposing "small state" faction wanted the eastern boundary set at the Sierra Nevada Mountains. The mountain range, they argued, was a natural boundary. They also pointed out that Congress would never accept such a huge state; moreover, the "large state" concept would include thousands of Mormon settlers in Utah who were not represented at the convention.

In the end, the delegates reached a compromise plan that created a state larger than the "small state" proposal but substantially smaller than the "large state" plan, agreeing on the present-day boundary of the Colorado River and north along an angle encompassing some areas east of the Sierra Nevada Mountains.

After some angry discussions, the delegates approved a design for the Great Seal of California. Various features were proposed and accepted as additions to the seal. When the addition of the grizzly bear was proposed, several Californio delegates stood up to oppose the motion. Mariano Vallejo suggested that the bear be shown as being under the control of a vaquero, with a lasso around its neck. The bear was approved without the lasso.

The California State Constitution was signed on October 13 and approved by voters on November 13, 1849. At that time, the voters elected two Congressmen, Edward Gilbert and George Wright. In December, the California legislature selected two U.S. Senators. (Prior to the adoption of the 17th Amendment to the Constitution in 1913, U.S. Senators were not directly elected by the voters.) John C. Frémont drew the "short" term of two years, and William M. Gwin got the full term of six years. Indeed, nearly a year before actual statehood, California had a functioning state government and full slate of elected officials, as if statehood had already been granted. By contrast, Arizona and New Mexico, both of which were annexed at the same time as California, would not become states until 1912, 62 years later.

However, before California could be admitted to the Union, the question of slavery had to be resolved by Congress. Over the previous decades, the Union had maintained a balance between "slave" states and "free" states. In the proposed state constitution, California requested admission as a "free" state, but the South was determined to block this proposal. For weeks, the issue was deadlocked in Congress. In an effort to reach a compromise, Senator Henry Clay proposed that California be admitted as a "free" state in exchange for a stronger Fugitive Slave Law, one that would return runaway slaves from the North back to their owners in the South. Both of these measures, as well as territorial status for Utah and New Mexico, were accepted as part of a series of proposals called the Compromise of 1850.

Finally, on August 13, 1850, the United States Senate passed the bill making California a state. On September 7, after some delay by southern states, the House of Representatives passed the same bill. On September 9, 1850, President Millard Fillmore signed the bill and officially welcomed California as the 31st state of the Union.

Statehood came at a time of tremendous population growth. Just prior to the Gold Rush, the population of California is estimated to have been about 15,000. By the end of 1850, it was about 100,000, and in 1852, the population soared to 250,000. Certainly, this growth occurred as a result of the Gold Rush, and its effect was primarily on the northern part of the state. However, the south experienced significant growth as well. When Los Angeles was incorporated as a city in 1850, it reported a population of 1,610. Ten years later, it had more than doubled to 3,700.

With statehood, the people of California sent their first slate of senators and representatives to Washington, D.C. As previously indicated, one of these first two senators to represent California in 1850 was John C. Frémont. While many thought his career was finished, the resilient Frémont had recovered from the humiliation of his court-martial. He had become a millionaire when gold was discovered on his ranch in Mariposa. He invested heavily in railroad construction, and in 1848 and 1849, led a private survey expedition to find suitable passes through the mountains for a railroad route from the upper Rio Grande to California. Exploiting his fame as the "Pathmarker of the Old West" and touting himself as a hero of California Independence, he served his two years as one of California's first two U.S. Senators.

In 1856, Frémont was the first Presidential candidate for the newly formed Republican Party. His running mate was William L. Dayton, and their campaign slogan was "Free Speech! A Free Press! Free Men! Freedom! and Frémont!" He ran as a firm opponent of slavery but lost to the Democrat, James Buchanan. Yet he had correctly assessed the political mood of the country, and his candidacy and

ABOVE:

John C. Frémont campaign ribbon, 1856, The Historical Society of Pennsylvania, Philadelphia;

RIGHT:

The Great American Buck Hunt of 1856, lithograph, The Historical Society of Pennsylvania, Philadelphia

campaign succeeded in uniting the electorate of the North and West against the South, foreshadowing the coming Civil War.

In 1861, at the outbreak of the Civil War, Frémont was commissioned a Major-General and given command of the Western Department of the Union Army, a jurisdiction that included the vital border state of Missouri. Missouri was one of the most fought-over states in the Civil War, as it controlled the important confluence of the Missouri and Mississippi Rivers. Like other border states, Missouri sent men to fight on both sides: 27 military units fought for the Union and 15 for the South. Being mostly sympathetic to the Union, Missouri nevertheless was legally a slave-holding state, and President Lincoln was concerned that many of its officials, including the governor, were actively urging the state to secede from the Union.

One of the first battles of the Civil War, on August 10, 1861, was the Battle of Wilson's Creek, called the Battle of Oak Hills by the Confederates, fought a few miles from Springfield. The Union Army, led by General Nathaniel Lyon, attacked a superior Southern force under Generals Sterling Price, Ben McCulloch and N. Bart Pearce. After a day-long battle in which General Lyon lost his life, the Union Army retreated. Thereafter, Missouri became the scene of constant guerrilla attacks, which the Union Army found difficult to subdue.

Feeling that President Lincoln was unable to stem the course of Southern sympathy toward border-state politics, Frémont took it upon himself, a few days after the Battle of Wilson's Creek, to put Missouri under martial law and issue a "Deed Of Manumission," which freed the slaves of one of Missouri's leading citizens. The proclamation read:

> Whereas, Thomas L. Snead, of the city and county of St. Louis, State of Missouri, has been taking an active part with the enemies of the United States, in the present insurrectionary movement against the Government of the United States; now, therefore, I, John Charles Frémont, Major-General commanding the Western Department of the Army of the United States, by authority of law, and the power vested in me as such commanding general, declare Hiram Reed, heretofore held to service or labor by Thomas L. Snead, to be FREE, and forever discharged from the bonds of servitude, giving him full right of authority to have, use, and control his own labor or service as to him may seem proper, without any accountability whatever to said Thomas L. Snead, or any one to claim by, through, or under him.

This brazen move was immediately revoked by President Lincoln, who feared that Missouri and other border states would quickly move to the Southern cause in fear of having their citizens' land and property confiscated by the Union. When Lincoln ordered Frémont to rescind the order, he refused. Lincoln then fired General Frémont, once again ending his military career.

After the Civil War, Frémont endured his exile from public affairs by devoting himself to railroad projects in the West. In 1878, he returned to public office when he was appointed Territorial Governor of Arizona, a post he held until 1883. In 1887, having lost the fortune he had made in gold mining in various other business deals, he retired to California. Frémont died on a visit to New York on July 13, 1890. Shortly before he died, he was reinstated to the rank of Major-General in the U.S. Army.

Samuel Colman, Mount San Antonio, San Gabriel Valley, *11¾ x 26½ in., North Point Gallery, San Francisco*

THE LAND COMMISSION

The Mexican War ended with the Treaty of Guadalupe-Hidalgo, signed on February 2, 1848. Under the terms of the treaty, the United States annexed most of the American Southwest, including California and the disputed area between the Nueces River and Rio Grande in Texas. As compensation, the U.S. paid Mexico the sum of $15 million. The treaty also stated that all Mexican citizens in these regions would be given the option of becoming American citizens or leaving the former Mexican territories. If they chose to stay, there was an agreement that all Mexican land grants would be respected.

In 1848, no one could have foreseen the immediate and considerable transformations that were coming with the Gold Rush. There was every expectation that statehood for California would follow the normal pattern and take several years to achieve. Before Congress would consider accepting California as a state, the territory had to be surveyed, boundaries had to be marked and all land claims and titles needed to be validated.

There were more than 800 grants for more than 14 million acres of land granted in California during the Spanish and Mexican periods. To study the situation and determine a proper course of action, the governor of California appointed Captain Henry W. Halleck, an officer in the military government of California, and in a separate move, the U.S. Secretary of the Interior sent William Carey Jones.

Halleck, who would later find fame as Union Army Chief of Staff in the Civil War, completed his work early in 1849. He stated that most Mexican land titles were imperfect because their boundaries were so vaguely defined, and that many other claims were clearly fraudulent. It was his opinion that the United States government could easily challenge and break most claims.

Halleck's findings bolstered the settlers and encouraged "squatters," people who took possession of what they believed to be unclaimed or disputed lands, hoping to establish legal occupancy. In the Sacramento Valley, the squatter problem was particularly rampant, especially the closer one got to the gold fields.

Sutter's immense tract of land, 50,000 acres given to him by Mexican Governor Alvarado in 1839, was overrun by several thousand gold seekers, who essentially established the city of Sacramento in just a few weeks. Squatting quickly led to violence, as Sutter moved to evict squatters from his settlement. Repeated efforts to drive out squatters led to riots and the deaths of several, including Mayor Harden Bigelow and Sheriff Joseph McKinney, who had attempted to enforce eviction orders.

Meanwhile, William Carey Jones, a brilliant Spanish-speaking lawyer who, like John C. Frémont, was a son-in-law of Senator Thomas Hart Benton, arrived in

TOP: *Herman Herzog*, Old Mexican Quarters, Los Angeles, *8 x 12 in., Garzoli Gallery, San Rafael, CA;*
BOTTOM: *Manuel Valencia*, First State Capitol, *DeRu's Fine Arts, Laguna Beach, CA*

Maurice Braun, California Hills, *1914, oil on canvas, 40 x 50 in., The Irvine Museum*

Monterey in September 1849, just as the Territorial Convention was in session and thousands of gold seekers crowded into San Francisco. Acting on orders from the Secretary of the Interior, he collected and classified all land grants and claims from both the Spanish and Mexican periods—carefully separating those given during the time of the Mexican War—as well as claims of mission lands, mining titles, island titles and Indian ownership of land. He worked quickly, as he had to complete his report before the end of the next session of Congress, in less than a year.

Overall, he found records of land titles to be current, but in some cases, titles were incomplete, in disarray or missing altogether. Accurate surveys of landholdings were nonexistent, as most grants were done on the basis of a *diseño*, a crude, hand-drawn map of the proposed grant. There were no record books prior to 1839, and there was no record book started for 1846, the year of the Mexican War, when former Governor Pico indulged in a massive, last-minute land giveaway. Jones also researched land records in Los Angeles, where Pico had relocated the capital of California, San Francisco, San Jose, San Diego and finally in Mexico City. He completed his report on schedule and sent it to President Millard Fillmore on April 10, 1850.

In the summary of his report, Jones put forth the opinion that, except for a few clear cases of fraudulent, last-minute Mexican grants, the land grants in California were "mostly perfect titles." Understandably, the Jones report was hailed by the Californios but repudiated by the American residents and newly arrived settlers.

In keeping with the Halleck and Jones reports, the United States Congress, early in 1851, debated two contradictory bills offered by California's first two Senators, John C. Frémont and William M. Gwin. Frémont, Jones' brother-in-law, offered a bill to accept all land claims in California as recorded by the Mexican government. Gwin, who sought to open California to new settlement, offered a substitute bill, which required that the U.S. government examine and confirm all claims. The huge size of many of the ranchos created suspicions among members of Congress, and there was a general feeling that California should be opened up to American settlement at the expense of the defeated Californios and their ranchos. Gwin's bill was passed on March 3, 1851, creating a three-person board to examine and decide on the validity of all claims. In spite of the Treaty of Guadalupe-Hidalgo, which specifically validated Mexican property rights in California and the Southwest, the burden of proving the validity of all land titles in California was now the burden of the property owners.

The Land Commission began its job in San Francisco in January 1852. Under its mandate, *"Each and every person claiming lands in California by virtue of any right or title derived from the Spanish or Mexican governments, shall present the same to the said commissioners when sitting as a board, together with such documentary evidence and testimony of witnesses as the said claimant relies upon in support of such claims."* Any landowner not appearing before the commission within two years automatically forfeited all claims.

The commission was authorized for three years, but two year-long extensions resulted, for a total of five years. All sessions were held in San Francisco, except for one term in Los Angeles. As the commission considered cases from one part of the state to the next, enterprising American law firms blanketed advertising space in local newspapers in advance. Claimants needed all the legal help they could get, as they were required to present deeds or other papers, many of which were long lost, and failing that, had to submit testimony from friends and relatives, show documents relating to length of tenure, land use, cattle tallies or any other evidence of continued tenure and use of property.

Hoping to break as many claims as possible, government lawyers appealed nearly every confirmed claim, no matter how valid and persuasive. The endless number of appeals caused many old family ranchos to be mortgaged in an effort to raise mounting legal fees to defend their claims. Even after the appeals were upheld, the average length of time to issue a complete and final patent by the U.S. government was 17 years. Protracted court proceedings and appeals by both sides, as well as the difficulty in getting approved surveys, added greatly to the already huge financial costs incurred by many Californians.

The dictates of the Land Commission bred conflict between American settlers and the Californio rancheros, an antagonism that lasted for more than a generation. Californios considered all squatters to be trespassers and lawless ruffians; settlers saw the great ranchos as lands won by conquest and thus open to victorious Americans.

When the work of the land commission was completed in 1856, it had processed 813 cases. Of those, 604 were finally confirmed, 190 were finally rejected, and 19 claims were withdrawn. One hundred and thirty-two of the rejected claimants chose to appeal the commission's findings in court, and of those, 98 won reversals. The government attorneys had the right to appeal as well. Of the 417 cases they appealed, only five were reversed.

One of the first claims to be decided was the Rancho Las Mariposas in central California, owned by John C. Frémont. Las Mariposas had in fact been the first case filed with the commission. The rancho was huge, encompassing ten square leagues, or about 70 square miles. It had originally been granted to Juan Bautista Alvarado in 1844, who in turn sold it to Frémont for $3,000 in 1846, in a transaction handled by Thomas Larkin. In 1849, gold was discovered on the property. After a long investigation and much litigation, title to the land, popularly referred to as the "ten million dollar rancho," was granted to Frémont in 1856.

Many of the successful claimants found theirs an empty victory, as they had to sell much of their land, cattle and possessions to pay for legal fees. For many, their newly confirmed land titles did not rid them of squatters. Senator Gwin, long the settlers' champion, even proposed a law to allow squatters to "homestead" private rancho lands by reimbursing owners with acreage from public lands. A similar law was passed in 1856, requiring landowners to pay for any improvements made by squatters, but a year later it was ruled unconstitutional.

Through the authority of the United States Land Commission, Joseph S. Alemany, Bishop of San Francisco, was able to challenge the Mexican Government's right to sell the old missions after secularization. Bishop Alemany was successful; all subsequent sales of former mission property were reviewed, and some were nullified. Early in 1865, President Lincoln signed a document that formally returned several of the missions to the Catholic Church. One of these was the Mission San Juan Capistrano, along with five small tracts of land surrounding it, which were expropriated from John Forster.

In the end, the history of how the Americans, in the form of the government, the Land Commission, the speculators and their lawyers, dealt with Mexican grants in California, according to Henry George in 1871, as quoted by Cleland, *"will be a history of greed, of perjury, of corruption, of spoliation and high-handed robbery, for which it will be difficult to find a parallel…It would have been better, far better, if the American government had agreed to permit these grant holders [the Californio rancheros] to retain a certain amount of land around their improvements, and [compensated them] for the rest the grants called for, by the payment of a certain sum per acre, turning it into the public domain."*

Thomas Hill, Mount Shasta, *1882, oil on canvas,*
13 x 21¼ in., Butterfield & Butterfield

The Modoc War

The so-called Modoc War of 1873 was the last outbreak of organized Indian resistance in California and the only time that the U.S. Army fought an Indian campaign in the state. The Modocs, who lived in present-day Modoc and Siskiyou counties, near the northeast corner of California just south of Oregon, occupied an area that included a large tract of lava beds formed by nearby Mount Lassen, an extinct volcano. Even though their land was of no particular interest to farmers and settlers, the Modocs were nevertheless forced to deal with immigrants who crossed their land by coming through Lassen Pass, one of the main routes for western migration in the mid-19th century. The growing numbers of immigrants led to repeated, and often violent, confrontations.

Ralph Davidson Miller, A View of Mt. Shasta, *oil on canvas, 20 x 26 in., Ronald J. Estep*

One of the earliest confrontations between Modocs and Americans occurred in 1846, when Captain John C. Frémont, who had been expelled from California by Colonel José Castro, was attacked by Klamath Indians along the Oregon border. Three of his men were killed, and in retaliation, Frémont mistakenly raided a nearby village of Modocs, killing several people. Thereafter, the Modocs steadfastly resisted any incursions on their land. The 1850s and 1860s were marked by a series of attacks on immigrant trains and miners, which in turn led to ruthless reprisals on Modoc villages.

Finally, in the early 1860s, the Modoc people, who had been greatly reduced in numbers by disease and war, were forcibly removed to a reservation in southern Oregon, in an area occupied by the Klamath Indians. When conflict erupted between the Modocs and Klamaths, Chief Kientepoos of the Modocs, popularly called "Captain Jack," led a group of his people back to California in 1869. This action was deemed a violation of the Modoc treaty with the U.S., and the Indian Agent ordered the Modocs to return to their reservation in Oregon. Not long afterward, further hostilities with the Klamaths forced a reluctant Captain Jack to return once more to California in the winter of 1872–73. When the U.S. Army sent 1,000 troops to evict the Modocs, Captain Jack took his people into the lava beds, where they hid in a series of natural caves and successfully held off all attempts to return them to Oregon.

The Modocs who hid in the lava beds consisted of only 53 warriors and about 100 women and children. Surrounded by a large force of well-armed soldiers, they nevertheless beat back all attacks and survived for several months by eating mice and bats they found in the caves. On January 17, 1873, the U.S. Army, under the command of General E.R.S. Canby, advanced in force into the lava beds, supported by succeeding volleys of cannon fire. The determined Modocs fought back, inflicting severe losses on the soldiers and forcing them to turn back.

Reluctant to suffer further losses, the army laid siege and decided to starve the Modocs into surrender. Incredibly, during the long siege, newspaper reporters were allowed into the lava beds to interview Captain Jack. The small, but highly persistent, band of Indians became known the world over, with extensive stories appearing in many newspapers, including the *London Daily News*. Finally, after several months of this standoff, both sides met and seemingly agreed to a peace conference.

On Good Friday, April 11, 1873, Captain Jack and four of his men met with General Canby and a delegation of government representatives. Regrettably, the Modocs had set a trap. When the peace conference started, Captain Jack produced a pistol and killed General Canby. A group of armed Indians appeared from hiding and attacked the other members of the delegation, killing at least one other person.

On April 15, the U.S. Army launched a final assault on the lava beds. Heavy fighting continued for several days, and on May 6, the Modocs abandoned their stronghold. Out of water and greatly outnumbered, they fled under cover of night and scattered into the mountains. By late May, most of the Modocs had been hunted

TOP: The Modoc War: Captain Jack's Cave, *BOTTOM:* The Modoc Indians in the Lava Beds, *from* London News, *1873, Private Collection*

down and killed or captured individually. On June 1, an exhausted Captain Jack was captured along with two warriors, five women and seven children. He was given a military trial and hanged on October 3, 1873.

The Modoc War was the costliest Indian campaign for the U.S. Army since the Seminole Wars of the 1830s. More than 1,000 soldiers had been sent to fight the Modocs, and of those, at least 80 had been killed in the war. The Modocs, who as a fighting force consisted of no more than 53 warriors, lost only 17 men, including the four leaders who were executed after the war. ❧

William Wendt, Sycamores, *oil on canvas,*
30 x 40 in., Private Collection, courtesy of
The Irvine Museum

CHAPTER 18

James Irvine I
Founder of
The Irvine Ranch

BY *Joan Irvine Smith*

My great-grandfather, James Irvine I, was born in Belfast, Ireland in 1827, of Scotch-Irish Presbyterian descent. His father was a man of modest income, and my great-grandfather was next-to-the-youngest in a family of nine children. In 1846, at the age of 19, he and his younger brother, William, emigrated to the United States. In later years he would write with deep feeling and understanding, *"I tell you, a boy cast upon the world with not a dollar in his pocket, with none within reach…but absolute strangers and without…a claim upon any of them, is in a position to appreciate the value of a helping hand."*

For two years, my great-grandfather worked in the Praslee Paper Mills in Molden Bridge, New York, until he caught Gold Fever and joined the stampede to California in 1849. He booked passage on a boat sailing to Chagres, on the east coast of Central America, and crossed the Isthmus of Panama by canoe, mule and on foot, which at the time could take as little as four days but most often took up to two weeks or more. In Panama City, on the west coast, he obtained passage to San Francisco on the Dutch sailing ship *Alexander Humbolt*. During the voyage, which took 101 days, he and his fellow passengers consumed *"hard beans and hardtack, mahogany beef and bilge water daily."* Among his companions were Collis P. Huntington and Dr. Benjamin Flint. The latter association eventually led to the creation of the Irvine Ranch.

Upon his arrival in California, my great-grandfather struck out for the gold fields, where for a time he filled the dual role of merchant and miner. In 1854,

Fortunato Arriola, Isthmus Ranch, 1866, Private Collection, courtesy of Montgomery Gallery, San Francisco

295

John Stobart, The Vicar of Bray in Yerba Buena Cove, San Francisco, in 1849, *Maritime Heritage Prints, Boston*

he bought an interest in a San Francisco commission house on Front Street, which had been opened by one of his kinsmen named John Lyons. The firm was renamed "Irvine and Company, Wholesale Produce and Grocery Mchts." As profits from the business were large, he invested in income-producing San Francisco real estate. He was a member of the Vigilance Committee of 1856, a staunch Republican and a significant figure in the Society of California Pioneers.

Eventually, my great-grandfather became a silent partner in a sheep-raising venture with Thomas and Benjamin Flint and their cousin Llewellyn Bixby. Like thousands of other young men, these three Maine adventurers had joined the Gold Rush in 1849, made a little money, returned home then come back to California to live. In 1849, they had come by sea; in May 1853, they left Keokuk, Iowa with a flock of nearly 20,000 head of sheep, 11 yokes of oxen, two cows, four horses and enough camping equipment to cross the continent. In eight months, by the exercise of constant vigilance and a large measure of good luck, the drovers brought their far-ranging flock to California without serious mishap. This daring venture laid the foundation of both a great industry and a great fortune.

E. Godchaux, Vue de San Francisco, *1851, gouache, 10 x 16 in., Garzoli Gallery, San Rafael, CA*

William Hahn;
ABOVE: Market Scene, Sansome Street, San
Francisco, 1872, *oil on canvas, 60 x 96 in.,*
Crocker Art Museum, Sacramento, CA;
RIGHT: Gibbs Warehouse and Government
Corral, San Francisco *(at Front and Vallejo*
streets, location of Irvine and Company store),
oil on canvas, 17 x 28 in.;
Maxwell Galleries, San Francisco

William Wendt;
TOP: Crystal Cove, 1912, oil on canvas, 28 x 36 in.;
BOTTOM: There Is No Solitude Even in Nature,
1906, oil on canvas, 34 x 36 in.;
Private Collection,
courtesy of The Irvine Museum

The three partners, under the name of Flint, Bixby and Company, then joined with Colonel W.W. Hollister to purchase the 54,000-acre Rancho San Justo in Monterey County, and rapidly expanded their holdings of both land and sheep.

Before 1860, the sheep industry yielded large returns; with the disruption of the cotton trade during the Civil War, the price of wool increased, bringing the California sheepmen still greater profits and producing substantial fortunes in a few years. Not long after the beginning of the Civil War, many of the large wool growers in Monterey, Santa Cruz and the adjacent counties decided to expand their operations further south and either purchase or lease some of the large cattle ranchos near Los Angeles.

Growth slowed during the 1860s. Westward migration declined as a result of the Civil War and renewed Indian attacks, and surveys of possible railroad routes to California were suspended. On the coastal side of the mountains, severe flooding inundated the Coastal Plain in 1861. Only a few years later, many of the large ranchero holdings were devastated by the Great Drought of 1863–64.

In 1864, my great-grandfather joined with Bixby and the Flint brothers to purchase three Mexican land grants in Los Angeles County: the Rancho San Joaquin, the Rancho Lomas de Santiago and a portion of the Rancho Santiago de Santa Ana, which was originally a Spanish land concession. Covering roughly 115,000 acres and reaching from the ocean to the San Bernardino County line, 23 miles long and eight miles wide, these three tracts of land, known then as Rancho San Joaquin, would eventually become the Irvine Ranch, comprising one-fifth of what is today Orange County.

By 1866, James Irvine I had become a very prominent citizen in San Francisco. Some years earlier, his father and mother had come from Belfast to live in Cleveland, Ohio, and my great-grandfather was well-acquainted in that city. That same year, he married Henrietta Maria (Nettie) Rice of Cleveland. The couple made their home at the corner of Folsom and Eleventh Streets, and the house with its furnishings cost more than $25,000. *"But it is a very comfortable one,"* my

Nettie Rice Irvine;
James Irvine I (1827–1886);
photographs, The Irvine Family Archives

Granville Redmond, Passing Shadows, *1907, oil on canvas, 33 x 53 in., formerly in the collection of James L. Coran and Walter A. Nelson-Rees, destroyed in the Oakland fire, 1991*

great-grandfather wrote, *"with a beautiful yard filled with shrubbery, flowers and clover, and there I take solid enjoyment."* In fact, he loved the location of his new home so much that in 1875, he built 14 or 15 houses near the site for rental purposes.

Nettie Rice came from a distinguished family. Her father, Harvey Rice, was an educator, lawyer, real-estate salesman, prolific author, and served in the Ohio legislature and senate. As a state senator, he took an active part in badly needed prison reform and sponsored the bill that established Ohio's public school system and school libraries. He became gratefully known to his fellow citizens as the "father of the common school system of Ohio."

Although my great-grandfather's San Francisco grocery and produce business was extremely profitable and his real-estate investments increased rapidly in value, his larger fortune lay in the ranch lands he and his associates in Flint, Bixby and Company had purchased in southern California. As his share in the properties was equal to that of his other three partners combined, he was the dominant figure in the group.

As had been previously agreed upon, he and his partners immediately stocked their newly purchased ranchos with thousands of head of sheep. In the summer of 1867, my great-grandfather visited the properties and returned to San Francisco more enthusiastic than ever. *"We rode about a good deal,"* he wrote, *"sometimes coming home in the evening after a thirty or forty mile ride, pretty thoroughly tired out, but we had to do it in order to see much of the ranch and the flock. We have been making further purchases of land adjoining ours. Now our tract contains about 101–115,000 acres. On one side, the line is nearly 23 miles long and the average width is nearly eight miles. So you can see there is considerable riding to be done, if one is to see much of it."*

Due to generous winter rains that year, my great-grandfather found ample feed on the ranges to support 200,000 head of sheep. At that time, the partners were grazing less than 30,000 but expected to increase the herd to 40,000 or 45,000 in the next six or eight months. Eventually, they hoped to raise the number to 100,000 head.

Undoubtedly as a result of his visit, my great-grandfather urged the purchase of a large number of additional sheep and stressed the importance of improving the standard of the flocks by adding thoroughbred bucks and ewes. A few months later, the partners imported 25 Spanish merino sheep—at a cost of $250 to $500 each—from the Sandwich Islands, now known as the Hawaiian Islands.

On October 16, 1867, my grandfather James Harvey Irvine was born. His father's happiness at the birth of a son and heir was cut short, however, as Nettie contracted puerperal fever, the dreaded curse of childbirth in that pre-antiseptic age. For a while, it was uncertain whether my great-grandmother would live or die. When the crisis passed, my great-grandfather could hardly find words to express his relief and gratitude. To Nettie's mother, he wrote: *"I am going to do all in my power to benefit or make her happy, I love her too dearly to do otherwise, and daily I feel grateful to you and her father for the wife you gave me, for I think a sweeter nature and lovelier spirit than hers, God never breathed into human form."*

In the winter of 1867–68, the rainfall was so abnormally high in southern California that both the Santa Ana and San Gabriel rivers changed their course and many roads became impassable. Although the sheep on the Irvine-Flint-Bixby ranges suffered to some extent from the severity of the weather, the lambs that spring numbered between 40,000 and 45,000.

In order to have a suitable place to stay and conduct business while he visited the Rancho San Joaquin, my great-grandfather commissioned a house to be built in 1868. The two-story frame house, which was also intended to house the ranch superintendent, cost $1,300 and was constructed near the old Sepúlveda compound. It was the first wooden house to be erected between Anaheim and San Diego. The finest house for miles around, the San Joaquin Ranch house had a kitchen, dining room, parlor, four bedrooms and a porch that ran around most of the house. It also had Chinese household help.

The First Ranch House, Rancho San Joaquin,
photograph, The Irvine Family Archives

As early as 1865, the 105-ton stern-wheeled river steamer *Vaquero* paid regular visits to San Joaquin Bay, known today as Newport Bay, mainly to collect hides, meat and tallow from the nearby ranchos. In 1868, the partners shipped their wool to San Francisco, then on to New York or Boston. That year, prices remained high, and my great-grandfather believed that when the ranches were fully stocked, they would yield a yearly net revenue of 20,000 to 30,000 pounds sterling.

Even a major earthquake—which occurred October 21, 1868, doing serious damage to San Francisco and killing a number of people—could not check my great-grandfather's enthusiasm. In a letter to one of his brothers, he gave a graphic description of the disaster:

> The ground sunk from a few inches to several feet, and in other places it opened and closed again, testing buildings severely. There was, of course, a general rush for the streets and elsewhere to get out of the way of the falling walls. Thousands of chimneys were either tumbled down, broken off at the roof, or twisted around. Some friends were at my house and we were at breakfast at the time. All felt the shake and were about to make a hasty retreat. I urged them to sit still, that it would be over in a few seconds. They did so for a short time, but the shock continued, becoming steadily more severe, until the house sounded as if it were being wrenched and ground to pieces. With one consent, all sprang to their feet and ran to get out of doors, in which they soon succeeded. I ran upstairs for Baby and the nurse, and when we got down it was all over. We all escaped

John Prendergast, San Francisco after the Fire, *1851, Oakland Museum of California, Gift of the Estate of Marjorie Eaton, by exchange*

Harvey Rice, c. 1870,
photograph, The Irvine Family Archives

injury, narrowly missing a lot of falling plaster that fell in the hall where we were running. After the shock, I went on an exploring expedition to see how the house had stood it and in nearly every room found abundant evidence of rough usage in the shape of fallen plaster, cracked walls, vases and other articles thrown down and in some cases broken. On ascending to the roof, I found the chimneys (of which there were four tall heavy ones) broken near the roof and some of them moved quite out of place. Fortunately, none of them fell down as in that case there is not much doubt but that they would have gone through the house, clear to the cellar before stopping, and ruined the house. They weighed three to four tons each above the roof. I have had them taken down and others, newer and lighter, and not so tall, put in their places, and now we feel much safer. Our house, like nearly all the residences here, is built of wood so there is not much damage to any part of it except the brick chimneys being thrown down. I would not live in a brick or stone house. I have felt many earthquakes before, but this one beats them all. I hope we shall have no more like it. The business portion of the city, built of bricks, stone and iron, suffered severely, but much less than I would have supposed.

The earth doesn't seem quite settled yet, from thirty to forty shakes have occurred since the heavy one (three of them within the last 24 hours) but none heavy enough to do any harm except to keep some people nervous.

Neither the earthquake, nor the severe epidemic of smallpox that followed, could check San Francisco's amazing growth. Agriculture had long since become more important than mining in California. The first transcontinental railroad was nearing completion, and manufacturing and building in San Francisco were never as active. On California, Montgomery, Bush and a few other streets, real estate was selling at $500 to $3,000 a front foot, and my great-grandfather's city properties had risen to nearly $200,000 in value. He thought of California as the *"most prosperous state in the Union"* and wrote in 1869 that though much of the land recently acquired by the partnership in southern California—which came to be known as the Rancho San Joaquin—was *"in active demand at $10 an acre and upwards,"* he and his associates had no intention of selling the property at that time, as prices were steadily rising.

After the completion of the transcontinental railroad in 1869, my great-grandfather's father-in-law, Harvey Rice, and his wife, Emma, traveled by rail from Cleveland to San Francisco. They left Ohio on September 6, and after making additional sightseeing trips along their route by stagecoach, arrived in San Francisco on October 6.

In his interesting little book, entitled *Letters from the Pacific Slope*, published in 1870, my great-great-grandfather gives a colorful account of their journey.

We arrived in San Francisco on the 6th early in the evening, crossing the bay in a steamer. The next day, we took a brief survey of our whereabouts, and found ourselves in the heart of a splendid city, only twenty years old yet looking mature, and destined to become the great central city of the commercial world. It is here that Europe, Asia and America will meet, shake hands and be good friends. Here they will concentrate their wealth, exchange commodities, gamble in stocks and test the comparative sharpness of their wits. In the course of a few days, after our arrival, we began to feel quite at home in the city. The citizens are candid, frank and polite to strangers and generous to a fault. They are proud of their city, and seem to think there is no other place in the wide world so delightful as California. In this opinion, I concur, so far as my brief experience extends. The general aspect of the city is peculiar. It looks as if it was constructed of sand hills and windmills, and in truth it really is.

William Coulter, View of San Francisco, 1874,
26 x 18 in., Dr. & Mrs. Edward H. Boseker

The city is located on the tip-end of a tongue of land, or peninsula, lying between the bay and the sea. It contains at this time, it is said, one hundred and seventy-five thousand inhabitants. This is a wonderful growth for a city but twenty years old, especially when we consider the fact that it has been twice almost entirely destroyed by fire [There were, in fact, six critical fires in San Francisco in the first three years of its existence, but the two Rice refers to were in January 1849 and October 1851]…The bay is amply sufficient in breadth and depth to accommodate the navies of the civilized world, and furnishes a line of dockage that might be extended the entire distance of forty miles…It may be truthfully said of the Pacific coast, generally, that for climate and productiveness of soil, it excels the world. For beauty of natural scenery and sunny skies, Italy does not compare with it. The air here is so pure and exhilarating, that it makes one feel, who breathes it, as if he were drinking champagne all the time. It is enough, perhaps to say that it is a wonderful country—a land of fruits and flowers enriched with mountains of gold…Yet, this modern paradise has its annoyances. In San Francisco, dense fog envelops the city until ten o'clock in the morning, strong winds prevail the rest of the day, drifting the sand into mounds and into your eyes so as to blind you. Still, by way of comparison, for all of this, you have here a cloudless sky for nine months of the year; a climate that is uniformly mild; and a vernal season that flings over the hills and the valleys a mantle of wild flowers, perfuming every breath of air you breathe. And yet, in California, it is gold that makes the man; the want of it, an outcast or an

View of San Francisco, 1853, *photograph, Oakland Museum of California Gift of Minna McGauley Stoddard*

John Gamble, Spring Once in a Lifetime
(Lupine and Owl's Clover), *oil on canvas,
26 x 40 in., Private Collection, courtesy of
The Irvine Museum*

outlaw. It is said there are at least seven thousand able-bodied men in San Francisco, who cannot find employment and probably more than twice that number roving about the state....It is, after all, a poor country for a poor man; but a good country for a man who has capital, nerve, and perseverance.

The more I see of this city, I am surprised with its peculiarities, nationalities and novelties. It is a modern Rome, built on not only seven, but seventy times seven hills. Some of these hills are large, and composed of granite; but the most of them are conical sand hills, which have been drifted into strange and novel shapes by the prevailing winds.

The windmills give to the general appearance of the city a feature that is as singular as it is repulsive to architectural taste. They are erected for the purpose of pumping water from wells to irrigate the lawns and gardens. By this means, the grounds occupied for residences are kept green, and the gardens made productive the year around. The poor classes cannot afford the luxury of irrigation and consequently the town plat for two-thirds of the year looks like a checkerboard or patch-bed quilt.

The commercial part of the city is located along the bay and built up in magnificent style, in blocks of stone, brick and iron, three and four stories high, and equal to the best business streets in the eastern cities. Most of the buildings are anchored or braced with iron bolts, so as to secure them against the action of earthquakes. The ground in this part of the town is level, being made land by grading the sand hills into the bay. The wholesale and retail stores are not only imposing in the fronts they present, but largely stocked with every variety of goods and products gathered from every clime.

Theodore Wores, The Candy Seller, *1884,*
oil on canvas, 41 x 27 in.,
Garzoli Gallery, San Rafael, CA

There is no city on the face of the globe, I think, in which the leading business men exhibit so much activity and intensity of purpose, so much rushing ahead in the streets, as in San Francisco. The business streets, from morning 'till night, are crowded with passing drays and men stepping on each other's heels, and jostling elbows at every angle, as if life were at stake. And more especially is this true on steamer days, so called from the sailing of the Panama steamers every two weeks, when all of the merchants are expected to settle balances with each other. In doing this, an unusual bustle is created in the streets and in the banks; hundreds of men are seen bearing hither and thither, sacks of gold coin on their shoulders, containing in some instances as much as they can conveniently lift. At almost every shop door, you will hear, in passing, the "musical ring" of twenty dollar pieces, as they are counted out in the adjustment of dues and demands. On one of these steamer days, I stepped into the Bank of California, where I saw more gold received and paid out and standing in cord piles, than I ever expect to see again. It took an army of clerks to count the money.

The various nationalities in San Francisco, make it an epitome of the civilized world. In fact, every civilized nation is represented here. The Irish pre-dominate and dominate. The Chinese are curiosities. They dress alike and look alike and are really a very shrewd people. Not much less than thirty thousand reside in the city. Some of them are merchants on a large scale, worth from thousands to millions of dollars, and are truly very intelligent and accomplished men. The Chinese population occupy, almost exclusively several of the business streets, and follow all sorts of trades and employments, from cooks to bankers.

Gold not only concentrates but begets talent. This is fully illustrated in the history of San Francisco. Here you will find, concentrated, more men who excel in every art and science than in any other city in the world containing the same population. This is true, whether you refer to genius and excellence, as exhibited in the pulpit, at the bar, on the bench, or at the counter, or in the workshop.

The trade annual commerce of San Francisco has become comparatively immense. In less than twenty years, the merchandise export trade had increased from one million and a half to twenty-two millions of dollars per annum. The gold exports average, for the last twenty-one years, nearly fifty millions of dollars per annum. Though the gold mines are less productive than formerly, the silver mines have largely increased their productions, and promise a still more liberal yield for the future.

William Hahn, Going to Market, *1873*
oil on canvas, 27 x 35 in., Garzoli Gallery,
San Rafael, CA

The markets are stocked throughout the year with the best of beef, mutton, wild game, fish and fowl, including every variety of fruits and garden vegetables. The gardens furnish strawberries, green corn, green peas, new potatoes, and other luxuries of this character, in abundance every month of the year. The fruits and vegetables are as excellent in quality as they are remarkable for size. Onions grown as large as tea plates, beets sometimes weigh from fifty to seventy-five pounds apiece.

The hotels overflow with strangers, coming and going, all on the rush. On some of the streets, nearly every other door opens

John Stobart, San Francisco, Embarking on
Voyage Home in 1850,
Maritime Heritage Prints, Boston

into a drinking saloon, gambling den or something worse. The gamblers dress richly and overload themselves with ostentatious jewelry. There is no place so safe that thieves do not "break through and steal." And yet there is as much good society to be found in San Francisco as in any other city of the same population. They are a social, genial, generous people, especially the better classes.

The city has natural advantages which cannot be taken away from her. She has no rival and need fear none. She sits majestic on her throne of hills and bathes her feet in the sea. Telegraph Hill is her flag-staff. It looks in the distance like a church spire and is built with dwellings to its apex. From its highest point floats the American flag, as a signal to ships at sea, seeking to enter the Golden Gate.

On November 6, they left San Francisco and *"after a voyage on the coast steamer of two days and a half, entered the Bay of San Pedro,"* where they were *"transferred to a small class steamer and taken seven miles up the bay to Wilmington,"* and then by rail to Los Angeles.

The City of the Angels is a unique old town, full of oddities and whimsicalities. Half the population is Mexican, the other half American, English, Scotch, Irish, German and the Lord knows what. Yet there is a goodly number of intelligent, refined and accomplished people, who reside here and give tone to society. The learned professions appear to be over-stocked, yet each is represented by some individuals of distinguished talent. The city, with few exceptions, is built in Mexican style and wears a dilapidated look. It contains a population, they say, of about 20,000. The roofs of the houses are generally flat and the walls adobe. It is situated at the base of the foothills, about thirty miles from the line of the sea coast, and extends into the plain for a considerable distance. It includes within its

Alexander Harmer, Chinatown, Los Angeles, 1886, oil on canvas, 19 x 30 in., The Irvine Museum

William Wendt, A Clear Day, *oil on canvas,
30 x 40 in., The Irvine Museum*

*limits many fine gardens, vineyards and orange groves. It is emphat-
ically the land of fruits and flowers, always fresh and fascinating. If
not the first, it is the second edition of the true Garden of Eden.*

*The climate here is the finest in the world, never too hot
and never too cold, but always equable and exhilarating. It never
rains except in winter; the fruit trees, the gardens, and the vineyards
are ever-flourishing, and co-mingling fruits and flowers in perennial
profusion. The winter rains are nothing more than genial showers.
In fact, the winter is like our spring, when the leaves of trees, and
the buds and the flowers burst into life, and the fields become green.*

From Los Angeles, which they regarded as their base or central point, my
great-great-grandparents

*made an excursion into the country and visited several of the most
extensive ranches within the circuit of a hundred miles, traveling in
an open carriage. A ranch is simply an old Spanish plantation, containing usually from 10,000 to 150,000 acres and sometimes more;
in or near the center of which stands an old flat-roofed house, built
of adobe, which is a large square mud brick, dried in the sun, instead
of being burned in a kiln. The house is generally constructed in the
shape of a parallelogram, enclosing an open court and having on
the outside an open portico. It is a queer looking sort of a mansion;
yet in the olden time, it possessed all the charms of a royal palace
in the estimation of the populace. It was in palatial residences of
this character, that the richer classes of the Mexicans and Spaniards
took their ease and lived in comparative luxury, until the war with
Mexico occurred when they were annexed to the United States.*

Granville Redmond, Tending the Flock,
oil on canvas, 12 x 18 in., Private Collection,
courtesy of The Irvine Museum

After the war, they attempted to adopt American habits and to live in American style. The result was, they became extravagant and soon so encumbered their estates that they were obliged to sell them at nominal prices. The Americans were the purchasers and obtained the lands, in many instances as low as ten cents an acre. Some of the large tracts thus obtained are now worth from five to fifty dollars an acre. They compose the best lands in California, and extend in a chain of valleys from San Diego to San Francisco, and even along the entire coast of the state. The appearance of these ranchlands in summer and the fall months is quite unlike the green fields we see in the eastern United States. Here the grasses acquire a rank growth after the rains in winter and during the early spring, and then become perfectly dry, still standing upright where they grew and thus remain for seven or eight months, during the rainless season, as dry and sweet as the best of hay preserved in a barn. While in this condition, these grasses are still rich and nutritive and afford abundant feed for the vast herds of sheep, cattle and horses that roam at large over the plains. In a word, Nature does the haying and leaves man with little to do, except to guard his flocks and herds and take it easy.

We visited several ranches and were not only politely received and entertained, but acquired an interesting though brief experience of ranch life.

Spending the greater part of a week on the Rancho San Joaquin, my great-great-grandfather described the great estate as follows:

This ranch consists of 110,000 acres [sic] and is stocked with 40,000 fine-wooled sheep. In extent, it is one of the largest ranches south of Los Angeles, being some twelve miles wide by twenty long [sic]. It is mostly valley land and stretches from the foothills to the sea. In some of the hills within its boundaries, mines of coal and quicksilver [mercury] have recently been discovered, which promise to become valuable. The ranch is amply watered by springs and a chain of small lagoons extending through it. Centrally, supposed to be a subterranean river, from the connection there is in the hidden currents that pass from one lagoon to another, and the tremulous character of the soil which seems to rest on the surface. In some places, if you thrust a pole through the turf, it disappears at once, and is never seen again. These lagoons terminate in a small bay, which extends from the ocean into the ranch about two miles. On the shore of this bay, I saw a camp of Mexican fishermen, who were engaged in manufacturing oil from the carcasses of sharks, which they catch in abundance along the sea coast. The Mexicans make this a profitable business. They go out to sea in small boats and catch the sharks by harpooning or shooting them, as they rise to the surface in their eagerness to swallow the bait flung to them. When caught, they are towed into the bay and so great is the number of their skeletons lying

Granville Redmond, Evening, *1903,*
oil on canvas, 33 x 70 in.,
The Irvine Museum, Gift of Ray Redfern

about the camp that the atmosphere throughout the entire vicinity for miles, is rendered impure and even offensive.

The sheep with which this ranch is stocked, are subdivided in flocks of three thousand to five thousand, and each division placed in charge of a shepherd, who watches over them, by day and by night, like the shepherds of old, but with this difference, perhaps, that he gathers the sheep into a corral or pen at night, and then betakes himself to his eight-by-ten board cabin, next the enclosure, and there cooks, eats and sleeps as best he can, with no other associates than his sheep and faithful dog. His life is truly a lonely one, and yet he seems happy in the companionship of his sheep and dog, who understand his signs and his whistle, and even the import of his words, and obey him with a child-like confidence in his superior wisdom and intelligence. The annual clip of wool from the sheep of this ranch, is said to be about 200,000 pounds. It is of the finest quality and sells at a high price in the eastern market. Add to the income from the wool the annual product of 20,000 lambs, and it is easy to see that wool growing is a very profitable business in California.

After leaving the Rancho San Joaquin, my great-great-grandparents went by carriage to Anaheim,

a beautiful little German city, "the loveliest of the plain." Situated on the banks of the Santa Ana River...it is a city of vineyards and takes the lead in California as a wine district. The quality of the wine is excellent, and the amount annually produced very large. The wine is sold by the pipe, and goes to the dealers in San Francisco, who bottle it and put it into the market. Much of it is shipped east.

In returning from the sheep ranch to this vine-clad city, we crossed several large rivers, nearly half-a-mile wide, but with channels dry as a sand desert. In this country, most of the rivers become dry in summer, or so low that the water, what little there is at different points, sinks and is lost in the sand; perhaps in underground currents. But, in the rainy season, the rivers often overflow their banks and flood the country, far and near, making it extremely dangerous to cross them with teams. As yet, there are no bridges or ferry boats. The quicksand in the beds of the stream, increase the danger of passing them. It often happens that horses, wagons, and all, go down, and sometimes are lost.

Southern California is almost entirely destitute of valuable timber. In some directions, you might do a hundred miles and not be able to cut a walking stick. There are, of course, no fences. Everybody's herds and flocks graze where they please, unless watched

William Wendt;
ABOVE: Saddleback Mountain, Mission Viejo,
1923, oil on canvas, 30 x 40 in.;
RIGHT: Santa Ana River, *oil on canvas, 25 x 30 in.;*
Private Collection,
courtesy of The Irvine Museum

William Wendt, Untitled (Wild Mustard),
1909, oil on canvas, 16 x 20 in.,
The Upchurch Collection,
photo courtesy of William A. Karges Fine Art,
Los Angeles and Carmel

by herders. It is bewildering to ride through the vast plain of tall grass and wild mustard, especially at this season of the year, when vegetation stands erect, though dead and dry as a stubble field. The mustard grows seven feet high, and when mature, resembles a field of ripened rye. It is of good quality and is often gathered and sold in the market at a handsome profit. Thousands of acres are densely covered with it and in traveling through it one is liable to get lost. The country is so level and smooth that you can drive a team in any direction you please. There are but few roads; in many parts of the country nothing more than trails or pathways. It seems to a stranger like an uninhabited land.

Wild game is very abundant. Innumerable squirrels, gray and black, burrow in the ground for want of trees, and may be seen running in all directions. The coyotes, a kind of wolf, are also numerous and destructive among the sheep. In addition to these, there are deer, wild cats, bears and lions, among the foothills and higher mountains, and acres of wild geese flying in the air, or feeding along the lagoons and water courses. There are two distinct varieties of geese, the white and the black. We also saw rabbits in abundance, multitudes of quails, hawks, crows and buzzards. Black birds in flocks follow the sheep and light on their backs, picking the grass seeds lodged in their wool, and riding along at leisure. The sheep submit with perfect indifference. It is a novel sight.

Besides all this variety of game, there are plenty of wild hogs roaming about the marshes and brush thickets. They belong to anybody who can catch or kill them. In some parts of this region, we saw hundreds of acres of corn, as stout as ever grew, for which there is no market. As many as 1,040 kernels have been known to grow in a single ear. Pork brings a high price, and so for want of tame hogs to consume the corn, the ranch men catch and fatten the wild ones, and thus make their corn crops available. Hunting and catching wild hogs is an exciting business, and requires skill and experience. They are pursued with trained dogs and lassoed.

From Anaheim, we returned by stage to this ancient City of the Angels. Myself, wife and a Englishman were the only passengers who took seats in the coach at Anaheim. The coachmen, accompanied with an armed guard, sat on the outside. The distance between the two cities is about forty miles, and the region through which we had to pass, is for the most part, wild and uninhabited. A few weeks prior to this time, the stage coach had been waylaid on this route, and all the passengers robbed of their money and other valuables... Pistols and pluck are the only safe-guards on which you can rely in such emergencies...It is never safe to go unarmed, or travel alone, especially if you are well dressed, or display golden ornaments.

My great-great-grandfather concludes his book recounting his journey by saying,

If you intend to make the trip, I should advise you to take along with you a basket of lunch, a flask of brandy, and a pocket pistol. If you have a wife, take her also; if you have none, marry at once, and

J. Bond Francisco, Out of the Dust, *oil on canvas, Private Collection*

make it your bridal trip. A gentleman who is accompanied by his wife, is sure of being treated with consideration; but if he travels without a lady in charge, he must expect to be regarded as of little more consequence than so much freight. A word to the wise ought to be sufficient.

Ernest Narjot, Under the Redwoods, Spout Farm, *Elisabeth Waldo-Dentzel Multicultural Arts Studio, Northridge, CA*

In 1869, James Irvine 1 sold part of his interest in his wholesale produce and grocery company to his brother William and an associate. Three years later, he withdrew entirely from active participation in the partnership and devoted his time to his San Francisco properties, his southern California holdings and his other large investments.

In his business affairs, my great-grandfather was known for his sagacity, sound judgment, sense of fairness and justice, and "exactitude even in the most trivial transactions." He was deeply concerned for the welfare of his parents, who were now living in Cleveland, Ohio, and his large family of brothers and sisters still living in Ireland. He advised them on many of their problems and from time to time, sent them money. On December 16, 1869, he wrote to his brother John that he had "been blessed with a great degree of prosperity" and knew of no better way in which to use his wealth than to aid others less fortunate and to share it with other members of his family. He added that he was going to set aside 500 to 1,000 pounds sterling annually for his kinfolk, and distribute it where he thought it was most needed, would do the most good or would confer the most happiness. My great-grandfather also financed a number of his brothers in different business ventures and came to the financial aid of friends and business associates.

His appreciation of the value of an education was typical of his Presbyterian Scotch-Irish upbringing and early environment. Referring to the children of one of his brothers, who were attending a good school despite family hardships, he thoughtfully wrote, "*Undoubtedly, in their more mature years, they will have more to thank their parents for and will feel more deeply and thoroughly grateful for the opportunity and the means afforded them for obtaining a good education, than for anything else that may or can be given them. That lasts and blesses for life, and to a certain extent commands success. It certainly aids it greatly, while a little or even a large sum of money may last but a short time and prove of little value while it does.*"

In 1869, the San Joaquin Ranch produced 70,000 pounds of wool, which brought around 30 cents a pound in Boston and New York. But in spite of these satisfactory returns, my great-grandfather found the property a constant source of minor irritations. Squatters began moving in onto the ranges, and the controversies between the landowner and the intruders became increasingly bitter, with the quarrels often leading to violence and bloodshed. Wages and ranch costs were rising; taxes on some of the property were getting out of hand; a trusted employee had taken to whiskey and gambling; and the business of the ranch "*was being greatly neglected.*"

In May 1870, a young man named Charles E. French accompanied Bixby from Boston to southern California and was persuaded to take the position of ranch superintendent at Rancho San Joaquin. He arrived there during an extended drought, when the landscape was desolate and not a blade of grass could be seen anywhere. In a letter to his wife, Emma, who had remained in Boston, he described the ranch as *"a God forsaken land with coyotes barking, wildcats screaming, and not a light to be seen anywhere in the darkness of the night."*

Added to French's other problems was the most constant annoyance of all—the fleas. The ranch house was situated at the main sheep camp, and the sheep were covered with fleas. Before his wife and daughter Gertrude arrived from Boston a few months later, French *"flooded the floors and plastered walls to get rid of these pests. At night, after undressing, a person jumped into bed as quickly as possible in order not to get them in the bed."*

When my great-grandfather came from San Francisco, he stayed in the San Joaquin ranch house with the Frenches. In the evening, he read poetry aloud to Mrs. French, a welcome break in the monotony of her isolation.

Soon after French's arrival in 1870, the ranch problems grew worse instead of better, as thousands of sheep and lambs began dying from lack of feed, due to the drought. By the following year, all but about 12,000 of the remaining sheep had been moved north to grazing lands in San Luis Obispo County. Those that remained were driven into the higher ranges of the Santa Ana Mountains, where they were held throughout the drought.

The loss of the sheep and the resulting loss in revenues caused my great-grandfather to urge every possible economy in ranch operations. "It's very, very dear cooking," he wrote to French, when an examination of the payroll showed that two Chinese were employed at $60 a month plus board, to cook for eight people. Fifteen dollars a month seemed to him an adequate wage for the ordinary employee, and he breathed more freely when the two Chinese cooks were dismissed.

Sheep Shearing, Irvine Ranch, c. 1890,
photograph, San Juan
Capistrano Historical Society

Wages on the Rancho San Joaquin for June 1870 came to $723, which seemed to my great-grandfather much higher than the prevailing rate on an ordinary sheep ranch. He wanted to know how many people were "supported on the ranch," hoping the payroll could be reduced to $500 a month. However, with 30 or 40 employees, this seemed impossible.

In those days, and for years thereafter, itinerant workers and "bindle stiffs," or hobos, roamed the southern California countryside in great numbers and often made pests of themselves at the ranches, large and small alike. The Rancho San Joaquin always supported more than its share of these individuals, and my great-grandfather urged French to find a way of lessening the nuisance.

When French became excited over the prospect of finding gold on the ranch, he sent an optimistic letter to my great-grandfather accompanied by a box of salted ore samples that had been given to him by a wily "old miner." My great-grandfather, who had begun his career in California as a prospector, replied in disgust,

> *In reference to your letter of the fourth inst., I hardly know what to say. This, however, I will say. If any more "gold miners" want to send cobblestones here by express, let them do it at their own expense.*
>
> *What kind of an opinion must the fellow have of you to attempt to palm-off on you such a cheap and bare-faced swindle? Had you used a knife at once, you would have discovered that the "golden fleece" was only rubble on the surface, and for this purpose a cobble stone (showing you to be wholly uninitiated) was as good as any other. But under no circumstances would such stones as you sent show any affinity for gold. If you want to see how it is done, just take any piece of rock and rub hard the edge of a twenty-dollar piece upon it...and you will have equally as good specimens as any the "old miner" gave you. I only hope he has not succeeded in wheedling you out of any of your money.*

Model of the Vaquero, Newport Harbor Nautical Museum, Newport Beach, CA

In September 1870, Captain Samuel Dunnells navigated his steamer *Vaquero* from the ocean into lower San Joaquin Bay and all the way into the upper bay, where he unloaded a cargo of lumber and shingles. When my great-grandfather heard the news, he hurried from his home in San Francisco to the Rancho San Joaquin and met with James McFadden and his brother Robert, at his newly constructed ranch house. They all agreed it really was "a new port," and gave it the name of Newport.

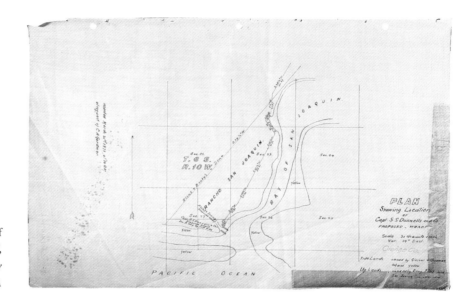

Plan Showing the Location of Capt. S.S. Dunnells and Co. Proposed Wharf, 1871, Rancho San Joaquin, *Sherman Library and Gardens, Corona del Mar, CA*

In 1873, the McFadden brothers, who already owned 4,000 or 5,000 acres of land that formerly belonged to the Rancho Santiago de Santa Ana, bought a small dock and warehouse on Newport Bay, where they began importing lumber and shipping out wool, grain and a few other agricultural products. Because of dissatisfaction with lighterage (barge transportation) charges and a delay in the settlement of an old account for damages, my great-grandfather and his partners transferred their wool-shipping business from the McFaddens' Newport Bay landing to Phineas Banning's new harbor of Wilmington.

As time passed, my great-grandfather became more and more enthusiastic about the region where the San Joaquin Ranch was located, speaking of it as the most delightful land he had ever seen, "either in California or outside of it." Quietly, he added numerous tracts of land in the "Santa Anas" and elsewhere in the area to the partners' landholdings, until he and his associates held an empire of nearly 120,000 acres of potential farmland of great fertility and value.

In the meantime, Los Angeles and the rich San Gabriel and Santa Ana valleys began to experience one of the first clearly defined real-estate booms in the history of southern California. Publicity and advertising—of which California had received a larger share than perhaps any other corner of the globe—were making the state widely known in Europe as well as in the United States. Immigrant companies were being organized in a number of countries to settle in California. The pioneer Anaheim Colony of 1857 was established on part of the Rancho San Juan Cajon de Santa Ana, but a number of later subdivisions were laid out on lands for-

William Wendt, When Fields Lie Fallow, *1931,*
oil on canvas, 40 x 50 in., Private Collection,
courtesy of The Irvine Museum

merly included in the Rancho Santiago de Santa Ana. As early as 1867, Columbus
Tustin and N.A. Stafford bought some 1,300 acres of this ranch for $2,000. Tustin
laid out a town on the eastern boundary of his tract, to which he gave the name
"Tustin City."

In 1869, two years after the founding of Tustin, William H. Spurgeon, the
"father of Santa Ana," bought another portion of the Rancho Santiago de Santa
Ana, divided part of it into residence and business lots, then gave the name of Santa
Ana to the new town. The valley irrigation system was in its infancy. Farmers were
just beginning to plant trees and vines. Melons and vegetables had to take the place
of fruit until the trees and vines began to bear.

In 1871, Andrew Glassell and Alfred Beck Chapman, members of one of
the leading law firms in Los Angeles, laid out still another town a few miles from
Rancho San Joaquin and called it Richland. The Richland Farm District, a tract of
600 acres surrounding the town, was surveyed and platted at the same time. The
land was advertised as being "beautifully located under the flow of the A.B. Chapman Canal…well-watered, sheltered, and above the influence of frost." The plots
in town were ten acres, and farm lots were 40 acres. The town of Richland is now
known as Orange.

When my grandfather James Irvine II was six years old, a brother, Harvey
Rice Irvine, was born, but the child died in infancy. A week after James turned seven,
his mother, Nettie Rice Irvine, died of consumption on October 23, 1874. At the time
of her death, her husband was 47 years of age. He buried his grief at the loss of his
beloved wife by immersing himself more deeply in the management of his various
properties and other investments.

At that time, the Rancho San Joaquin was used only for pasturing sheep. Around 1875, French asked permission to do "a little farming on his own responsibility and at his own risk." My great-grandfather gave his guarded consent saying, "I have no objection to your farming all you want…It will not be a bit of expense to the ranch. Indeed, I would like much to see a little farming done there, but we must not add to current expenses which are already beyond endurance. You see, I am a little afraid of the cost of the experiment."

Six months later, my great-grandfather informed French that he was willing to have parts of the ranch devoted to tenant farming, provided the tenants assumed all the risk and expense of the venture. He would not, however, advertise that land was for rent.

In March 1876, the Southern Pacific Railroad persuaded the government to bring suit to invalidate the partners' title to a portion of the Rancho Lomas de Santiago, one of the grants that made up the Rancho San Joaquin. If successful, the suit would throw the land into question in the public domain and enable the railroad to obtain a right-of-way across the ranch. The case, however, was dismissed on April 22, 1878.

In 1876, my great-grandfather acquired his partners' interest in the Rancho San Joaquin for $150,000. No sooner had he secured full ownership of the ranch than the historic drought of 1876–77 dried up the ranges and devastated the grazing industry, destroying the sheep of southern California almost as effectively as the similar drought of the mid-1860s had destroyed the range cattle industry.

That same year, my great-grandfather instructed French to find a more suitable location for a ranch headquarters, one that was closer to civilization. The location decided upon was near Tustin City and the stage depot. Construction soon began on the country-style Georgian frame house that would serve as both the Irvine family home and the ranch office on Rancho San Joaquin.

The 130-mile Seeley & Wright stage line, from Los Angeles to San Diego, was started in 1866 after my great-grandfather gave Alfred L. Seeley permission to run the stage across the ranch. The stage road, and also the telegraph line through the ranch, followed El Camino Real, the historic road first used by Gáspar de Portolá and the Spanish missionaries in the late 1700s. Part of the road lay in an old streambed, close to the foothills of the Santa Ana Mountains, and the sandy bottom was a very hard pull for the horses, which were forced to slow to a walk. This was the most dangerous stretch of the journey. If bandits planned to rob the stage, this was where they would strike. The Seeley & Wright stage line advertised that they would deliver passengers from one destination to another inside of 24 hours; 23 if there were no broken wheels or axles, if the team didn't run away, and if robbers didn't hold up the stage.

In 1877, Nettie Irvine's younger brother, James Stephen Rice, came to California from Cleveland, Ohio, due to his ailing health. Rice, with his wife and two children, moved into the San Joaquin ranch house and, among other businesses,

  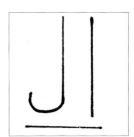

joined in a hog-raising venture with my great-grandfather. The hog farm was located where the University of California-Irvine is today, and was in operation for more than 75 years. Rice and his family lived at the San Joaquin ranch house for only one year before moving to Tustin. After they moved, a cooking wing was added to the house and it became the cattle foreman's home, as in addition to raising sheep, the Rancho San Joaquin also ran a substantial number of cattle. These were the descendants of the vast herds that had grazed there during both the mission and rancho periods.

Uncertain boundary lines and long-delayed court decisions encouraged squatters to move in on the property. My great-grandfather's attorneys and French were kept busy dealing with the trespassers. Such disputes often led to newspaper attacks on the large landholdings in southern California. The December 31, 1881 issue of the *Santa Ana Herald* took occasion to criticize my great-grandfather for both evading his rightful taxes and failing to contribute to the settlement and prosperity of the county by refusing to subdivide and sell off his land.

> *The liveliest town in southern California this winter is Santa Ana…*
> *A new brick hotel has been built…more business is transacted in*
> *Santa Ana than in any other town along the coast. The township*
> *contains the following tracts of land: the San Joaquin Rancho of*
> *48,833 acres; the Santiago de Santa Ana, 62,516 acres; Lomas de*
> *Santa Ana* [sic]*, 48,226 acres; Canyon de Santa Ana, 13,326 acres.*
> *The Lomas and San Joaquin Ranches are as yet uninhabited, except*

Herding cattle at the Rancho San Joaquin,
The Irvine Family Archives

32-Horse Harvester, Irvine Ranch, *photograph,*
San Juan Capistrano Historical Society

by herders and one home ranch-house. They reach clear across the county, from the ocean to the San Bernardino line, 20 miles long and 9½ miles wide [sic].

We traveled through the rancho, the property of James Irvine of San Francisco, a distance of nearly 12 miles, during which we saw no house nor found any improvement. Of the San Joaquin Rancho of 48,900 acres, one-third is level and well adapted to cultivation. There are three Artesian wells on the tract and the whole is susceptible of irrigation by Artesian water. Mr. Irvine's adjoining rancho, the Lomas de Santiago, containing 47,000 acres, contains about 9,000 acres of fine wheat, and fruit land, but is wholly uninhabited…At present, there are only about 35,000 head of sheep upon them and it is estimated that about 100,000 sheep could be fed there each year. This immense estate, so dreary and so desolate, presents a vivid contrast to the adjoining rancho, which has been made to blossom like a rose in its beauty and luxuriance. The Santa Ana Rancho, which was originally granted to the Yorba family, has been cut-up and sold out into tracts upon which thousands of happy homes may be found, including the towns of Santa Ana, Orange and Tustin City, three of the prettiest and most prosperous places in California.

In 1882, my great-grandfather undertook to subdivide and sell part of his share of the Rancho Santiago de Santa Ana and a portion of the Rancho San Joaquin. According to Robert Glass Cleland, *"The soil [in the Santa Ana Valley] was as rich as the Land of Goshen. Corn grew so tall that a man could scarcely reach the lowest ear on the stalk with an ordinary walking stick, and production often ran as high as a hundred and twenty-five bushels an acre. A yield of two hundred and twenty-five sacks of potatoes an acre and pumpkins that weighed two hundred pounds or more were not uncommon."*

The land was divided into 40-acre farms. A main highway through the property and lateral roads were constructed, and the parcels were sold on the installment plan. However, when some of the purchasers failed to complete the required payments, my great-grandfather was compelled to enter into considerable litigation. One such case, which had begun two years earlier, was with the McFadden brothers and involved two long, drawn-out suits over the ownership of land; it lasted for at least five years.

By the mid-1880s, the semi-frontier conditions were rapidly giving way in the Santa Ana Valley, as elsewhere in southern California, to a more advanced social and economic order. The completion of the Southern Pacific Railroad to Los Angeles in 1876, and the coming of the Santa Fe Railway nine years later, changed the agricultural outlook for the Los Angeles-Santa Ana Basin, brought about a large influx of population, stimulated the subdivision of many large landholdings and ushered in the great boom of 1886–88.

But my great-grandfather, founder of the Irvine Ranch, was not able to participate to any degree in these new developments, as he died in San Francisco on March 15, 1886. His heirs-at-law were his 18-year-old son, James II, and his second wife, Margaret Byrne Irvine, who he had married five years earlier.

Under the provisions of his father's will, my grandfather James Irvine II had to be 25 years of age to claim his inheritance. In 1887, the Trustees of the estate put the Irvine Ranch up for public auction. On April 16, 1887, the Trustees "offered and agreed to sell" at least 100,000 acres of the Irvine Ranch in Los Angeles County at public auction. The bidding began at $1,300,000 and had reached $1,385,000 when the timekeeper became confused as to which of the two bidders had made the final bid. When the decision was challenged in court, the judge ruled that neither bidder was entitled to the land. Though the Trustees refused either offer, they soon renewed their efforts to sell the property, either as a whole or in separate parcels.

Under the Irvine-Flint-Bixby Partnership, the property had been used almost entirely for the pasturage of sheep, but by 1878, a small amount of the land had begun to be devoted to tenant farming. Although sheep-raising continued as an important business long after the death of James I, the large flocks of earlier years had dwindled and been replaced by a substantial number of cattle. Much of

TOP: James Irvine II (1867–1947) in military school uniform at Adelbert College, Cleveland, Ohio; BOTTOM: James Irvine II; The Irvine Family Archives

the range land was leased to outsiders, and the Irvine Ranch was fast undergoing a radical transition from a grazing and pastoral stage to a farming economy that characterized the general agricultural development of most of southern California.

By the close of 1888, more than 5,000 acres of the Irvine property had been leased in relatively small tracts for raising hay and grain. In addition to grain farming, more and more land was being put under cultivation. A small vineyard was set out, chiefly for home use, and the Trustees made a strong effort to establish the olive industry as one of the major interests of the ranch, without success. A walnut orchard, irrigated at first by tank wagon, was also set out, and more than 11,000 eucalyptus or "gum trees" were planted for both wood and windbreaks; a few orange trees were also set out, but used only for home consumption.

On August 1, 1889, after several attempts, Orange County broke off from Los Angeles County. In December that year, *"the heavens broke loose"* as the *Santa Ana Weekly Blade* exclaimed, and continual rain caused serious floods in many parts of southern California. The Los Angeles, San Gabriel and Santa Ana rivers went on a wild rampage. Bridges, railroad tracks, houses and farmlands were washed away, according to Cleland.

The Trustees continued their efforts to sell the ranch, but negotiations dragged on and time ran out. In 1893, my grandfather James Irvine II came into full possession of the property. He retained complete control and direction over the ranch until his death, well over half a century later, on August 24, 1947.

On June 4, 1894, James Irvine II incorporated his holdings as the Irvine Company, under the laws of the State of West Virginia. Eventually, my grandfather would transform the Irvine Ranch into one of the great agricultural empires in the world. But this is another story. ॐ

William Wendt, Laguna Hills, *1928, oil on canvas, 25 x 30 in., Private Collection, courtesy of The Irvine Museum*

John Gamble, Joyous Spring, *oil on canvas, 26 x 20 in.,*
Private Collection, courtesy of The Irvine Museum

TIMELINE OF CALIFORNIA & WORLD EVENTS

BY *James Irvine Swinden*

CALIFORNIA EVENTS	YEAR	WORLD EVENTS
Native Americans live and prosper for more than 14,000 years along the west coast of North America in what is now California.	1453	Mehmed II of the Ottoman Empire captures Constantinople, destroying what remains of the Byzantine Empire, and effectively curtails European trade with the Orient. The Hundred Years' War between England and France ends with the English being expelled from most of France.
	1455	The War of the Roses begins in England between the Royal Houses of York and Lancaster. The Gutenberg Bible is printed in Germany using the new invention of movable type.
	1469	Ferdinand and Isabella marry, uniting their Spanish Kingdoms of Aragon and Castile.
	1483	Dominican Monk Tomás de Torquemada becomes Grand Inquisitor of the Spanish Inquisition. Jews and Muslims in particular suffer under his cruelty.
	1485	The War of the Roses ends and Henry VII begins the Tudor Dynasty as King of England.
Chinese and Japanese ships had been visiting the west coast of North America for about 1,500 years in search of seals, otters and abalone.	1492	Italian master mariner Christopher Columbus, with the backing of Ferdinand and Isabella I of Spain, makes the first of several voyages to the Americas.
	1499	Portuguese navigator Vasco da Gama returns from India with a rich cargo of spices after becoming the first European to sail around the tip of Africa. This begins the Portuguese dominance of trade in India.

1502   Montezuma II becomes Emperor of the Aztec Empire.

1503   Canterbury Cathedral in England is completed after 436 years of work.

Leonardo da Vinci paints the *Mona Lisa*.

1510

Portuguese author Garcí Ordoñez de Montalvo writes *Las Sergas de Esplandian* describing a mythical island called "California," of which the Spanish explorers believed Baja California to be the southern tip.

C. 1510   Spanish explorer Juan de Grijalva is introduced to tobacco, which becomes one of the most valuable exports from North America.

1512   Michelangelo Buonarroti completes the painting of the Sistine Chapel, the largest painting in the world at the time.

1513   In search of the Fountain of Youth, Spanish explorer Juan Ponce de León lands on the east coast of Florida at what is now St. Augustine. Arriving on Easter Sunday, he names Florida after Pascua Florida, the Spanish name for Easter Sunday.

Spanish explorer Vasco Núñez de Balboa leads an expedition across the Isthmus of Panama and discovers the Pacific Ocean, which he names "Mar del Sur," or South Sea.

1517   The Protestant Reformation is born when German monk Martin Luther nails his 95 Theses to the door of Wittenburg Cathedral. His criticism of the Roman Catholic Church ultimately fractures the Christian World.

1519   Conquistador Hernando Cortez conquers the Aztec Empire.

Portuguese navigator Ferdinand Magellan leads the first expedition to circumnavigate the globe. Magellan is killed by natives in the Philippines, but his ship continues on and proves that the earth is round.

	1521	San Juan, Puerto Rico founded by Spanish Conquistadors.
	C. 1530	The potato is discovered by Spanish Conquistador Jiménez de Quesada while exploring the Andes.
Conquistador Hernando Cortez sends the first expedition into the Gulf of California in search of pink pearls, but it fails as the Spaniards are attacked and massacred by natives.	1532	Italian writer Niccolo Machiavelli publishes *The Prince*, a study in ruthless political tactics.
	1533	Spanish Conquistador Francisco Pizarro executes the Inca Emperor Atahualpa and plunders Cuzco, thus completing the conquest of Peru.
Spanish explorer Francisco de Ulloa attempts to find the Strait of Anián, the mythical "Northwest Passage," by sailing north into the Gulf of California.	1539	The first printing press in the New World is set up in Mexico City by Spanish printer Juan Pablos.
Portuguese sailor and adventurer Juan Rodríguez Cabrillo leads a Spanish expedition along the west coast of North America and discovers San Diego Bay.	1542	
	1543	The Inquisition under Pope Paul III brings heretics to trial and begins burning them at the stake in an attempt to stem Protestantism.
		Polish astronomer Nicolaus Copernicus publishes his theory of a sun-centered solar system.
	1547	Ivan the Terrible is crowned Czar of Russia and opens trade with England.
	1558	Elizabeth I becomes Queen of England and The Elizabethan Age begins.
	1565	Spanish explorer Pedro Menéndez de Avilés establishes the settlement of St. Augustine, the oldest continuously occupied European city in North America.
Manila galleons begin bringing Chinese goods from the Philippines to Mexico, where they are then sent to Europe and sold at a tremendous profit.	C. 1565	
Sir Francis Drake cruises the Pacific Ocean in search of Spanish galleons and lands a little north of San Francisco, claiming the territory for England.	1579	

	c. 1580 Philip II of Spain sends the first black slaves to St. Augustine when the Spanish fail to develop a work-force from Native Americans and white immigrants.
	1582 Pope Gregory XIII adopts the new Gregorian Calendar in place of the old Julian Calendar, which had become inaccurate.
English captain Thomas Cavendish captures the Manila galleon *Santa Ana* off Cabo San Lucas.	**1587**
	1588 The Spanish Armada is defeated by England, beginning the long decline of Spanish power in Europe.
	1592 William Shakespeare first appears in London as a playwright.
During the second half of the 16th century, Dutch pirates begin preying upon the Manila galleons off the coast of California.	**1598** Henry IV, King of France, issues the Edict of Nantes at the end of the Wars of the Religions, allowing the Huguenots to practice Protestantism.
	1600 Zacharias Janssen of Denmark invents the compound microscope.
	The British East India Company is chartered and acquires extremely favorable trading rights in India.
	c. 1600 The Black Death, or Bubonic Plague, kills more than 33,000 people in London.
In search of a safe harbor in California to protect the Manila galleons, Spanish adventurer Sebastián Vizcaíno discovers Monterey Bay.	**1602** The Dutch East India Company is formed to counter the closing of the Oriental spice market by the Portuguese.
	1605 Spanish novelist Miguel de Saavedra Cervantes pens *Don Quixote de la Mancha*.
	1607 Jamestown becomes the first permanent English settlement in America.
	1609 Galileo Galilei constructs the first astronomical telescope.
	1611 The King James version of the Bible is first published in England.

1613	Czar Mikhail Romanov is crowned in Russia, beginning the 300-year Romanov Dynasty.
1619	The first African slaves are brought to Virginia.
1620	The Pilgrims land in Plymouth, Massachusetts.
1624	Dutch colonists purchase Manhattan Island for $24 worth of trinkets.
1637	French philosopher René Descartes, recognized by many as the father of modern philosophy, publishes *Discourse on Method*.
1642	The English Civil War begins. Lord Protector Oliver Cromwell ultimately prevails and executes Charles I, thus bringing to an end a monarch's claim to "rule by divine right." Dutch artist Rembrandt van Rijn paints *The Night Watch*.
1643	Louis XIV of France is crowned and reigns as the "Sun King" for 72 years.
1644	The Ch'ing Dynasty begins and rules as the last Chinese monarchy until 1912.
1648	The Taj Mahal is completed by Mughal emperor Shah Jahan.
1664	French playwright Jean-Baptiste Poquelin Molière writes one of his most famous satires, *Le Tartuffe*. English mathematician Sir Isaac Newton discovers the Law of Gravity.
1680	Italian Antonio Stradivari opens his own shop and begins making his famous violins.
1682	French explorer Robert Cavelier Sieur de La Salle claims the Mississippi River Valley for France and names it Louisiana.

Italian Jesuit Father Eusebio Francisco Kino attempts to establish the first mission in Baja California at La Paz, but fails due to lack of water in the region.

The first successful mission is founded in Baja California by Italian Jesuit Father Juan María Salvatierra at Loreto. The Jesuits go on to establish 23 additional missions in Baja California from 1697 to 1767.

1683   The Chinese capture Taiwan from the Dutch.

1694   The Bank of England is founded and later helps the country's financial stability by issuing the first English banknotes.

1697

1700   The Great Northern War begins with Russia, Poland, Denmark and England allied against the Swedish Empire.

1701   The War of the Spanish Succession begins when France and Spain unite against England, Holland and the Holy Roman Emperor.

English agriculturist Jethro Tull invents a mechanical seed-planting drill that revolutionizes farming.

1707   Mount Fujiyama erupts for the last time in Japan.

C. 1710   China outlaws Christianity.

Physicist Daniel Gabriel Fahrenheit invents the mercury thermometer.

1712   Twelve black slaves are executed in New York after rebelling and killing six whites.

A Nantucket fisherman captures a sperm whale, initiating the whaling industry in North America.

1715   The Jacobites rise up in Scotland to restore James Stuart to the English throne, but are defeated the following year.

1716   Shogun Yoshimune builds the first irrigation projects and allows Western books to be brought into Japan.

1718   French-Canadian explorer Jean-Baptiste Sieur de Bienville establishes the City of New Orleans.

Edward Teach, also known as Blackbeard the Pirate, is hunted down and killed in North Carolina.

1719   English author Daniel Defoe writes *The Life and Strange Surprising Adventures of Robinson Crusoe.*

1721   The Great Northern War ends in victory for Russia. St. Petersburg is built by Peter the Great as Russia's new capital and "Window on the West."

Irishman Jonathan Swift writes *Gulliver's Travels*, a biting satire of England's political system.

1727   German chemist J. H. Schulze discovers that silver salts will darken when exposed to light, thus laying the foundation of photography.

1729   Diamonds are discovered in Tejuco, Brazil, causing an invasion of prospectors.

C. 1730   English Lord Charles Townshend develops the system of rotating crops, thereby greatly increasing the agricultural productivity of farmlands.

Nearly three million people starve to death in Japan due to famine.

1731   The first circulating library is founded by Benjamin Franklin in Philadelphia.

1733   French philosopher and author François-Marie Arouet de Voltaire publishes his *Letters Concerning the English Nation*, exalting English philosophy and science that will characterize French Enlightenment.

1739   English clockmaker John Harrison perfects the chronometer, which allows navigators at sea to calculate longitude accurately for the first time.

1740   Austrian Archduchess Maria Theresa lays claim to the Hapsburg lands and precipitates the War of the Austrian Succession, which ultimately involves almost every major European country.

c. 1740	English composer George Frederic Handel composes the hymn "Joy To The World."
1742	Swedish astronomer Anders Celsius invents a new temperature scale that establishes 0° as the freezing point and 100° as the boiling point of water.
1750	The Industrial Revolution begins in Britain.
1751	While flying a kite in a thunderstorm, Benjamin Franklin discovers the principles of electricity and lightning. French encyclopedist Denis Diderot publishes his *Encyclopédie*.
1753	King Alaungapaya of Burma makes Rangoon his capital.
1756	The Seven Years' War begins with France, Austria, Russia, Saxony, Sweden and Spain on one side, and England, Prussia and Hanover on the other. Eventually the conflict spreads beyond Europe, with battles being fought in North America and India. Frederick the Great of Prussia emerges as a brilliant military leader and establishes Prussia as a significant European power.
1759	The English under General James Wolfe capture Quebec City and force the French out of Canada. Irish brewer Arthur Guinness begins making beer in Dublin.
c. 1760	The Great Famine of Bengal claims more than ten million lives.
1763	The Seven Years' War ends with the signing of the Treaty of Paris. France loses most of its colonial territories and Britain ranks supreme as a colonial and maritime power.

1765 Left with an enormous national debt after the Seven Years' War, the British Parliament passes the Stamp Act to help pay for maintaining British troops in the American colonies.

British jurist Sir William Blackstone begins publishing his *Commentaries on the Laws of England*, which has a significant impact on legal thought both in Britain and America.

King Carlos III of Spain orders that all Jesuits in New Spain and the Philippine Islands be arrested and expelled. Control of the missions in Baja California is then assumed by the Franciscan Order.

1767 English astronomers Charles Mason and Jeremiah Dixon survey the boundary between Pennsylvania and Maryland. Known as the Mason-Dixon Line, it is used before the American Civil War to designate the boundary between "slave" and "free" states.

Franciscan Father Junípero Serra and Baja California Governor Gaspar de Portolá are selected to establish a series of missions and presidios to protect Spanish interests in California. An expedition is mounted and the first California mission is founded in San Diego.

1769 Scottish inventor James Watt develops the first steam engine.

Monterey is founded with the dedication of the new Mission by Father Junípero Serra and establishment of the Presidio by Governor Gaspar de Portolá. In all 21 missions would be built along El Camino Real.

1770 British soldiers fire on a crowd in Boston, killing five people. American patriotic leaders quickly label this event the Boston Massacre to gain support for their cause.

1773 English explorer Captain James Cook is the first to cross the Antarctic Circle. Later he explores the coasts of Australia, New Zealand and the Hawaiian Islands.

Doctor Samuel Johnson completes *A Dictionary of the English Language*.

Antonio Bucarelli, Viceroy of New Spain, orders a series of coastal expeditions to determine if Russia or Britain had established any permanent settlements in California, however none were found.

1774

Spanish explorer Juan Bautista de Anza travels 700 miles from Tubac, Arizona, to Mission San Gabriel, opening an inland route that briefly allows Spain to establish a reliable supply line to Alta California.

In retaliation for abuses by Spanish soldiers, the Indians of San Diego rebel and burn the Mission to the ground.

Father Junípero Serra dedicates the Mission San Juan Capistrano.

Spanish explorer Juan Bautista de Anza leads the first group of Spanish colonists to Alta California.

The Pueblo de Nuestra Señora la Reina de Los Ángeles de Porciúncula, now called Los Angeles, is founded.

Yuma Indians attack Spanish settlements and garrisons near the Colorado River, effectively closing the Juan Bautista de Anza Trail for many years and forcing the Spanish to once again supply California by sea.

King Charles III of Spain confers the first royal land permits, which ultimately become the great ranchos of California.

French scientist Comte de la Pérouse visits Monterey while on a scientific expedition.

1775 The American Revolutionary War begins with the "shot heard round the world" when British troops and Colonial militia fire upon one another at the Battles of Lexington and Concord.

1776 The Declaration of Independence is signed by members of the Continental Congress in Philadelphia, declaring the 13 colonies to be free and independent states.

C. 1780 *The Empress of Canton* becomes the first American ship to be received in China, thus initiating trade between the two countries.

French chemist and physicist Antoine-Laurent Lavoisier writes the first chemistry textbook, *Elements of Chemistry*.

1781 The American Revolution ends with the surrender of British General Charles Cornwallis at Yorktown, Virginia.

1782 Austrian composer Wolfgang Amadeus Mozart creates his classic opera *The Marriage of Figaro*.

1784

1786

1788 The United States Constitution is ratified and becomes the fundamental law of the nation.

The first convicts arrive in England's penal colony at Botany Bay, now known as Sydney, Australia.

1789 The French Revolution begins when a Parisian mob of peasants storms the Bastille prison.

C. 1790 Jacob Schweppe establishes the first carbonated beverage company in Geneva, Switzerland.

1792	Denmark abolishes the trading of slaves.
1793	American inventor Eli Whitney invents the cotton gin, which revolutionizes the cotton industry in the southern United States.

	Louis xvi of France is guillotined in the Place de la Concorde.
1795	The British Royal Navy orders that all its vessels carry a lime juice ration after Scottish physician James Lind discovers that fresh citrus fruits will cure scurvy.
1796	English physician Edward Jenner discovers that cowpox can be used as a vaccine against smallpox, thus laying the foundation for the science of modern immunology.
	Scottish poet Robert Burns writes "Auld Lang Syne."
	Bavarian printer Aloys Senefelder invents lithography in Munich.

1799	French troops under Napoléon i discover the Rosetta Stone, which ultimately leads to the deciphering of Egyptian hieroglyphics.
1800	The electric battery is invented by Italian physicist Alessandro Volta.
	America's John Chapman begins spreading apple seeds throughout the Midwest and becomes known as Johnny Appleseed.
	The Royal College of Surgeons is established in Britain.
1803	The Louisiana Territory is purchased from Napoléon i of France by President Thomas Jefferson for $15 million, effectively doubling the size of the United States.
	American pioneers Meriwether Lewis and William Clark set out on their expedition of the newly acquired Louisiana Territory.

Reconstructed
Bastion or Block House
built in 1811 by Russians.
Fort Ross, Calif.

In search of provisions for the Russian fur trappers in Alaska, Nikolai Petrovich Rezanov sails into San Francisco harbor, and contrary to official Spanish policy, is supplied with food.

Ivan Kuskov of the Russian-American Fur Company erects a Russian settlement on Bodega Bay north of San Francisco in order to secure a reliable source of food for Russian trappers in Alaska.

The Russians build Fort Rossiya, now known as Fort Ross, north of Bodega Bay, to aid in the transport of supplies to Alaska.

An earthquake strikes Mission San Juan Capistrano, collapsing the bell tower into the main part of the church, destroying the largest and grandest church in California.

1804	Napoléon 1 crowns himself Emperor of France. Over the next eight years he will go on to lead France through her greatest period of military conquest.
	French chef Nicolas Appert discovers that food can be preserved in hermetically sealed containers.
1805	English naval hero Horatio Nelson dies at the climax of his greatest victory, when he defeats the combined French and Spanish fleets at the Battle of Trafalgar.
1806	English poet Lord Byron privately publishes *Fugitive Pieces,* but the Church of England immediately suppresses the poems on moral grounds.
	American David Melville uses coal gas for the first time for lighting in Newport, Rhode Island.
1807	Egyptian governor Muhammad Ali defeats a British expeditionary force and establishes himself ruler of Egypt.
1809	
1810	Revolutionist Simón Bolívar takes the first steps in the liberation of South America from Spanish rule by joining the Venezuelan Revolution.
1812	The War of 1812, between the United States and Britain, is sparked by the impressment of American sailors.
	Swiss Orientalist John Lewis Burckhardt rediscovers the ancient city of Petra, in what is now Jordan.
1813	British novelist Jane Austen pens *Pride and Prejudice.*
1814	American lawyer and author Francis Scott Key writes "The Star-Spangled Banner" while watching Fort McHenry being bombarded by British ships during the War of 1812.

French pirate Hippolyte de Bouchard conducts a series of raids along the California coast from Monterey to San Juan Capistrano.

Mexico gains independence from Spain, and California becomes part of the Republic of Mexico.

Mexican authorities open California's ports to foreign vessels and a brisk trade develops for hides, tallow and horn.

1815	British, Dutch and German troops defeat Napoléon I of France at the Battle of Waterloo, thus bringing to an end the Napoleonic Wars.
	The Indonesian volcano Tambora erupts, killing more than 10,000 people. Another 80,000 will die due to disease and famine as a result of the volcanic ash.
1816	French physician R.-T. Laënnec invents the stethoscope, which greatly enhances the observations of cardiac and pulmonary functions.
1817	Parkinson's disease is first described by English physician James Parkinson.
1818	*Frankenstein* is published by English author Mary Shelley.
	Chile declares its independence from Spanish rule after José San Martin defeats the Spanish at Chacabuco.
1819	Florida is ceded to the United States by Spain.
	Chocolate is first produced commercially in Vevy, Switzerland.
	The steamship *Savannah* crosses the Atlantic Ocean in 24 days, ushering in a new mode of transportation.
1820	"Rip Van Winkle" is published by American humorist Washington Irving.
	The fundamentals of electric currents are discovered by French physicist André-Marie Ampère.
1821	British chemist-physicist Michael Faraday invents the electric motor.
1822	

Mountain man Jedediah Strong Smith leads the first group of fur trappers from Bear River Valley, Utah, across the Rocky Mountains and into California, arriving at Mission San Gabriel.

California Governor José Maria de Echeandía passes the Declaration of Emancipation making all Indians Mexican citizens and begins the secularization of the California missions.

Mexico secularizes all remaining mission property in California.

1823 The Monroe Doctrine is presented by President James Monroe and proclaims that the United States will not tolerate further colonization of the American Continents by any European powers.

1824 Ludwig van Beethoven, who has become totally deaf, performs his Symphony No. 9 in Vienna for the first time.

1825 The Erie Canal is completed between Albany and Buffalo, New York and brings tremendous growth to the cities along its route and the development of the lands around the Great Lakes.

The New York Stock Exchange opens.

1826 The first permanent photograph is produced by French scientist J.-N. Niepce.

1829 The Greek War of Independence ends and Greece is finally free after 400 years of Ottoman rule.

South America erupts in revolution and Bolivia, Peru and Venezuela declare their independence from Spain.

The game of poker is invented by sailors in New Orleans.

1831 Nat Turner leads a bloody slave uprising in Virginia, during which approximately 70 whites and 100 blacks are killed before it is suppressed.

French author Victor Hugo writes his epic romantic novel *The Hunchback of Notre Dame.*

1833 English mathematician Charles Babbage puts forth the idea of an "analytical engine," which ultimately leads to the development of the calculator.

Franco-Polish composer Frédéric Chopin composes his Piano Concerto in E Minor, which becomes one of the greatest musical pieces of the Romantic movement.

Californio Juan Bautista Alvarado successfully leads a revolt to make California briefly an independent state. Even though California is still technically part of Mexico, the revolt greatly reduces Mexican authority over the Californios.

American William Wolfskill plants the first commercial orange grove in Alta California, thus pioneering California's fruit-growing industry.

1834 The system of raised point writing is invented by French teacher Louis Braille.

1835 Danish writer Hans Christian Andersen publishes his *Fairy Tales*.

1836 President Santa Anna of Mexico leads an army to put down a rebellion in Texas and kills all the defenders of a converted mission fort called the Alamo. Subsequently, Texas gains its independence when Sam Houston wins the Battle of San Jacinto.

1837 The rules of probability are established by French mathematician Siméon-Denis Poisson.

The Morse Code is invented by Alfred Lewis Vail, who is American inventor Samuel Morse's assistant.

1839 The Opium War erupts between China and Britain when a Chinese official tries to stop the importation of opium into Canton.

Vulcanized rubber is invented by Philadelphia hardware merchant Charles Goodyear.

1840 American sailor and author Richard Henry Dana publishes *Two Years Before the Mast*, exposing the harsh conditions under which sailors worked.

The afternoon ritual of serving tea is introduced in Britain by the Duchess of Bedford.

1841

1842 Hong Kong is ceded to Britain at the conclusion of the Opium War and will not be returned to China until 1997.

1843 "A Christmas Carol" is penned by English author Charles Dickens.

French artist and ornithologist John James Audubon begins sketching wild animals and birds and becomes one of the most famous naturalist painters.

American immigrant John Augustus Sutter completes Sutter's Fort at the strategic convergence of the American and Sacramento rivers. Sutter's Fort ultimately becomes an important frontier outpost controlling the immigration routes from both Oregon and Nevada.

American Lt. John C. Frémont, guided by frontiersman Christopher "Kit" Carson, leads a "survey expedition" to California and becomes a central figure in the American conquest of California.

American William B. Ide initiates the Bear Flag Revolt in Sonoma by declaring a republican form of government and raising the California Bear Flag, on which California ultimately bases its state flag.

Commodore John D. Sloat lands American marines and sailors at Monterey, hoists the American flag and proclaims California to be a portion of the United States. Over the next six months, American sailors and soldiers fight the Californios in a series of engagements up and down the state.

The Donner Party of American immigrants becomes trapped in the deep snows of the Sierra Nevada Mountains and only 45 out of the original 87 members of the party survive the ordeal.

California becomes an American possession with the end of the Mexican-American War.

American James W. Marshall discovers gold while constructing a sawmill northeast of Sutter's Fort. This

1844 American Brigham Young becomes the head of the Mormon Church after prophet Joseph Smith is lynched. Young leads the great migration west to Utah, where he directs the settlement of Salt Lake City.

French author Alexandre Dumas writes his romantic adventure story *The Three Musketeers*.

1845 American writer and poet Edgar Allan Poe pens his famous poem "The Raven".

Famine strikes throughout Europe when the potato crop fails. The Irish are particularly hard hit and begin to leave their homeland for America, Australia and Canada.

1846 The Mexican-American War begins when the United States admits Texas to the Union and American troops are ordered to the Rio Grande.

The rules of baseball are first set down by New York surveyor Alexander Cartwright.

1847 German social philosopher and revolutionary Karl Marx, who decries religion as "the opium of the people," publishes *The Communist Manifesto* with Friedrich Engels.

1848 American feminists Elizabeth Stanton and Lucretia Mott open the first Women's Rights Convention in the United States in Seneca Falls, New York.

King Louis Philippe is forced from the throne of

begins the California Gold Rush, which not only brings great prosperity to the state, but also results in a tremendous population explosion.

American William Henry Aspinwall founds the Pacific Mail Steamship Company, which carries mail to Oregon by way of Panama and California.

The Territorial Convention opens in Monterey and results in the adoption of the California State Constitution.

California petitions and becomes the 31st state in the Union.

The 1st Vigilance Committee in San Francisco is established to maintain public order, but is itself a law unto its own. Other towns also create local vigilance committees, which were little more than organized mobs.

The Land Commission, authorized by the United States Congress, begins hearing cases to establish the rightful owners of the more than 800 land grants made during the Spanish and Mexican periods.

Mexican Joaquin Murieta, the celebrated California bandit, is tracked down and killed after eluding authorities for five years.

France when Parisian workers and students seize the city during the February Revolution. The Third Republic is declared and Louis-Napoléon Bonaparte becomes President of France.

1849 The Sikhs are defeated by British troops, and Britain expands its control of India to include the Punjab.

As news spreads of the discovery of gold, people from Europe and the Orient make their way to California to participate in the Gold Rush.

1850 Chinese mystic Hung Hsiu-Ch'üan leads the Taiping Rebellion against the Ch'ing Dynasty. The rebellion, which will last for 15 years, ultimately leads to intervention by Western armies.

The sewing machine is patented by American inventor I. M. Singer, and Bavarian-American Levi Strauss introduces blue jeans to the American public.

1851 *Uncle Tom's Cabin*, written by American author Harriet Beecher Stowe, is a huge success as the anti-slavery movement grows in the North.

American gun maker Samuel Colt introduces his mass-produced revolver, which is an immediate success with British military leaders.

1852 An automatic safety device is developed by American inventor Elisha Gray to prevent the fall of hoisting machinery. This invention ultimately leads to the development of the elevator.

1853 Japan reluctantly agrees to enter into a trading relationship with the United States after Commodore Matthew Perry enters Edo Bay with his Pacific Squadron.

English scientist George Cayley makes the first glider flight and becomes known as the founder of aerodynamics.

	1854 The Crimean War commences when Russia seeks to claim territory from Turkey. Britain and France come to Turkey's aid, and ultimately Russia will be forced to withdraw.

1854   The Crimean War commences when Russia seeks to claim territory from Turkey. Britain and France come to Turkey's aid, and ultimately Russia will be forced to withdraw.

English nurse Florence Nightingale ministers to the wounded in the Crimean War by setting up a barracks hospital.

American author Henry David Thoreau publishes his most famous work, *Walden, or Life in the Woods.*

1855   Scottish missionary David Livingstone names Victoria Falls on the Zambezi River in honor of Queen Victoria.

1856   Soldiers returning from the Crimean War introduce cigarettes to Europe.

Californio Juan Flores leads a gang of escaped convicts called the "Manillas" on a ruthless and terrifying raid of San Juan Capistrano. The entire gang is eventually captured and hung.

1857   The British are taken by surprise when the Sepoy Mutiny of Indian soldiers erupts in Bengal. The revolt is put down the following year and the British Crown takes control of India from the East India Company.

1858   Berlin doctor Rudolf Virchow develops the idea that "the cell is the basic unit of all life."

French schoolgirl Bernadette has visions of the Virgin Mary at Lourdes, France.

The Comstock Lode is discovered in Washoe, Nevada and for a short time, miners leave California to mine silver across the state line.

1859   *On the Origin of Species by Means of Natural Selection, or the Preservation of Favored Species in the Struggle for Life* is published by English naturalist Charles Darwin.

American abolitionist John Brown leads a raid on the Federal Arsenal at Harper's Ferry, Virginia. He is quickly captured by United States troops under the command of Colonel Robert E. Lee, convicted of treason and hung.

1860   The Pony Express starts mail service between Missouri and California, but will become obsolete with the completion of the transcontinental telegraph the following year.

1861	Confederate forces fire on Fort Sumter in Charleston Harbor, South Carolina, thus beginning the American Civil War.

Russian serfs are emancipated by Czar Alexander II.

1862	After General Robert E. Lee is defeated at the Battle of Antietam, President Abraham Lincoln issues the Emancipation Proclamation declaring free all slaves held in the South.

1863	General George Gordon Meade defeats the Army of Northern Virginia at the Battle of Gettysburg, which turns out to be the high watermark of the Confederacy.

The Mexican throne is offered to Austrian Archduke Maximilian after French forces occupy Mexico City.

Many of the large landowners become bankrupt due to the Great Drought of 1863–1864. The cattle business is ruined and ranchers turn to raising sheep instead.

1864	The Geneva Conventions are adopted by 26 nations, specifying the treatment of prisoners of war, military wounded and civilians trapped in war zones.

President Abraham Lincoln authorizes an order returning several of the California missions to the Catholic Church.

1865	The American Civil War comes to an end when General Robert E. Lee surrenders to General Ulysses Grant at Appomattox, Virginia. The five-year conflict claims the lives of over 600,000 American soldiers on both sides. President Abraham Lincoln is assassinated shortly afterward.

The natural laws of heredity and genetics are discovered by Austrian botanist and Augustinian monk Gregor Johann Mendel.

Alice's Adventures in Wonderland is penned by English writer and mathematician Lewis Carroll.

1866	Prussian prime minister Otto von Bismarck orchestrates the Austro-Prussian War in his attempt to create a single German nation.

Dynamite is invented by Swedish engineer Alfred Nobel. The immense fortune derived from his discovery will later fund the Nobel Peace Prize.

War and Peace is written by Russian author Leo Tolstoy.

1867 The United States purchases Alaska from Russian Czar Alexander ii.

Southern California experiences its first real estate boom.

1868 American printer and journalist Christopher Sholes is issued a patent for the typewriter.

A major earthquake occurs in San Francisco, causing enormous damage and a great many deaths. The city, however, remains resilient and continues its unprecedented growth.

The University of California formally opens in Oakland with 38 students. In 1873 it will move to Berkeley, which will become the largest of the system's nine campuses.

1869 France completes the Suez Canal, which allows ships to pass to and from the Mediterranean Sea and the Indian Ocean.

The Central Pacific and Union Pacific Railroads meet at Promontory Point, Utah, completing the Transcontinental Railroad.

An anti-Chinese riot breaks out in Los Angeles leaving 19 Chinese dead and dozens hurt.

1871 The Franco-Prussian War concludes with France ceding Alsace and part of Lorraine to a united German Empire under Prussia's Emperor Wilhelm i.

"The Greatest Show on Earth" is created by American showman P. T. Barnum and opens in Brooklyn, New York.

The Chicago Fire destroys most of the inner city.

The Modoc War erupts in Northern California when the Modoc Indians resist being returned to their reservation in Oregon. After a costly campaign by the U.S. Army, the Modoc leaders are finally captured and executed.

1873 Civil war continues in Spain as supporters of the monarchy battle those of the First Spanish Republic.

San Francisco's famous cable streetcars are put into operation to deal with the city's hilly streets.

1874 The first show of French Impressionists is held in Paris by the artists themselves when their works are rejected by the art establishment.

The historic drought of 1876–1877 literally burns up the ranges and nearly destroys the sheep industry of Southern California.

1875   The Suez Canal comes under British control through the efforts of British Prime Minister Benjamin Disraeli.

1876   The telephone is invented by Scottish-American scientist and inventor Alexander Graham Bell.

United States Army officer Lt. Col. George Armstrong Custer is defeated and his entire command killed by Native American Indians at the Battle of the Little Bighorn.

The Philadelphia Centennial Exhibition, which is held to celebrate the nation's centennial and reunification after the Civil War, attracts millions of visitors from all over the world.

Maurice Braun, Untitled, San Diego Back Bay,
oil on canvas, 25 x 30 in., Private Collection,
courtesy of The Irvine Museum

BIBLIOGRAPHY

American President Lines. "APL Narrative History and Timeline." http://www.apl.com/history/timeline/timeline.htm

Astrov, Margot, ed. *American Indian Prose and Poetry*. New York: Capricorn Books, 1962.

Bancroft, Hubert H. *History of California*. Vol. 2–5. San Francisco: The History Company, 1884-90.

Bean, Walton. *California, An Interpretive History*. New York: McGraw-Hill Book Co., 1973.

Bear Flag Sesquicentennial Home Page. "Bear Flags of Sonoma." http://www.vom.com/bearflag/sobearfl.htm

Black Culture Day Committee, California Department of Parks. "Pio Pico State Historic Park." http://www.whittierbiz.com/info/pico.htm

Blomquist, William A. *Dividing the Waters: Governing Groundwater in Southern California*. San Francisco: ICS Press in association with The Center for Self Governance, 1992.

Breschini, Gary S. "Coastal Navigation and Exploration of the Monterey Bay Area." Monterey County Historical Society. http://users.dedot.com/mchs/coastalnav.html

California State Parks. "Pio Pico State Historic Park." http://www.calparks.ca.gov/south/angeles/ppshp551.htm

Campbell, Leon G. "The First Californios: Presidial Society in Spanish California, 1769-1822." In *The Spanish Borderlands*. Edited by Oakah L. Jones. Los Angeles: L.L. Morrison, 1974.

Caughey, John Walton. *California*. New York: Prentice-Hall, 1940.

Channel Islands National Park. "Cabrillo's Ship Model." http://www.nps.gov/chis/cabrillo.htm

Chapman, Charles C. *Charles C. Chapman: The Career of a Creative Californian, 1853-1944*. Edited by Donald H. Pflueger. Los Angeles: Anderson, Ritchie & Simon, 1976.

Chapman, Charles E. *A History of California: The Spanish Period*. New York: Macmillan, 1930.

City of Escondido, Calif. "San Pasqual Battlefield." http://www.escondido.ca.us/visitors/uniquely/battle/index.html

Cleland, Robert Glass. *Pathfinders*. California series. San Francisco: Powell Publishing Co., 1929.

___. *A Letter from a Gold Miner*. San Marino, Calif.: Friends of the Huntington Library, 1944.

___. *El Molino Viejo*. San Marino, Calif.: Ward Ritchie Press, Huntington Library, 1950.

___. *The Cattle on a Thousand Hills: Southern California 1850-1880*. San Marino, Calif.: Huntington Library, 1951.

___. *The Irvine Ranch*. San Marino, Calif.: Huntington Library, 1952.

___. *This Reckless Breed of Men: The Trappers and Fur Traders of the Southwest*. New York: Alfred A. Knopf, 1963.

Cleland, Robert Glass, and Osgood Howell. *March of Industry*. California series. San Francisco: Powell Publishing Co., 1929.

Conroy, William B. "The Llano Estacado in 1541." In *The Spanish Borderlands*. Edited by Oakah L. Jones. Los Angeles: L.L. Morrison, 1974.

Convis, Charles L. "Father Payeras' Diary of a Trip to Fort Ross in 1822." *The Far Westerner, the Quarterly Bulletin of the Stockton Corral of Westerners* 30:2 (April 1989).

Cruz, Lucille Branch. "History of the Santa Ana Mountains." In *Proceedings of the Conference of Orange County History, 1988*. Orange, Calif.: Chapman College, Department of History, 1989.

De Anza, Juan Bautista. "Journal of California Expeditions." In *The American Frontier*. Edited by Robert V. Hine and Edward R. Bingham. Boston: Little, Brown & Co., 1972.

Doti, Lynn Pierson, and Larry Schweikart. *California Bankers, 1848-1993*. Needham Heights, Mass.: Ginn Press, 1995.

Driesbach, Janice T., Harvey L. Jones, and Katherine Church Holland. *Art of the Gold Rush*. Oakland Museum of California, Crocker Art Museum and University of California Press, 1998.

Dumke, Glenn S. *The Boom of the Eighties*. San Marino, Calif.: Huntington Library, 1944.

Eldredge, Zoeth Skinner. "General Mariano G. Vallejo (1808-1890)." Museum of the City of San Francisco. http://www.sfmuseum.org/bio/vallejo.html

Engelhardt, Fr. Zephyrin. *San Juan Capistrano: The Jewel of the Missions*. Los Angeles: The Standard Printing Co., 1922.

___. *Mission San Carlos Borroméo: The Father of the Missions*. Santa Barbara, Calif.: Mission Santa Barbara, 1934.

Englebert, Omer. *The Last of the Conquistadors: Junípero Serra*. Translated from the French by Katherine Woods. New York: Harcourt, Brace & Co., 1956.

Engstrand, Iris W. "Scientists in New Spain: The Eighteenth Century Expeditions." In *The Spanish Borderlands*. Edited by Oakah L. Jones. Los Angeles: L.L. Morrison, 1974.

___. "San Diego: Its Spanish and Indian Heritage." In *The Cross and the Sword*. Edited by Jean Stern. San Diego: Fine Arts Gallery of San Diego, 1976.

Frémont, John Charles. "Reports on Expeditions." In *The American Frontier*. Edited by Robert V. Hine and Edward R. Bingham. Boston: Little, Brown & Co., 1972.

Garza, Roberto. "Pío de Jesús Pico." Pamphlet, *History Alive!* Chautauqua. San Francisco, Los Angeles and San Diego: California Council for the Humanities, The Sesquicentennial Project, n.d.

Gleason, Duncan. *The Islands and Ports of California*. New York: Devin-Adair Co., 1958.

Gould, Stephen. "Orange County Before it was a County." In *Proceedings of the Conference of Orange County History, 1988*. Orange, Calif.: Chapman College, Department of History, 1989.

Gregg, Josiah. "The Santa Fe Trade." In *The American Frontier*. Edited by Robert V. Hine and Edward R. Bingham. Boston: Little, Brown & Co., 1972.

Gudde, Erwin G. *California Place Names: A Geographical Dictionary*. Berkeley and Los Angeles: University of California Press, 1949.

___. *Bigler's Chronicle of the West*. Berkeley and Los Angeles: University of California Press, 1962.

Hallan-Gibson, Pamela. *The Golden Promise: An Illustrated History of Orange County*. Northridge, Calif.: Windsor Publications in association with the Charles W. Bowers Memorial Museum, 1986.

___. *Two Hundred Years in San Juan Capistrano*. Norfolk, Va.: Donning Co., 1990.

___. "Mission San Juan Capistrano." In *Romance of the Bells: The California Missions in Art*. Irvine, Calif.: Irvine Museum, 1995.

Hardwick, Michael R. "Se Fundaron un Pueblo de Españoles" (A Village of Spaniards Was Founded). Hispanic Heritage in the USA. http://coloquio.com/galvez/funderon.html

Hawgood, John A., ed. *First and Last Consul, Thomas Oliver Larkin and the Americanization of California: A Selection of Letters*. Palo Alto, Calif.: Pacific Books, 1970.

Heizer, Robert F., and Albert B. Elasser. *The Natural World of the California Indians*. Berkeley: University of California Press, 1980.

"The History of how California Became a State." http://www.ccnet.com/~laplaza/calhist.htm

Holliday, J.S. *The World Rushed In: The California Gold Rush Experience*. New York: Simon & Schuster, Touchstone, 1981.

___. *Rush for Riches: Gold Fever and the Making of California*. Oakland, Calif.: Oakland Museum of California; Berkeley, Los Angeles and London: University of California, 1999.

Horan, James D., and Paul Sann. *Pictorial History of the Wild West*. New York: Crown Publishers, 1972.

Horgan, Paul. "The Mountain Man." In *The American Frontier*. Edited by Robert V. Hine and Edward R. Bingham. Boston: Little, Brown & Co., 1972.

Humble, Richard, and the Editors of Time-Life Books. *The Explorers.* Alexandria, Va.: Time-Life Books, 1978.

Hutchinson, W.H. *California: Two Centuries of Man, Land, and Growth in the Golden State.* Palo Alto, Calif.: American West Publishing Co., 1971.

Jackson, W. Turrentine. "Wagon Roads West." In *The American Frontier.* Edited by Robert V. Hine and Edward R. Bingham. Boston: Little, Brown & Co., 1972.

Johnson, Paul C. *Pictorial History of California.* New York: Crown Publishers, Bonanza Books, 1970.

Katz, Bob. "Juan Bautista de Anza." *DesertUSA.* http://www.desertusa.com/mag jan98/jan_pap/du_anza.html

Kronzek, Lynn C. *Los Angeles: A Place of Possibilities.* Carlsbad, Calif.: Heritage Media Corp. in association with the Los Angeles Conservancy, 1998.

Latino Heritage Month Web Site. "Joaquin Murieta: California's Chicano Geronimo." http://www.latinoheritage.org/ joaquinrstory.html

Leadabrand, Russ. *A Guidebook to the Sunset Ranges of Southern California.* Los Angeles: Ward Ritchie Press, 1965.

Lee, Ellen K. *Newport Bay: A Pioneer History.* Newport Beach, Calif.: Newport Beach Historical Society, 1976.

Lemonick, Michael D., and Andrea Dorfman. "The Amazing Vikings." *Time,* May 8, 2000, 68–74.

Levy, Jo Ann. *They Saw the Elephant: Women in the California Gold Rush.* Norman, Okla. and London: University of Oklahoma Press, 1992.

Library of Congress. "Cabrilho's Discovery of California." http://lcweb.loc.gov/rr/hispanic/ portam/cabrilho.html

Liebeck, Judy. *Irvine: A History of Innovation and Growth.* Houston: Pioneer Publications, 1990.

Lillard, Richard G. *Eden in Jeopardy: Man's Prodigal Meddling with his Environment, the Southern California Experience.* Westport, Conn.: Greenwood Press, 1966.

Matthews, Miriam. "Los Angeles and its Founders." *Los Angeles Black Tourist Guide.* http://www.afgen.com/founders. html

McCall, Lynne, and Rosalind Perry, comps., *California's Chumash Indians.* San Luis Obispo, Calif.: EZ Nature Books in association with the Santa Barbara Museum of Natural History, 1986.

McCawley, William. *The First Angelinos: The Gabrielino Indians of Los Angeles.* Banning and Novato, Calif.: Malki Museum Press and Ballena Press, 1996.

McIssac, Colin H. *A History of the Santa Barbara Mission, from the Founding, 1786, to the Earthquake, 1925.* Revised by Rev. Augustine Hobrecht. Santa Barbara, Calif.: Schauer Printing Studio, 1926.

McRae, Bennie J., Jr. "Major Generals John C. Fremont and David Hunter versus President Abraham

Lincoln." *Lest We Forget.* http://www.coax.net/people/lwf/fhl_pol.htm

Meacham, Alfred B. "The Tragedy of the Lava Beds." In *The American Frontier*. Edited by Robert V. Hine and Edward R. Bingham. Boston: Little, Brown & Co., 1972.

Miller, Gerald J. "The Missions: A Story of Romance & Exploration in California." In *Romance of the Bells: The California Missions in Art*. Irvine, Calif.: Irvine Museum, 1995.

Moorhead, Max L. "The Soldado de Cuera: Stalwart of the Spanish Borderlands." In *The Spanish Borderlands*. Edited by Oakah L. Jones. Los Angeles: L.L. Morrison, 1974.

Moratto, Michael J. *California Archaeology*. Orlando: Academic Press, 1984.

Museum of the City of San Francisco Web Site. http://www.sfmuseum.org

Neuerburg, Norman. "The California Missions in Art: 1786-1890." In *Romance of the Bells: The California Missions in Art*. Irvine, Calif.: Irvine Museum, 1995.

O'Flaherty, Joseph S. *Those Powerful Years: The South Coast and Los Angeles, 1887–1917*. Hicksville, N.Y.: Exposition Press, 1978.

Pacoima (Calif.) Chamber of Commerce. "History of Pacoima." http://www.pacoima.net/History/history.html

Paddison, Joshua, ed. *A World Transformed: Firsthand Accounts of California Before the Gold Rush*. Berkeley: Heyday Books, 1999.

Palmer, William A. "Juan Forster." *Costa D'Oro Magazine*, Winter 1999.

Panama Railroad Web Site. "History of the Panama Railroad." http://www.trainweb.org/panama/history1.html

Pattie, James Ohio. "A Trapping Expedition." In *The American Frontier*. Edited by Robert V. Hine and Edward R. Bingham. Boston: Little, Brown & Co., 1972.

Petersen, Martin E. "San Diego: The Legend of Saint Didicus." In *The Cross and the Sword*. Edited by Jean Stern. San Diego: Fine Arts Gallery of San Diego, 1976.

Porter, Kenneth. "The American Fur Company." In *The American Frontier*. Edited by Robert V. Hine and Edward R. Bingham. Boston: Little, Brown & Co., 1972.

Pourade, Richard F. *The History of San Diego: The Explorers*. San Diego: Union-Tribune Co., 1960.

___. *The History of San Diego: The Silver Dons*. San Diego: Union-Tribune Co., 1963.

___. "Juan Rodriguez Cabrillo, Discoverer of California." In *The Spanish Borderlands*. Edited by Oakah L. Jones. Los Angeles: L.L. Morrison, 1974.

Priestly, Herbert Ingram. *José de Gálvez, Visitor-General of New Spain (1765–1771)*. 1916. Reprint, Millwood, N.Y.: Kraus Reprint Co., 1974.

Rawls, James J. *Indians of California: The Changing Image*. Norman, Okla. and London: University of Oklahoma Press, 1984.

Rawls, James J., and Walton Bean. *California: An Interpretive History*. New York: McGraw-Hill Book Co., 1993.

Ressler, John Q. "Indian and Spanish Water-Control on New Spain's Northwest Frontier." In *The Spanish Borderlands*. Edited by Oakah L. Jones. Los Angeles: L.L. Morrison, 1974.

Rice, Harvey. *Letters from the Pacific Slope: First Impressions*. New York: D. Appleton and Co., 1870.

Ridge, John Rollin [Yellow Bird]. "Joaquín Murieta." In *The American Frontier*. Edited by Robert V. Hine and Edward R. Bingham. Boston: Little, Brown & Co., 1972.

Robinson, W.W. *Ranchos Become Cities*. Pasadena, Calif.: San Pasqual Press, 1939.

___. *Land in California*. Berkeley, Los Angeles and London: University of California Press, 1979.

Rolle, Andrew. *California: A History*. Wheeling, Ill.: Harlan Davidson, 1998.

Roske, Ralph J. *Everyman's Eden: A History of California*. New York: Macmillan, 1968.

Ross, Alexander. "Fur Hunters of the Far West." In *The American Frontier*. Edited by Robert V. Hine and Edward R. Bingham. Boston: Little, Brown & Co., 1972.

Rush, Philip S. *Historical Sketches of the Californias*. San Diego: Philip S. Rush, 1953.

Saunders, Charles Francis, and Father St. John O'Sullivan. *Capistrano Nights: Tales of a California Mission Town*. New York: Robert M. McBride and Co., 1930.

Schiesl, Martin J. "The Evolution of the Irvine Ranch from Agriculture to Suburbanization." In *Proceedings of the Conference of Orange County History, 1988*. Orange, Calif.: Chapman College, Department of History, 1989.

Schmutz, Richard A. "Jesuit Missionary Methods in Northwestern Mexico." In *The Spanish Borderlands*. Edited by Oakah L. Jones. Los Angeles: L.L. Morrison, 1974.

Scott, Ray. "The Grizzly Bear and Recreation in Early California." *The Far Westerner, the Quarterly Bulletin of the Stockton Corral of Westerners* 10:3 (July 1969).

Shinn, Charles H. "Mining Camps." In *The American Frontier*. Edited by Robert V. Hine and Edward R. Bingham. Boston: Little, Brown & Co., 1972.

Shumway, Burgess McK. *California Ranchos*. San Bernardino, Calif.: Borgo Press, 1988.

Simmons, Marc. "Settlement Patterns and Village Plans in Colonial New Mexico." In *The Spanish Borderlands*. Edited by Oakah L. Jones. Los Angeles: L.L. Morrison, 1974.

Slayton, Robert A., and Leland L. Estes, eds. *Proceedings of the Conference of Orange County History, 1988*. Orange, Calif.: Chapman College, Department of History, 1989.

Sleeper, Jim. *Bears to Briquets: A History of Irvine Park, 1897-1997*. Trabuco Canyon, Calif.: California Classics, 1997.

Smith, Frances Rand. *The Architectural History of the Mission San Carlos Borroméo*. Berkeley: California Historical Survey Commission, 1921.

Smith, Joan Irvine, and Jean Stern. *Reflections of California*. Irvine, Calif.: Irvine Museum, 1994.

Spicer, Edward H. *A Short History of the Indians of the United States*. Malabar, Fla.: Robert E. Krieger Publishing Co., 1983.

Starr, Kevin. *Inventing the Dream: California Through the Progressive Era*. New York and Oxford: Oxford University Press, 1985.

Stern, Jean. "A Brief History of the Spanish Southwest." In *The Cross and the Sword*. Edited by Jean Stern. San Diego: Fine Arts Gallery of San Diego, 1976.

___. "The California Missions in Art: 1890-1930." In *Romance of the Bells: The California Missions in Art*. Irvine, Calif.: Irvine Museum, 1995.

Thacher, John. "Christopher Columbus: On the Indians." In *The American Frontier*. Edited by Robert V. Hine and Edward R. Bingham. Boston: Little, Brown & Co., 1972.

Turner, Geoffrey. *Indians of North America*. New York: Sterling Publishing Co., 1992.

Utley, Robert M. *A Life Wild and Perilous: Mountain Men and the Paths to the Pacific*. New York: Henry Holt and Co., 1997.

Villagrá, Gaspár. "The Oñate Expedition." In *The American Frontier*. Edited by Robert V. Hine and Edward R. Bingham. Boston: Little, Brown & Co., 1972.

Waid, Beverly Henrickson. "The Picos in California." In *Proceedings of the Conference of Orange County History, 1988*. Orange, Calif.: Chapman College, Department of History, 1989.

Walker, Doris I. *Dana Point Harbor/Capistrano Bay: Home Port for Romance*. Dana Point, Calif.: To-The-Point Press, 1995.

Warner, Barbara R. *The Men of the Bear Flag Revolt and their Heritage*. Sonoma, Calif.: Arthur A. Clark Co. in association with the Sonoma Valley Historical Society, 1996.

Weaver, John D. *El Pueblo Grande: A Non-Fiction Book About Los Angeles*. Los Angeles: Ward Ritchie Press, 1973.

Wilson's Creek National Battlefield. "The Battle of Wilson's Creek." http://www.nps.gov/wicr/batlhist.html

Index

California, State of
    admission of, 283
    Constitution signed, 282
    Constitutional Convention of, 276–77, 281-82
    eastern boundary decided, 281
    Great Seal of, 282
Captain Jack (Chief Kientepoos), 292
Carrillo, José Antonio, 180, 197, 201, 202, 276
    exile by Governor Victoria, 178
Carson, Christopher "Kit", 186, 191, 213, 230, 232
Castillo, Edward D., 35
Castro, José, 200, 202, 215–19, 228, 292
    named military commandant, 204
    revolt against Governor Micheltorena, 204
cattle industry, 139, 140. *See also* rancho era
    effect of Great Drought on, 180, 194, 208, 299, 321
Cavendish, Thomas, 59, 60
Chagres River, in Panama, 259–260
Channel Islands, 27, 54, 78, 85
Chapman, Charles Edward, 20
Chief Kientepoos. *See* Captain Jack
cholera, 262, 264
Cíbola, legend of, 49, 50–51, 54
citrus industry in California, 194
Clay, Henry, 282
Cleland, Robert Glass
    account of *Forster vs. Pico*, 209
    description of 1889 flood, 325
    description of California's Golden Age, 139
    description of horse classifications, 148
    description of Land Commission, 289
    description of rancho life, 140, 155, 164

description of Rancho San Juan, 135
description of rodéo, 142
description of Santa Ana Valley, 324
description of Secularization Act of 1833, 133
Cody, William Frederick (pseud. Buffalo Bill), 255
Colonization Act of 1824, 134
Columbus, Christopher, 43–44
Compromise of 1850, 282
Conception, Point, 19, 61, 85
Coronado, Francisco Vasquez de, 50–51, 53–54
Cortez, Hernando, 48–51, 52
    search for pearls in California, 49
Costansó, Miguel, 26, 27, 77, 79
    account of Indian hunting and fishing methods, 26
Crespí, Juan, 74, 78, 82–85, 93, 98

D

Dana, Richard Henry, 172–75, 179
Davis, William Heath, 146, 173
de Anza, Juan Bautista. *See* Anza, Juan Bautista de
de Bouchard, Hippolyte. See Bouchard, Hippolyte de
Dead Man's Island, 229
Dead Miner, The, 249
Declaration of Emancipation, 132
Diaz, Bartolomé, 44
Diputación, 117, 177–178, 197–198, 200–2
diseño, 127, 287
    mapping of land grants, 135
Donner Party, 182, 237–38, 269, 272
Drake, Sir Francis, 57–58

E

earthquakes, 85, 112, 302–3, 305

PUBLICATIONS BY THE IRVINE MUSEUM

Selections from The Irvine Museum

Reflections of California:
The Athalie Richardson Irvine Clarke Memorial Exhibition

Impressions of California: Early Currents in Art 1850–1930

Romance of the Bells: The California Missions in Art

Palette of Light:
California Paintings from The Irvine Museum

California Impressionists:
A Presentation of The Olympic Games Cultural Olympiad
(co-published with the Georgia Museum of Art)

All Things Bright and Beautiful:
California Impressionist Paintings from The Irvine Museum

Guy Rose: American Impressionist
(co-published with the Oakland Museum of California)

The Life and Art of Paul de Longpré